# Data Publics

Data has emerged as a key component that determines how interactions across the world are structured, mediated and represented. This book examines these new data publics and the areas in which they become operative, via analysis of politics, geographies, environments, and social media platforms.

By claiming to offer a mechanism to translate every conceivable occurrence into an abstract code that can be endlessly manipulated, digitally processed data has caused conventional reference systems which hinge on our ability to mark points of origin, to rapidly implode. Authors from a range of disciplines provide insights into such a political economy of data capitalism; the political possibilities of techno-logics beyond data appropriation and data refusal; questions of visual, spatial and geographical organization; emergent ways of life and the environments that sustain them; and the current challenges of data publics, which is explored via case studies of three of the most influential platforms in the social media economy today: Facebook, Instagram and WhatsApp.

*Data Publics* will be of great interest to academics and students in the fields of computer science, philosophy, sociology, media and communication studies, architecture, visual culture, art and design, and urban and cultural studies.

**Peter Mörtenböck** is Professor of Visual Culture at TU Wien's School of Architecture and Planning, and Professorial Research Fellow at Goldsmiths College, London.

**Helge Mooshammer** is an architect and cultural theorist based at Goldsmiths College, London and TU Wien. He is Co-Director of the Centre for Global Architecture.

## Routledge Research in Design, Technology and Society

*Series Editors: Daniel Cardoso Llach (Carnegie Mellon University, USA) and Terry Knight (Massachusetts Institute of Technology, USA)*

*The Routledge Research in Design, Technology and Society* series offers new critical perspectives and creative insights into the roles of technological systems and discourses in the design and production of our built environment. As computation, software, simulations, digital fabrication, robotics, 'big data,' artificial intelligence and machine learning configure new imaginaries of designing and making across fields, the series approaches these subjects critically from enriched socio-material, technical and historical *perspectives*—revealing how conceptions of creativity, materiality and labor have shifted and continue to shift in conjunction with technological change.

**Computer Architectures**
Constructing the Common Ground
*Edited by Theodora Vardouli and Olga Touloumi*

**Data Publics**
Public Plurality in an Era of Data Determinacy
*Edited by Peter Mörtenböck and Helge Mooshammer*

For more information about the series, please visit: https://www.routledge.com/Routledge-Research-in-Design-Technology-and-Society/book-series/RRDTS

# Data Publics

Public Plurality in an Era of
Data Determinacy

Edited by Peter Mörtenböck and
Helge Mooshammer

LONDON AND NEW YORK

First published 2020
by Routledge
2 Park Square, Milton Park, Abingdon, Oxon OX14 4RN

and by Routledge
52 Vanderbilt Avenue, New York, NY 10017

*Routledge is an imprint of the Taylor & Francis Group, an informa business*

© 2020 selection and editorial matter, Peter Mörtenböck and Helge Mooshammer; individual chapters, the contributors

The right of Peter Mörtenböck and Helge Mooshammer to be identified as the authors of the editorial material, and of the authors for their individual chapters, has been asserted in accordance with sections 77 and 78 of the Copyright, Designs and Patents Act 1988.

*British Library Cataloguing-in-Publication Data*
A catalogue record for this book is available from the British Library

*Library of Congress Cataloging-in-Publication Data*
Names: Mörtenböck, Peter, 1966– editor. | Mooshammer, Helge, editor.
Title: Data publics : public plurality in an era of data determinacy / edited by Peter Mörtenböck and Helge Mooshammer.
Description: London ; New York : Routledge, 2020. | Series: Routledge research in design, technology and society ; volume 2 | Includes bibliographical references and index.
Identifiers: LCCN 2020007314 (print) | LCCN 2020007315 (ebook) |
Subjects: LCSH: Social media. | Social interaction. | Information theory. | Communication.
Classification: LCC HM741 .D39 2020 (print) | LCC HM741 (ebook) | DDC 302.23/1—dc23
LC record available at https://lccn.loc.gov/2020007314
LC ebook record available at https://lccn.loc.gov/2020007315

ISBN: 978-0-367-18472-8 (hbk)
ISBN: 978-0-367-51344-3 (pbk)
ISBN: 978-0-429-19651-5 (ebk)

Typeset in Sabon
by Apex CoVantage, LLC

# Contents

# Acknowledgments

The making of this publication has been embedded in a long-term research project based at the Institute of Art and Design at TU Wien and conducted in collaboration with the Visual Cultures Department at Goldsmiths College, University of London. The latter has generously hosted an inspiring public research forum which has been pivotal in shaping the direction and outcomes of this project. For supporting this gathering in London in January 2017, which brought together voices from around the world working in such diverse fields as architecture, digital and cultural studies, sociology, political theory, philosophy, and the arts, we would like to thank, in particular, Simon O'Sullivan for welcoming this research so warmly as Head of the Department of Visual Cultures. The organization of this international gathering as well as the research for and the production of this book would not have been possible without the financial support provided by the Programme for Arts-based Research (PEEK) initiated by the Austrian Science Fund (FWF: AR 371), for which we are truly grateful. Many of the authors represented in this publication already participated in this exchange of ideas, approaches, and outcomes, and we would like to take this opportunity to thank all our contributors for their ongoing encouragement and commitment.

Furthermore, we are indebted to numerous colleagues and friends for engaging with the issues raised in this book and advancing our understanding of them by hosting or contributing to talks, seminars, and conferences; inviting and commenting on related journal articles and book contributions; and sharing critical observations and fruitful conversations. Among many others, we wish to thank Ross Exo Adams, Dani Admiss, Alessio Antoniolli, Gerald Bast, Katherine Carl, Teddy Cruz, Helena Doudová, Angelika Fitz, Fonna Forman, Christian Frieß, Elaine Gan, Matthew Gandy, Paolo Gerbaudo, Stefan Gruber, Ayesha Hameed, Maroš Krivý, Peter Lang, Robert Leckie, Tom McDonough, Juan Pablo Molestina, Susan Moore, Christina Nägele, Gerald Nestler, Praba Pilar, Joshua Portway, Heidi Pretterhofer, Vyjayanthi Rao, Scott Rogers, Irit Rogoff, Esther Romeyn, Andreas Ruby, Andreas Rumpfhuber, Evelyn Ruppert, Susan Schuppli, AbdouMaliq Simone, Beverley Skeggs, Douglas Spencer, Christian Teckert, Christoph Thun-Hohenstein, Tom Trevatt, Matias Viegener, Cecilia Wee, and Simon Yuill. Their generous invitations and comments have been indispensable to the process of refining the editorial framing of this publication.

Many students in studio and seminar courses have further contributed with their work to sketching out the global picture of emergent data-scapes. We also owe a debt of gratitude to Carmen Lael Hines for her invaluable help with communicating with our contributors, editing chapter drafts, and preparing the manuscript for production, as well as to Joe O'Donnell for his skillful copy-editing of the texts. Sincere thanks are also due to Daniel Cardoso Llach and Terry Knight, editors of the Routledge Research in Design, Technology and Society series, for their enthusiastic embrace of this project. Suzanne Richardson and Grace Harrison, editors at Routledge, deserve special acknowledgment for guiding the realization of this publication with such care and precision.

# Contributors

**Ezekiel Dixon-Román** is an associate professor in the School of Social Policy & Practice at the University of Pennsylvania. His interdisciplinary scholarship is focused on the cultural studies of quantification and critical theories of difference, and he is the author of *Inheriting Possibility: Social Reproduction & Quantification in Education* (University of Minnesota Press, 2017).

**Matthew Fuller** works at Goldsmiths, University of London. He is author of such books as *How to Sleep: The Art, Biology, and Culture of Unconsciousness* (Bloomsbury, 2017), *How to Be a Geek: Essays on the Culture of Software* (Polity, 2018), and, with Olga Goriunova, *Bleak Joys, Aesthetics of Ecology and Impossibility* (University of Minnesota Press, 2019).

**Jennifer Gabrys** is Chair in Media, Culture and Environment in the Department of Sociology at the University of Cambridge and Visiting Professor in the Department of Sociology at Goldsmiths, University of London. She is Principal Investigator on the project AirKit, and she leads the Citizen Sense project, both funded by the European Research Council. She is the author of *Program Earth: Environmental Sensing Technology and the Making of a Computational Planet* (University of Minnesota Press, 2016) and *Digital Rubbish: A Natural History of Electronics* (University of Michigan Press, 2011) and co-editor of *Accumulation: The Material Politics of Plastic* (Routledge, 2013). Her recent and forthcoming books include *How to Do Things with Sensors* (University of Minnesota Press Forerunners series, 2019) and *Citizens of Worlds: Open-Air Toolkits for Environmental Struggle*. Her work can be found at citizensense.net and jennifergabrys.net.

**Benjamin Gerdes** is an artist, writer, and organizer working in video, film, and related public formats, individually as well as collaboratively. He is interested in intersections of radical politics, knowledge production, and popular imagination. His work focuses on the affective and social consequences of economic and state regimes, investigating methods for art and cultural projects to contribute to social change. His projects emerge via multiple articulations from long-term research processes conducted in dialogue with activists, trade unionists, architects, urbanists, geographers, and archival researchers. Exhibitions and screenings include the Centre Pompidou, National Gallery of Art (US), New Museum (US), Rotterdam International Film Festival, and the Tate Modern. Publications include *October*, *Public*, *The Journal of Aesthetics + Protest*, *Incite!*, and *Rethinking Marxism*. He currently leads a professor group and seminar on logistics and infrastructure at the Royal Institute of Art in Stockholm.

**Stephen Graham** is Professor of Cities and Society at Newcastle University's School of Architecture, Planning and Landscape. He has an interdisciplinary background linking human geography, urbanism, and the sociology of technology. His books include *Splintering Urbanism* and *Telecommunications and the City* (both with Simon Marvin) and the *Cybercities Reader*; *Cities, War and Terrorism*; *Disrupted Cities: When Infrastructures Fail*; and *Infrastructural Lives* (with Colin McFarlane). Professor Graham's 2011 book *Cities Under Siege: The New Military Urbanism* was nominated for the Orwell Prize in political writing and was a *Guardian* book of the week. His latest book – *Vertical: The City from Satellites to Bunkers* (Verso) – was published in 2016. Another *Guardian* book of the week, it was in the books of the year lists of both the *FT* and the *Observer*.

**Lev Manovich** is one of the leading theorists of digital culture worldwide, and a pioneer in the application of data science for analysis of contemporary culture. Manovich is the author and editor of 13 books including *AI Aesthetics*, *Theories of Software Culture*, *Instagram and Contemporary Image*, *Software Takes Command*, *Soft Cinema: Navigating the Database*, and *The Language of New Media*, which was described as "the most suggestive and broad ranging media history since Marshall McLuhan". He was included in the list of "25 People Shaping the Future of Design" in 2013 and the list of "50 Most Interesting People Building the Future" in 2014. Manovich is a Presidential Professor in the PhD program in Computer Science at the Graduate Center, CUNY, and a director of the Cultural Analytics Lab that pioneered analysis of visual culture using computational methods. The lab created projects for the Museum of Modern Art (NYC), the New York Public Library, Google and other clients.

**Louis Moreno** is an urbanist and theorist based in London, whose research examines the socio-spatial ramifications of finance capitalism. He is a lecturer in the Department of Visual Cultures and the Centre for Research Architecture, Goldsmiths University of London. His PhD at the Urban Laboratory, University College London analyzed the impact of financialization on changes to the urban form of the postindustrial city. Louis is a member of the research collective freethought, which co-curated the Bergen Assembly 2016 in Norway.

**Peter Mörtenböck** is Professor of Visual Culture at TU Wien and Research Fellow at Goldsmiths College, University of London. His current work focuses on urban speculation, global resource consumption and new data publics. Together with Helge Mooshammer, he has published numerous books, including, most recently, *Informal Market Worlds: The Architecture of Economic Pressure* (with Teddy Cruz and Fonna Forman, nai010 Publishers, 2015) and *Visual Cultures as Opportunity* (Sternberg, 2016). Their forthcoming book *Building Capital: Urban Speculation and the Architecture of Finance* investigates the architectural signification and facilitation of investment processes that have crystallized around global economic crises.

**Helge Mooshammer** is an architect and theorist based at TU Wien and Research Fellow at Goldsmiths College, University of London. He has initiated numerous international research projects around questions of (post)capitalist economies and urban informality. Mooshammer is one of the founding directors of the Centre for Global Architecture (www.global-architecture. org), an interdisciplinary initiative established to study the planetary changes affecting spatial production today. His recent and forthcoming book publications together with Peter Mörtenböck include, amongst others, *Informal Market Worlds: The Architecture of Economic Pressure* (with Teddy Cruz and Fonna Forman, nai010 Publishers, 2015), *Visual Cultures as Opportunity* (Sternberg, 2016) and *Building Capital: Urban Speculation and the Architecture of Finance* (forthc.).

**Luciana Parisi** is Professor in the Program in Literature at Duke University (NC). Her research is a philosophical investigation of technology, information sciences, and computation. In 2004, she wrote *Abstract Sex* (Continuum Press) and in 2013, she published *Contagious Architecture* (MIT). She is currently working on a new manuscript on the metaphysics of automation, computational logic, and machine thinking.

**Ravi Sundaram** is a professor at the Centre for the Study of Developing Societies (CSDS), Delhi. In 2000 he founded the well-known Sarai program at the CSDS along with Ravi Vasudevan and the Raqs Media Collective. Sundaram is the author of *Pirate Modernity: Media Urbanism in Delhi* (Routledge, 2010) and *No Limits: Media Studies from India* (Oxford University Press, 2015). Sundaram's essays have been translated into various languages in India, Asia, and Europe. He is currently finishing his next book project, *Events and Affections: Post-Public Media Circulation*.

**Ignacio Valero** has a PhD from UC Berkeley. He is presently an associate professor at California College of the Arts/San Francisco and formerly held the following positions: Professorial Research Fellow, TU Wien; Dean, School of Fine Arts, CCAC; Presidential Advisory Council (environment), new Colombian Constitution; Acting Director & Deputy Director, Colombian Environmental Agency-INDERENA; Latin American Coordinator, CIFCA/UNEP, Madrid; Coordinator, Sierra Nevada de Santa Marta Eco-Development Pilot Project; Environment/Science/Technology, COLCIENCIAS; and Sustainable Development Consultant IDB/US – AID/UNDP. His current research includes EcoDomics, affective platform capitalism/psycho-power/the *emotariat*, artificial aesthetic(s)/media/design; and social movements/common(s)/post-capitalist markets/post-growth.

# Introduction

*Peter Mörtenböck and Helge Mooshammer*

## Data is not a property but a relation

The rise of data to become a key component of encounter and interaction has profoundly changed both the way we live our daily lives and how the world operates globally. By claiming to offer a mechanism to translate every conceivable occurrence into an abstract code that can be endlessly manipulated – copied, amplified, distorted – digitally processed data has caused conventional reference systems such as proximity and distance, size and scale, which hinge on our ability to mark points of origin, to rapidly implode. If, for the postmodern subject, as famously argued by Fredric Jameson in 1991, it had become impossible to locate itself in space and time (*Postmodernism: or, The Cultural Logic of Late Capitalism*, p. 44), then this is even more true for 21st century citizens faced with data-driven environments that champion the disruption of existing social, economic, and political orders. Being made to believe that life today means that anything can happen anywhere anytime, feelings of confusion, agitation, and anxiety have become dominant features in the way we relate to one another and to the world around us.

With this volume we seek to respond to this experience of disorientation and fear of heteronomy by probing the social, political, and economic coordinates of data now crucial to concepts of governance and the imagination of the civic. What new ways of thinking do we need to open up to address the daunting complexity involved in defining what currently constitutes public space and political economy? The rapid expansion of non-physical spaces within the 30 years that have passed since Jameson made his prescient observation means that what now counts as extended realms of the public domain impacts both the gathering of data and a multitude of publics. Can this fundamental tension force practices of understanding to emerge that are dedicated to an expanded awareness of data as a new arena of public life?

## Beyond data anxiety

We need to acknowledge the sheer forcefulness with which the acceleration of data has come to constitute one of the most powerful transformative experiences in the modern world. In many arenas of everyday life, we take advantage of the expanded possibilities and increased speed with which we can connect, exchange, and interact beyond our immediate physical environment. Yet, besides improved convenience and heightened enjoyment, one of the most dominant phenomena accompanying this change is fear. Fear of malign forces accessing our inner privacy. Fear that arbitrary interests may take control of our movements, thoughts, and choices without us ever being aware of it. At the same time, there is a widespread sense of worry about the uncontrollability of the digital sphere, whose incessant growth seems to elude every established mode of governance.

These concerns bring to mind the uncontrollable nature that Elias Canetti attributed to what he called the "open crowd", a social entity he saw emerging in 19th-century urban upheavals and in 20th-century mass societies (Canetti, 1962). Canetti's figure of the crowd has become the epitome of collective entities forming in the wake of political destabilizations and the withering away of state sovereignty in late modernity. Consequently, the crowd and its alleged aim to grow indefinitely by seizing everyone within reach have variably been subject to both contempt and political manipulation. Throughout the decades, populist movements have readily exploited the intense investment of collective desires associated with crowds, packs, hordes, mobs, gangs, and other types of politically unsettling social subjects. The radical corruption and exploitation of desire that Deleuze and Guattari placed at the root of fascism's appeal to the masses (Deleuze and Guattari, 2004), to mention just one of many examples, went hand in hand with a systematic assault on the constitution of political order. Such encroachments on the tradition of sovereignty have not only thrown into relief significant moments of overcoming what Canetti diagnosed as a profound human fear of being touched by the unknown, but also highlighted much wider ambivalences threatening the stability of the physical, psychological, and ideological boundaries of subjectivity and what constitutes a collective entity.

Forms of representation that have hitherto enabled social entities to manifest themselves in action – nation-states, political parties, regulatory authorities, professional associations, unions, etc. – are increasingly losing their traction, giving way to new forms of sociality that are not contained by traditional notions of the people or the public. Competing kinds of global social fabric seem to be emerging that are neither homogenous in terms of composition and experience nor constitutive of more even geographical development. The enthusiasm and relationships sometimes generated by such acts of becoming (or multiplicities in Deleuzian terms) (Deleuze and Guattari, 1980, trans. 1987) and the territories they constitute are challenging the old static and universalizing notion of the public, promising to provide solutions that better fit the evolving needs of populations. In the wake of this transformation, familiar conventions of government reliability have given way to a default governmentality designed to induce citizens to internalize the goals bestowed upon them.

While there is still a great deal of hope, especially with regard to digital initiatives, in the potential of democratic, participatory, and bottom-up political transformation to confront the persistence of growing global inequality, ongoing processes of neoliberalization and their effort to disrupt and dismantle existing public institutions also hinge upon the active mobilization of people in the digital realm. The dissolution of social contracts is increasingly being banked on in the corporate production of algorithmically controlled environments that regroup and aggregate dissociated singularities into value-oriented profiles for a better "user experience" and, by extension, higher profit margins. The redefinition of citizens as entrepreneurial consumers has become the ultimate objective under the spell of neoliberal rationality, with competition implemented as the defining characteristic of human relations.

It is therefore vital to discuss the quality of emerging forms of online civic cooperation not just in relation to the excitement of short-term, spontaneous, and open-ended experiments, but with regard to the gap between the modest scale of such attempts and the global crisis that they seek to address, as well as with regard to the need to stabilize these attempts in a project that requires long-term coordination, binding rules, and stable institutions (Brenner, 2017, pp. 128–146). Such multiplicities are prone to be targeted, corrupted, and exploited by powerful actors within the digital network economy, eager to build profitable "social infrastructures" in the name of a truly global society. Both the use of techniques of governmentality elaborated by Michel Foucault in *Security, Territory and Population* (1977–78, ed. 2007)[1] and the technological devices of data capture applied to emergent socialities via mobile devices, sensors, and digital platforms can be seen as turning the openness and connectedness of irreducible multiplicities into qualities that are responsive to political and economic valorization. Amidst these shifting imaginaries of belonging, order, and security vis-à-vis the self's social environments, our inherited notion of the public is transformed by processes of fragmentation, financialization, and datafication.

## Data citizens: emerging socialities and sovereignties

While under the auspices of modernity, the public sphere was largely elaborated through spatial analogies that foreground a physically tangible division between the public and the private, between rights of ownership, control, and usage, the contemporary public sphere of data can no longer be comprehended in such terms – as a static, albeit progressively opaque, environment that we simply traverse. A universalizing order, where everyone and everything is placed in relation to one another, has been superseded by a system of dynamic management, in which socio-economic currencies such as access, belonging, and potential are folded into each other. Increasingly "user generated", today's data publics bring with them a profound blurring of the capacities, roles, and motivations of different actors. From digital citizenship to peer-to-peer networks and from online community services to virtual support groups, there is an increasing range of sites that are data dependent or data driven and in which individual, commercial, and governmental agendas and interactions are becoming increasingly blurred. Traditional power apparatuses of national governments are confronted with the global reach of digital providers. Citizens become enlisted in the self-servicing of the social, cultural, and infrastructural fabric of societies.[2] And affective capital such as desire and identification, fear, and rejection turn into the most decisive currency determining the fate of new technologies and their associated economies.

The public of these new data publics is thus a multi-faced figure. In that it is implicated in its own generation, conventional political paradigms such as the protection of rights or the division and demarcation of powers fall short when it comes to engaging with the dynamic realities of the digital realm. The trivialization of friendship, intimate bonds and emotional attachment through social media has reshaped traditional ideas of conviviality and companionship in favor of abstract patterns of social connectivity that can be quantified, valorized, and monetized according to each user's unique performance level. And in much the same manner, work is no longer a specific place determining one's professional life but a constant demand for labor-performing tasks embedded in the development of a new social fabric. Informal organization in the form of short-lived, direct, and unstable agreements is thus coming to constitute a dominant way of life in which work, culture, education, and the social are beginning to orientate themselves to global economic interests and their mechanisms to such a degree that the market orientation of social relations Karl Polanyi saw as a corollary of the industrial and bourgeois political revolution (Polanyi, 1947)[3] is becoming an all-encompassing idea.

With government agencies seeking to befriend us, tech companies in search of the next market luring us into conversations with AI-enabled chatbots, and maverick politicians utilizing the emotional charge of popular internet memes, traditional sources of truth and belonging are being eclipsed by a new mode of public interaction, one shaped by the logics of interface technologies, instant consumption, and short-term alliances. What we are going to leave behind in one way or another are Western traditions of political thought in which the notion of the public is bound up with distinct models of democracy and the nation-state. This includes ideas of territorial belonging, the stability of political institutions, reliable rules and legislation, and other state-centered instruments that have traditionally formed the basis of the assertion of political claims through the concept of citizenship. The rise of data regimes to the forefront of civic life has highlighted a critical shift in our understanding of notions of mobility, citizenship, and land use, which are now seen as interrelated, flexible, and contingent practices rather than as defined by administrative or regulatory means. It has also shown how new modes of citizenship are being produced at the intersections of international corporate interests, the differentiated exercise of state power, and the contingent struggles of citizens themselves (Ong, 2006) and thereby extending the concept of citizenship beyond the idea of the enjoyment of territorialized rights. Along with the erosion of nationally and territorially bound citizenship and the bottom-up struggle for new forms of cultural, social, and economic participation, rendering into data all aspects of our life has brought about new kinds of public spheres that offer variegated access to a range of on-demand services (transportation, logistics, marketplaces, education, food, etc.), fusing political and economic interests with processes of subject formation.

In his unfinished 1930s novel *The Man Without Qualities*, Robert Musil wrote that "Before the law all citizens were equal, but not everyone, of course, was a citizen" (1953). Musil's 20th-century concept of the citizen is only applicable in modified form to the strangely unresolved hybridities confronting us today: the subject without qualities of the 21st century is characterized by the question not of whether someone counts as a citizen but of *which components* of citizenship are part of an individually claim-able package. The life without qualities can no longer hope for stability, especially given the permanent erosion of the prospect of overcoming crisis situations by means of a decisive event. Mobility has become a fundamen-tal constant of globalization and with it the compulsion to be constantly cognizant of the accumulation of strategic values that make one a worthy citizen. A discourse of citizenship has thus taken shape that is almost exclu-sively orientated to the ability of citizens to contribute to economic growth. Central to this transformation is the destabilization of previously exclusive links between nation-state territories and citizenries in favor of a "contrac-tualization" of citizenship aligned to the quid pro quo principles of market relations (Somers, 2008) – economic viability, efficiency requirements, com-petitive pressures, and terms of trade. The way in which labor forces are absorbed into economically successful regions and how profit can be gener-ated with them are increasingly shaped by neoliberal strategies seeking to implement and exploit conditions of permanent crisis (economic, social, or environmental) and exception. The creation of zones governed by various forms of sovereignty, the flexible bestowal of graduated legal titles, and the specification of immigrant contingents based on professional qualifications are some of the consequences of this development (Ong, 1999).

In addition to these factors, the situation has been exacerbated by coun-tries contesting traditional forms of citizenship through digital residency schemes that allow citizens from one country to acquire additional trans-national digital identities in another country. To expedite the increasing de-territorialization of government functions, e-residency programs are promoted along with the creation of data embassies for the storage of sov-ereign data, government clouds, and government-friendly cloud regions. Estonia's e-residency program is one such pathfinding digital gateway that offers entrepreneurs access to business opportunities across the European

Union by using a government-issued digital ID card to establish and manage companies online. The program sells the right to enter a market that would otherwise be closed to the buyer but does not confer to the purchaser any rights pertaining to citizenship, physical residency, or entry to a particular country. Although it is argued that the potential for public participation is enhanced (and its geographical reach expanded) by these new forms of data citizenship, the democratic qualities of public life are reduced from full citizenship based on the conviction of being equal to the rest and having the same rights and obligations to a status based on different models of entrepreneurial ecosystems, elastic enclaves focused on citizens' capacity to contribute to economic growth.

## The rise and enclosure of user-generated publics

What the ongoing redefinition of citizens as users, participants, consumers, entrepreneurs, or investors demonstrates is that the way we inhabit and relate to increasingly complex spaces today, including non-physical and technologically augmented spaces, has set in motion an extended concept of the public, one that seems to be much more in sync with new forms of digital, transnational communication, with new technological knowledge and skills, with newly emerging institutional protocols, and with the flexibility of changing beliefs and persuasions. The erosion of a state-centered notion of the public, along with the explosive growth of mobile and social media, has given rise to an increasing acknowledgment of multiple, co-existing publics, hegemonic as well as marginalized ones. The way we tend to encounter the plurality of such publics today is no longer in relation to clearly defined political projects (or open-ended discursive relationships) but in terms of spatialized and embodied forms of lived experiences and everyday practices.

Many authors, including Judith Butler (2015), Noam Chomsky (2012), Michel Feher (2018), and Evgeny Morozov (2012) have pointed out how "data publics" have played a vital role in political protest movements over the last few years and how new forms of political assembly in urban centers are linked to the use of new digital communication technologies as well as to their capacity to address very specific demographics. From the Arab Spring uprisings and the struggle of the Occupy movement to the Me Too campaign and the Black Lives Matter movement, cloud-based software, social media, and mobile applications have enabled large sectors of urban populations to be part of the game. These new forms of publics have also shown that some of the digital platforms that seem instrumental in voicing public concerns are also increasingly important arenas of economic governance. Be it Facebook, Twitter, Instagram, or other social media sites – these platforms are part of one of the fastest growing markets in today's global capitalism, offering almost unfiltered access to millions of lives as well as to all the creative ideas and activities that form the basis of today's publics. In economic terms, these media and technology platforms form an unparalleled asset class that expands the existing venture-capital ecosystem by combining financial interests and purposes of governance into a heady cocktail of strategic intelligence tools.

Against this background, it is easy to observe how the increasing plurality of publics and their particular inclinations and activities have become a distinct form of capital, one that can be put on the market or turned into political currency the moment it emerges, by mining and clustering the data that constitute particular *kinds* of publics. This is where the appeal of analytical methods and decision-making tools such as predictive analytics, forecast modeling, and machine learning comes in, and explains the force with which these technologies have started to mold the values, ambitions, fantasies, fears, and desires of citizens around a new set of logics. Caught between ideas of emancipation and exploitation, new socialities are emerging that are self-generated but know little about themselves, while others seem to know a lot about how to exploit their structures, their ambitions, and their desires. Mounting calls for users of digital platforms to start policing content themselves reflect the fact that these platforms are becoming an ever more expansive force thanks to the exploitation of extra-economic components such as trust, shared assumptions, belief systems, social bonds, and emotional attachment – components that are turned into measurable practices by platform providers to ensure values really are "lived" and open up new market opportunities. Technology-enabled platforms are key to how we are enrolled in embracing the new imperative of being good and productive digital citizens. They have become a widely adopted means of enclosure utilized to manage and manipulate the complexities involved in the constitution of data publics.

For all these reasons, our collective ambition needs to go well beyond conventional arguments centering on data appropriation and data refusal. We need to challenge the understanding of data as contested entities that can be adequately settled by concepts of ownership and control, especially in light of political initiatives aiming to establish new frameworks for data governance. Most government responses attempting to conquer rising fears of data among the populace have so far focused on measures relating to the distribution and enforcement of rights attached to data that can be defined as the property of someone or something. Most notable in this context, at the time of editing this volume, have been the actions of the European Commission and Parliament around the implementation of the so-called "General Data Protection Regulation" (GDPR). In force since May 2018, the GDPR's main intentions are stated as "people having more control over their personal data" and "businesses benefitting from a level playing field" (European Commission, 2018).[4] Throughout the regulation, the GDPR keeps linking references to the fundamental rights and freedoms of natural persons with an insistence on ensuring an unrestricted flow of personal data within the EU internal market (EU Regulation, 2016).[5] This dual objective is clearly no coincidence but ensues directly from a growth-oriented economic assessment, in which the spread of data fear (i.e., an increasing reluctance to engage in data-generating and processing situations, whether these arise through contact with public authorities such as hospital trusts or with private businesses) is recognized as a significant obstacle hampering the "strengthening and the convergence of the economies within the internal market".[6] Hence, the repeatedly reiterated emphasis on a strong and coherent data protection framework, backed by strong enforcement, in order to create "the trust that will allow the digital economy to develop across the internal market".[7]

In everyday reality, the application of the GDPR has triggered the birth of a whole new market of service providers offering fee-based data management to public and institutional bodies, including universities, hospitals, local housing authorities, and infrastructure providers, as well as to private companies, who are all anxious to minimize their exposure to the new legal and potentially severe financial risks. Similarly, rather than feeling they have gained rights through the establishment of the GDPR, most individuals primarily see it as exposing them to further responsibilities on top of their existing tasks as dutiful economic subjects. This sense of being overwhelmed, of lacking the necessary tools and being forced to surrender supposedly personal rights to profit-seeking consultancies points not only to practical flaws in these efforts, but also to significant effects engendered by the definition of data applied in this context. Prevalent neoliberal policy approaches, which perceive publicized fears of technological change as an economic hindrance, are directed toward curbing and reining in such uncertainties through actions of control and demarcation. The underlying bias toward seeing economic growth as irrevocably founded on the expansion of trade[8] propels a stubborn vision of data as a form of property.

These views are prioritized for obvious reasons. Irrespective of the use of the adjective "personal", the framing of data as property is designed to pave the way for a neat and frictionless transition of data into a tradable commodity with a monetary value. From the perspective of the market, the conception of property as a *characteristic* is just a short step away from the conception of property as a *commodity*. Both conceptions indicate a particular relationship of belonging, a process stabilized through legal, cultural, ideological, and economic conventions. However, it is this step from property being contingent on numerous variables, which help describe its character, to property being contingent solely on its exchange value that allows for the packaging of complex social and political tasks into abstract tradable entities. Here, the artifice of approaching data regulation as a combined legal matter of citizens and markets creates an operational terrain in which obligations to protect the fundamental rights of natural persons can be brought into line with demands for unhindered market flows. As a result, data fear becomes an issue of risk management, facilitating as well as being facilitated by the business of an unrestricted market.

## Dispossessing data

The blurred distinction between the rights of social subjects and the rights of private property has long been at the heart of struggles that confront the ideological bias of modern legal theory toward conceiving every aspect of the human subject as property owned by the individual (Hardt and Negri, 2004). These struggles have intensified in recent years, rallying against the softening of boundaries between human needs and property demands advanced by the enclosure of data as property. To counter the idea of "possessive individualism" (Macpherson, 1962),[9] a different relation between the One and the Many has been advanced over recent decades, one that is based neither on the idea of (subjective and material) property owned by the individual nor on state control, but on the idea of the commons. Acknowledging the irreducible multiplicity of movements, networks, and socialities that are emerging in activist, bottom-up initiatives on- and offline, this model is based on the concept of multiple forms of commonality constituting the foundation of the singularity of social subjectivities (Hardt and Negri, 2004, p. 202). When thinking about ways of counteracting the ongoing dynamics of data enclosure, we can take our clue from the concept of the commons and reframe the notion of data in a way such that data is not understood as property but as a relation – a fairly simple proposition, but one that has far-reaching ramifications.

As a mode of meaning-making, data comes into being only in a situation of exchange, in an encounter with an element outside ourselves, with something or someone "other". Data is constituted in that moment of encounter as a means of expressing, describing, and navigating this transitory situation. To put it differently, rather than being a piece of property, data is both a way and a form of articulating a relation. What is therefore at stake is not so much the question of what value we put on data but how we value the relations that underpin the generation of data. That is to say, what matters is not what price we demand for our personal data but how we care for our relations unfolding in the social sphere. If we accept that data is not at all a form of personal property, something that belongs exclusively to us, but is the result of a collective effort, we can start to think about different forms of care and about different forms of institution that can take care of these relations.[10] Rather than treating data as a stimulant of the neoliberal market economy, we might then begin to understand it as the intermediation of a new type of commons, as something that is collectively generated, managed, and cared for.

Continuing this line of thought, we can also discern that for data to come into being requires some kind of interface that records and acknowledges our interactions with someone or something else. This interface can take on many forms, ranging from our individual memory to the reference systems of cultural norms and values, and from artistic interpretations to globe-spanning recording machines. As a differentiating relation, data is generated at the intersection of a moment of encounter and an interface recognizing and seeking to delineate the elements involved in this encounter. Such critical encounters enable those involved to continuously constitute and reconstitute themselves, examining one another's perspectives and reflecting oneself in or as another. What we want to propose here is that it is these moments of encounter, the moments of interaction and recognition, in which we can locate the constitution of "data publics".

For this sphere to emerge, we need some kind of framework that provides the background against which a particular set of data – socially, temporally, and spatially contingent processes – can be exposed and recognized. Contemporary cities, for instance, function as such interfaces, requiring us to ask how they are set up to produce and deliver particular forms of recognition and, by extension, particular sets of data. Are the workings of our cities biased to (re)produce such forms of recognition that render us legitimate or illegitimate through particular modes of categorization such as racializing data practices. Are the institutional metabolisms of our cities geared toward specific sets of interests? Are they, for instance, skewed toward imperatives of productivity, prioritizing forms of recognition in which only our capacities to work matter? How fast can we move from A to B; how readily can we become available as a work force?

If we want to argue for the proposition of data as relation and not as property, it is crucial to reflect upon the structures and terms of recognition that are in place in cities and other environments, the performativity of data and its potential to yield different kinds of subjectivities as well as the character of relations recognized by data-mining techniques. In this context, it might prove fruitful to go beyond the immediate, digital technology–aided sites of recognition – electronic cameras, embedded sensors, signal processing devices, etc. – within the urban fabric as such and raise more fundamental questions about the persistent desire and need for the recognition of emerging data publics and their struggle against the conditions of data capture that cause certain groupings, movements, or socialities to be advantaged and others disadvantaged. This is a struggle that puts the finger on what Judith Butler has aptly described as the hegemony of an unequal distribution of recognizability: i.e., the relations of power that determine the structure and "realness" of data by recognizing particular relations as valuable while disregarding others. This kind of recognition, Butler suggests, "becomes a problem for those who have been excluded from the structures of political representation, and who will be denied access to such structures" (Willig, 2012). Indeed, many new technologies of data capture, analytics, and reporting impose schemes of recognition that determine our individual recognizability and hence limit the possibilities for many lives and relations to be recognized as real. They produce the norms and conventions that make human beings recognizable and exploit the vulnerabilities that enable recognition in the first place.

While in Butler's terms the subject is never generating data outside of the boundaries that determine what can become an object of recognition, since the scene of recognition is always preconfigured by powers and norms pre-existing interpersonal encounters, the power of subversive resignification lies precisely in the expropriability of the dominant discourse (including the discourse that renders data itself as property), in its failure to give a full account of who we are (Butler, 2005). And while there is a need to insist on a fundamental opacity, impenetrability, and shared blindness about ourselves and on the impossibility of absolute and complete recognition (Butler, 2010), there is simultaneously no way to deny that generating data in performative acts of relating to one another has a "plastic action" (Wittig, 1985) upon the real, provoking conditions of plasticity that are subject to alteration through continuous communicative practice. The relationality that lies at the core of data is both reinforcing and undermining who we are and what we know about ourselves. But it cannot be sustained in its invariable plurality if there is no movement beyond the logic of owning and disowning, movement that engenders an unbiased and equal distribution of recognizability.

The schemes of recognition that are currently in place in everyday inter-pretative frameworks in the form of data capture infrastructures do little to acknowledge the intrinsic demand formulated by this plurality. Determining the usefulness and uselessness of data by deciding who or what is wor-thy of recognition, whose relations are recommended to be endorsed, and whose communications are irrelevant to the further development of digital environments, prevailing apparatuses of data capture tend to reinforce the norms and conventions that support existing operations of power. For a more democratic and pluralistic vision of cohabitation to emerge, it is there-fore vital to challenge the politics underpinning the current schemes that regulate and distribute recognizability and to shift the debate from questions of appropriation to the quality of relations created in our encounters. In this shift, taking care of data ceases to be a question of enclosure, ownership, and control but a process in which alterity and its sphere of becoming can be understood as the commons of multiple data publics. It is this struggle *for* and *against* recognition that lies at the heart of emerging data publics. This struggle manifests our involvement in political processes that seek to redefine practices of engaging with the unbounded diversity of ourselves and our encounters. It helps us think through the various natures of these relations: how they come into being, what propels their development, and how they are embedded in flows of affect and desire, as well as in the logics of speculative economies.

## Dataism and the legitimacy of claims

An important part of the motivation behind compiling this volume is the heightened awareness of the way in which the algorithmic strategies of today's global techno-capitalism are intervening in the fabric of our every-day experience, and of how they are tying the management of future life so closely to computation and digital media. Day after day, we are seeing the emergence of new forms of data analytics, dataveillance, and algorithmic governance, and these technologies are bringing into focus the complex links between digital companies, platforms, intermediaries, governments, and users. While there is still a considerable lack of transparency about how these links are forged through distinct sets of operations, through the creation of hybrid data environments, new governmental techniques, and new technological devices, their impacts are becoming ever more tangible and pronounced: we are living in a time when not only has a global market orientation taken hold of everything we do, but an all-encompassing *data mentality* has become an imperative for the new citizen. A kind of "dataism" seems to be emerging as the new religion that one needs to embrace in order to be part of the production and accumulation of value, whether in terms of new modes of environmental data gathering, the development of political constituencies, or the mining and quantifying of previously unquantifiable categories such as trust, appreciation, and attitude.

In response to this situation, it is necessary not only to shed light on newly emerging routines and protocols in the context of a global-data and communication economy, but also to develop new perspectives on what constitutes "public awareness", "the public domain", and "the public interest" in an increasingly post-institutional world. What is therefore vital when attempting to retain the term "public" in some way is to stress the plurality and data dependency of new social entities arising in this context. Rather than universalizing, harmonizing, and homogenizing these pluralities, it is necessary to highlight the conflicts embedded in this process as well as the new forms of sovereign power that are beginning to stake their claims on the future.

Of central importance here is the decay of truth as a key parameter of our cultural condition, evidenced by the rise of "fake news" and "alternative facts" as part of a fast-spreading post-truth culture. This development has enormous implications for our sense of a shared reality and our ability to communicate across social and cultural divides. Most recently, we have been confronted by a number of events that make it almost mandatory to address the profound sense of ambiguity, if not anxiety, about contemporary publics that is emerging today: if we think of the growing strength of populist movements across the globe since the 2007–2008 financial crisis – for instance, if we think of Trump's ascent to the US presidency and the mistruths swirling around Britain's Brexit vote or if we think of the selection of "post-truth" as 2016's international word of the year – all these instances and the debates they have provoked seem to suggest that the notion of the public has become less stable, less predictable, and less trustworthy than it once was. The bourgeois fear of the masses appears to have given way to an elitist fear of the public. Contemporary notions of the public have become entangled with a sense of manipulation that is seen as linked to an increasingly computational world and especially to unprecedented levels of data collection, analysis, and dissemination by private as well as governmental entities. The ubiquitous and often obscure character of these processes has raised substantial doubts regarding the relationship between our becoming embedded in data environments and the computational shaping of new public spheres.

What is missing in this situation are new analytical tools and forms of critical engagement capable of transgressing the suffocating binary of either demanding control of data or fearing how endemic it has become to the operation of today's public realms. The development of such means will require a broader conversation about how the acceleration of data is undermining conventional political paradigms of citizen rights and civic participation, about how we can face these new challenges, and about how new forms of publics might emerge beyond the techno-capitalist vision of an information society. The increasing sense of manipulation associated with today's data publics has already led to game-changing effects: we can see how the lingering feeling of distrust *by* the public toward their political institutions has turned into a distrust *of* the public and its opinions. This change has tremendous repercussions for the entire political system, for its foundation in the articulation of a *public will*. It seems that under the aegis of data capitalism, this *public* can no longer be trusted. What is at stake is no longer the *political representation* of the public but the *legitimacy of claims* being made through (rather than in the name of) it – which is in the end a fundamentally political question, but one that now seems to be escaping and overruling established political institutions in favor of new models of political and economic leadership.

In critically examining the conceptual potentialities and limits of emerging data publics, together with their empirical performance, the edited collection *Data Publics* seeks to provide a significant and original intervention into critical data studies and to advance understandings of the operation of digital life and the interconnections between contemporary social, cultural, and media theory. In this context, the fundamental aim of our authors is to provide crucial evidence for nothing less than a new understanding of civic participation within the algorithmic estate. The 12 chapters that comprise this collection boldly investigate the political implications of hybridized data environments, chart the emergence of data capitalism, experiment with new visual and cultural modes of transgressing the digital public realm, and speculate about new models of governance in the context of self-generating data publics. All these topics are approached from very different perspectives, but they together help to fashion a common framework for understanding emerging data publics through the lens of multiple scales that extend from the body to its locality, from urban habitats to global flows, and beyond to the cosmos.

## Politics, environments, platforms

Section I (Politics) of this book offers insights into the political economy of data capitalism and the political potential of techno-logics that go beyond today's polarized views on data appropriation and data refusal. Contributing to an examination of the growing interlinkages between the technological and governmental paradigms shaping contemporary life, Matthew Fuller's opening chapter, "In praise of plasticity", explores the notion of "plasticity", the capacity to reformat parameters of operation through processes of experimentation and learning. In recent years, the corresponding concept of perpetually integrating feedback loops into the coded grammar of machine systems has encroached on many areas of daily life through the principle of algorithmic optimization. Increasingly, new technologies are being employed to imprint plastic actions on the real in order to serve particular economic gains and political ends, as seen, for instance, in the spread of "flexible" on-demand work arrangements such as zero-hour contracts, which allow for an externalization of economic risk into the social. On the other hand, the idea of advancement through "plastic" structural adaptation has also become a highly influential leitmotiv in contrasting visions of socio-political transformation.

Echoing the "plastic" workings of this school of thinking itself, Fuller explores and traces its ontology across three different contexts: Gordon Pask's work on cybernetics, the field of machine learning, and the political disposition of anarchism. The latter, in Fuller's analysis, is understood as "a political approach that emphasizes flows of information, not merely as a means of equitable distribution and democratic access, but as a process also of transformation". From early anarchist voices onward, this ethics of action and struggle has been articulated as the necessity to continuously reappraise every aspect of political protocol. Yet in practical terms, the complex textures and granularities of everyday realities pose multiple difficulties for upholding a truly egalitarian political structure in progress, producing and engendered by constitutive publics.

How, for instance, can self-initiated operations maintain manageable work arrangements; how can they grow and expand without reproducing limiting and self-defeating structures? And perhaps most crucially, how can a form of organization be devised that ensures a capacity to truly recognize a problem in all its dimensions rather than simply dealing with representations or mediations of it. Interested in the affinities between the different fields of cybernetics, machine learning, and anarchism, Fuller identifies an emphasis on "under-specification" as one possible way of learning how to face these dilemmas. Drawing on Pask's work on un-preprogrammed technologies, as articulated, for instance, in his collaboration on Cedric Price and Joan Littlewood's *Fun Palace* project – a responsive architecture attuned to users' changing needs and desires – Fuller argues that under-specification opposes mere functionalism and points instead to maximally open structures and minimally predetermined forms. As problems continuously mutate, it becomes imperative to maintain the "widest degree of redundancy or requisite variety in decision-making". Such an orientation toward a conversational perspective, Fuller suggests, can open up ways of resisting instrumentalizing forms of plasticity, unleashing instead the creative energies of plastic becomings as they impact and reflect on both processes of individuation and collective expression.

Luciana Parisi and Ezekiel Dixon-Román's chapter, "Data capitalism, sociogenic prediction, and recursive indeterminacies", resonates with Fuller's interest in machine learning. Interrogating the naturalizing effects of a data-centric worldview championing the predictive intelligence of machines, Parisi and Dixon-Román direct their inquiry toward the radical transformations inflicted by data capitalism. At the core of these attempts to self-pose capital as ontology, they detect "a new mode of machinic production that preserves within itself the future value of data". Yet this shift from data to algorithmic modeling not only heralds a new computational sovereignty, but also serves to reaffirm a heuristic regeneration of power, thus perpetuating regimes of sociogenic coding and racialization of the world.

In their quest for potential openings to challenge data capitalism's epistemological project, Parisi and Dixon-Román delve deeply into the modalities of recursive thinking by machines. By way of suggesting that automation can include both contingency and chance, they raise the question of whether "automated systems can be taken to act against the anthropomorphic biases of modeling".

Is there scope for "including wider margins of indeterminacy and ultimately overturning sociogenic programming all together"? Or have learning systems of intelligence already absorbed within themselves the horizon of the unthought and unknown, essentially eradicating all possibilities to reach beyond the planet's colonization by Western man? Parisi and Dixon-Román warn against a fatalistic viewpoint of an all-overriding techno-determinism. Instead, they argue for a more nuanced approach that at once engages the transformative scope of incomputables in redefining what a machine can do whilst also addressing the implicatedness of automated systems in the ontopower of data capital.

Ignacio Valero shares this dual objective of, on the one hand, insisting on a thorough analysis of the evolving nature of contemporary capitalism and, on the other, pushing for ways to make alternatives thinkable. Driven by this spirit of not wanting to concede to established boundaries, Valero's chapter, "*Emotariat* accelerationism and the republic of data", embarks on a highly sensitive exploration of what it is that makes us participate in the spreading of new forms of capitalist exploitation and destruction. To this end, the chapter opens with a crucial examination of the mobilizing effect of desire, both as the "raw material" targeted by today's rapidly proliferating passion economy and as an entry point for resurrecting the virtues of communality and solidarity. With regard to the former, further elaborating his concept of the "*emotariat*", Valero alerts us to how at the heart of contemporary wealth accumulation lies the ability to control and exploit the labor of emotional investment. Data technologies are key to this, offering boundless flexibility for the willful manipulation of the supply and demand of libidinal energies. As Valero reminds us, quoting Srnicek, today's "*dividualized* algorithms act as libidinal enclosure platforms. Their erotic, libidinal repression lights up a torch which like climate-induced wildfires threatens to engulf the entire body organic and body politic of the planet".

Whilst explicitly addressing the widening repertoire of instruments being deployed to enslave contemporary subjectivities, Valero is equally eager to tease out the more fundamental tensions underlying people's conceptions of their relation to the cosmos, its creation, and their place within it. Only when recognizing the mythological engine at work in liberal, capitalist modernity can we truly engage with our complex and contradictory libidinal involvement in it and channel analysis into a vision of change. Laying out potential pathways toward imaging alternative futures, Valero, too, calls upon the incomputable and unaccountable. Rallying a roster of critical voices, he makes clear that new technologies can reach well beyond their appropriation as tools of domination and are imbued with a decisive democratic potential to become socially innovative and politically disruptive. Indeed, looking at the plethora of movements emerging from outside Western epicenters, Valero encourages us to acknowledge, cherish, and learn from other desires already vigorously emergent that are informing both alternative concepts and practical realities, all the while steadily enriching a glocalized *EcoDomic* aesthetic(s) of the common(s).

Section II of this book (Environments) extends this debate by anchoring the often intangible worlds of data in questions of visual, spatial, and geographical organization. It connects these discussions with a closer analysis of emergent ways of life and the environments that sustain them. The widespread invisibility of data and associated technologies plays a significant role in casting their impact as benign and as merely another logical step in the gradual science-led improvement of our daily lives, which we have become accustomed to over a century marked by the advance of the mass consumer-goods market. A case in point is the growing number of satellites orbiting in space, which, being so far out of sight, are hardly ever considered to be part of everyday life. As Stephen Graham's chapter, "Unearthly domain: the enigmatic data publics of satellites", reminds us, this is rather paradoxical, given that so much of "valuable" human activity on Earth is now measured, guided, and implemented via satellite-controlled GPS data. What this blindness obscures is the steady erasure of established conventions. Far beyond an increased convenience in the execution of daily routines, the spheres opened up by novel global navigation and communication systems are causing fundamental shifts in economic, social, political, and spatial paradigms, triggering seismic ruptures in humans' understanding and organization of life on Earth, changes we have yet to become conscious of.

A key transformation in this context, and one that is taking place under the radar, as it were, relates to the way we locate ourselves as human beings in space. This, in turn, is heavily dependent on our perception of space itself, of the manifestation of space along a particular perspective and sets of clear and stable coordinates. Stephen Graham identifies a number of realignments at work in contemporary visual cultures, which are being reinforced by what is assumed to be the infinite technological capacity of new means of reconnaissance such as drones and satellites and which deserve our increased attention. One such realignment has to do with recalibrating the weight of horizontal and vertical vectors of space when it comes to determining the possession of power, a shift of focus from the land-bound parameters of nation-states to the time-dependent reach of orbital infrastructures, many of them linked to the operations of different sections of the global military-industrial complex. When these activities are brought into the realm of public visibility, the pretense of a god-like vision from above afforded by this vast data-scape of sensing and imaging is called upon to turn every occurrence on Earth into a targetable object of satellite-led intervention. Through a detailed study of the proliferating grip of this vertical view on our lives today, from the dawning weaponization of inner space to its commodification through Google Earth, Graham not only lays bare the military bias of this imperial gaze from above but also, importantly, decodes the inherent constructedness of data-based omniscience.

Descending from Graham's analysis of "above", Jennifer Gabrys's chapter, "Sensing air and creaturing data", grounds its analysis on a critical study of the role data plays in our knowledge and experience of the Earth's atmosphere. While Graham's chapter focuses on new alliances appropriating mastery of the vertical, which affect how we as humans locate ourselves in space, Gabrys reorients this sense of the vertical to explore how data technologies are transforming the logics of relational scales but, in her case, the relationship between individual data collection and spaces of data interpretation. She explores the disjunctive relation between the individual body experiencing data and the spaces where this data gets stored, processed, and shaped into communicable bits, whether as news stories, scientific reports, or data sets steering algorithmic operations in a wide range of contexts, from financial markets to on-demand services and social media platforms. As a consequence of this gap between data collection and data interpretation, a majority of data – although directly related to everyday experiences such as the environmental pollution of concrete locations, an example that provides the context for Gabrys's analysis – is rendered inactionable, not least for individual citizens. In response, an increasing number of initiatives have sprung up which seek to challenge this discrepancy between immediate experience and the availability of accountable information. So-called "citizen sensing" movements point the way to a strategy of shifting practices of data production and interpretation from the monopole sphere of scientific and policy experts to spaces with infinite numbers of participants. The crucial question here is whether this intervention can constitute more than merely the replacement of one group of stakeholders by another and whether, as a change of practice, it could herald the arrival of an entirely new quality with regard to the scope and meaning of data.

On the one hand, citizen sensing clearly expands the horizon of data recording. More than just a complementary add-on, citizen data has the capacity to change the makeup of data-scapes from within, shifting what is understood as center and periphery. On the other hand, rather than simply detecting what is already out there, Gabrys suggests, citizen sensing needs to be recognized as acts of creation that can alter the perception and experience of environments. Gabrys uses the term "creaturing data" to describe how citizens' engagement with computational-sensing technologies is bound up with the generation of new milieus, relations, entities, occasions, and interpretive registers of sensing. This notion of "creatured data" highlights how, beyond the accumulation of more or different data, citizen data can become a decisive factor in the creation of environments of relevance. By giving rise to new entities and perspectives, "creatured data" actualizes our world(s) precisely as a process of experience. Analyzing the implications of such practices of co-production in relation to concrete research experiments, Gabrys's chapter provides a crucial contribution to one of the main objectives of this volume: namely, to begin to comprehend how data is constituted and engendered through moments of encounter and what momentum such encounters can generate.

Benjamin Gerdes's chapter, "Offsite: data, migration, landscape, materiality", engages with the generative capacity of moments of encounter to aid our understanding of data constitution and the politics this constitution conveys and engenders. This chapter, experimental in its approach, interweaves paratactic research notes for a film essay about Gerdes's opportunity to tour two data centers in the Stockholm region of Sweden. Moving between narrative modes of research notes, video description, and acute analysis, Gerdes juxtaposes three recently developed phenomena in Sweden: the state-sponsored opening of several world-class data centers in rural parts of Northern Sweden, the recent restrictions to refugee resettlement and overall migration procedures, and the growth of informal recruitment of migrant labor in the berry-picking industry. He gradually unfolds, through juxtaposition, how these three phenomena link to and iterate from one another. Through his encounters with these concepts, Gerdes proposes questions of "selective migration" and the political mechanisms of Sweden's cherished concept of *allemansrätten* ("freedom to roam" or "right of public passage"). He considers which groups have priority within this freedom to roam, what kinds of exclusions exist at the heart of this "freedom", and who builds and controls the environments that are to be "roamed". He considers policies that restrict refugee resettlement alongside the placement of the entire country of Sweden on Airbnb, proposing that despite seeming paradoxical, they are instead two sides of the same coin, shaping how we understand the politics of access, environmental construction, and data relation. Open-armed policies toward companies like Facebook developing massive data centers in rural areas of Sweden and people treating rural areas of Sweden as their personal Airbnb bookings – rural areas that, in their remoteness, were once tactically opened to refugees – become monuments to a regime of oppressive, selective "open-ness". The style and structure of Gerdes's chapter embody the themes indicated by the situations he makes visible for intentionally multifaceted interpretation. Aiming to challenge a "site-by-site mode of inquiry" typical of academic approaches to studying data, borders, infrastructural privatization, and built environment, Gerdes instead "questions the contours" of each of these phenomena by describing them alongside one another, moving between scalar modes to indicate what these issues of data, migration, and built environment say about the disoriented scalar system in which we presently situate ourselves as subjects.

In his chapter, "Fracking sociality: real estate and the new urban architecture of the internet", Louis Moreno connects the question of how data production actively shapes environments with the key site of contemporary economic development – the city. Tracking the sometimes blurry architectural traces in the genesis of computational technologies, Moreno sets out to explore what urban systems the new global players of data capitalism like Google, Facebook, and WeWork are beginning to develop in order to implement particular kinds of ecologies. Described by their masterminds as "environments that . . . make ideas happen and go out into the world", the flip side of these supposedly socially embracing spaces catering holistically to our quest for a rich and fulfilled life is an ever more advanced furnishing of urban space with surveillance devices programmed to sense, track, and mine every move and behavior of a carefully chosen and monitored population. Moreno sees this new type of urban space as more than a mere representation of digital capitalism and seeks to identify and critique those "architectonic practices that bind the accumulation of capital in space to the communication of information in time (and vice versa)".

To this end, he juxtaposes a long-growing cultural unease about the dissolution of once familiar spatially marked orders, such as the distinction between private and public, with the need of capital to build environments through and in which its operations can become naturalized. The rise of real estate to both a hyper-performing asset class and determinant urban planning tool exemplifies this alignment of everyday life with the logics of financial capital. At the heart of this transformation, Moreno argues, lies the task of optimizing and synchronizing the circulation of people, labor, information, capital, profit, and so forth, but in a way that renders much of this circulation opaque, camouflaging it with a veneer of altruistic aesthetics. What we are witnessing now, he argues, is the readjustment of these alignments to the new possibilities of capital accumulation afforded by data technologies that can direct, filter, and absorb circulations in space in entirely new ways. With computational capacities now extending to the recognition and quantification of and predictions about not only material events but all sorts of immaterial aspects, such as social preferences, cultural tendencies, and individual and collective behaviors, it is no longer just the built environment as such but urban life in all its forms and expressions which gets traded and fetishized on speculative auction markets. However, as Moreno reminds us, this is not a purely technologically determined and thus "already lost" process; rather, what these developments call for is a comprehensive critique of the (transformative) moral and aesthetic systems that underpin capitalist appropriation by design.

Section III of this book (Platforms) concludes this debate by locating it in a variety of empirical contexts and by exploring the current challenges of data publics through influential platforms in the social media economy today. Mörtenböck and Mooshammer, expanding on the opaque circulations of the city as described by Moreno, turn their attention to new structures of supposedly porous relationalities within the city. The claim to break down debilitating hierarchies of outmoded forms of social and economic organization by allowing for unhindered, direct, relational interaction is frequently promoted as a primary selling point of the rapidly expanding breed of platform-based enterprises. Following the idealized model of "disruptive technologies", which prioritizes the simple fact of change itself over long-term values, many of these investor-backed so-called start-ups are targeting key components of urban life – from transport infrastructures to the organization of work and from the realignment of government-citizen relations to numerous services that have to do with taking care of oneself, such as housing, food, and leisure.

Mörtenböck and Mooshammer embed their analysis of this kind of "platform urbanism" in a wider genealogy of the role of urban development within the evolution of capitalism. They point out how over the last decades speculation *with* the building blocks of urban societies has been surpassed by forms of city-making purposely designed *for* speculative markets, of which platform urbanism can be seen as one of the latest incarnations. Under these conditions, which are deeply entrenched in the competitive mind-sets of financial markets, urban spaces, and the social practices unfolding within and through them, are perceived not just as asset classes but as variables within a larger set of parameters that need to be managed in such a way as to achieve whatever is deemed "best performance" in the eyes of investors. Reflecting on the urban typologies employed in the recent wave of large-scale campuses erected by the ruling tech giants in California's Silicon Valley, Mörtenböck and Mooshammer detect two significant trends through which platform mentalities imprint themselves on urban space: first, a collapse of scale, in which the imaginary of personal happiness is interpolated with a technological, corporate, and governmental restructuring of urban environments of vast dimensions, and second, orchestrated moves to cement these transformations through the modeling of all-encompassing worlds, in which one company takes care of each and every need. Any visions challenging these monopole cities, Mörtenböck and Mooshammer argue, would have to start with reconsidering the structural logics of platforms. If platforms' key assets are the provision and control of access, then what is at stake is the question of how to organize access to access.

In the following chapter, "The aesthetic society: or how I edit my Instagram", Lev Manovich explores how these platform technologies have had a profound impact on the emergence of global visual cultures. Due to their ability to level certain restrictions of space and time, these devices of connectivity have opened the door to a collectively produced visual iconography of hitherto unknown dimensions. In this context, Manovich is concerned with the specific case of Instagram, the way it has given rise to a particular form of popular photography, which he calls Instagramism, and how this mode of cultural expression sits within a hegemonic genealogy of social norms, political orders, and artistic styles. In Manovich's interrogation of the democratic potential of such a mass movement, the key questions become: what visions of the world are offered by this new phenomenon of Instagramism, and how can such globally shared modalities of production be conceptualized vis-a-vis widely attested monopole strategies of highly capitalized tech corporations? With regard to the latter, Manovich proposes the terms *aesthetic society* and *aesthetic worker* in order to grasp the coalescence of social and economic values operative in the promotion of 21st century lifestyle subjectivities.

At the heart of Instagramism, Manovich locates a global digital youth class traversing ever-changing landscapes of structured cultures, wherein different aesthetics are often characterized in opposition to each other, employed as a means of expressing tribal aspirations and belonging. The purpose of designed Instagram photos, then, is to act as evidence of "immersion in life": a life that is meaningful and satisfying. Hence, a demonstration of "being in the scene" has become key to the composition of Instagram aesthetics. Manovich identifies a range of different strata, which overlap and blur in these demonstrations of real life, ranging from a preference for mood and atmosphere over concrete events to an emphasis on improvisation and strategies of defamiliarization. What most of them have in common is a break with long-standing conventions of binary orders such as natural/artificial, high/low culture, etc. In doing so, Instagramism follows in the footsteps of many other new digitally enabled, disruptive spheres, happily ignoring long-standing rules or obligations associated with context while unashamedly raiding its environments for whatever might be of interest at the moment. This attitude fuels an obsession with capturing the here and now that needs to be constantly replenished. Echoing the concern of many other authors in this volume about time as the increasingly all-determining factor for "survival" in today's rapidly evolving data-scapes, Manovich alerts us to how in contemporary visual aesthetics, too, as exemplified by Instagram feeds, content (i.e., the substance and meaning of singular events) is increasingly losing traction compared to the relevance of the sequence (i.e., how things occur in relation to an endless mass of other things). Grappling with the implications of this disjuncture matters if we truly want to understand how contemporary realities, in which not just millions of fashion-hungry young people, as on Instagram, but everybody participates, are shaped simultaneously by the techno-logics of new communicative infrastructures and the ever evolving ways in which they are used.

Ravi Sundaram's concluding chapter, "Publics or post-publics? Contemporary expression after the mobile phone", acts as a pertinent reminder of the global impact of and seismic shift of power tectonics engendered/ provoked by the rapid spread of mobile media devices. As capacities to generate, share, and circulate audio-visual captures and representations of public events expand from the monopole of so-called legitimate bodies (government agencies, established news outlets, etc.) to unlimited numbers of individuals who happen to be at a certain place at a particular time, long-standing orders of authority over the distribution of information, the interpretation of right and wrong, and the certification of truth are also called into question. Crucially, Sundaram focuses his analysis of these transformative processes on the impulses driving individuals' participation in the creation of such new strata of collective engagement. As he points out, throughout modernity, concepts of collective formation have often been torn between opposing assertions of violent, uncontrollable, inherently illogical aggregations of anarchic masses on the one hand and a lulled passive public kept apathetic in their private spaces by manipulative consumer media on the other. Yet today, against the backdrop of increasingly sensor-equipped environments geared toward feeding calculative infrastructures and operations, these concepts fail to grasp the complex interaction and simultaneous segregation of content and process/performance at work in contemporary media-oriented theaters of power.

As Sundaram highlights, what we are confronted with today is a situation of blurred boundaries and hierarchies, in which public affect is no longer manageable through top-down governance but has turned into a fiercely contested marketplace of atmospheric media, which in turn is heavily reliant on generating and maintaining forms of multifaceted attachment both through infrastructural means and socio-aesthetic enmeshments. Being particularly concerned with the post-colonial context of countries like India, Sundaram examines recent tendencies to "informalize" modes of governance by way of appropriating third-party media channels for the dissemination of strategically and tactically placed messages. This interaction between structures of power and social media platforms controlled by global corporations, Sundaram stresses, does not just illustrate another step in the advancement of neoliberalism but heralds a significant paradigm shift in the relationship between representation and order. In an environment in which the value of experience is given precedence over everything else, the search for constant updates, a default setting of continuous circulation in which the present is rendered as a series of disruptive events, begins to override everything else. In this state of indeterminacy, spheres of intimate and public life become blurred, concepts of truth are suspended, and the closure of representation is deferred indefinitely. Similarly, collective attachment is no longer structured around pre-constituted entities but unfolds through splintered moments of experience. These developments pose fundamental challenges when it comes to the conceptualization of notions of public in our era of personalized mobile media: when private messaging groups become the primary source of information "every action is now potentially public", giving rise to new forms of "post-public" agglomerations. However, as Sundaram, referencing Miriam Hansen, suggests, this crisis condition of new media might also trigger groundbreaking ideas for a new "political ecology of the senses".

## Notes

1 In a Foucauldian sense, the term "techniques of governmentality" refers to processes through which populations shape their own conduct according to particular aims and expectations. More often than not, these processes are not directly initiated by governments but relayed within the guise of intermediaries and institutions.
2 For further reading, see Lilly Irani's *Chasing Innovation: Making Entrepreneurial Citizens in Modern India* (2019).
3 Reprinted in Dalton, *Primitive Archaic and Modern Economies* (1968).
4 Aiming to make Europe fit for the digital age, the European Commission's official website describes the regulation as "an essential step to strengthen individuals' fundamental rights in the digital age and facilitate business by clarifying rules for companies and public bodies in the digital single market". European Commission, "Data Protection in the EU".
5 "The proper functioning of the internal market requires that the free movement of personal data within the Union is not restricted or prohibited for reasons connected with the protection of natural persons with regard to the processing of personal data". REGULATION (EU) 2016/679 OF THE EUROPEAN PARLIAMENT AND OF THE COUNCIL, L 119/1.
6 Ibid, article (2), L 119/1.
7 Ibid, article (7), L 119/2.
8 Evidenced, for instance, in the GDPR's stipulation that "flows of personal data . . . are necessary for the expansion of international trade". Ibid, article (101), L 119/19.
9 In his contribution to modern liberal democratic theory C. B. Macpherson introduced the term "possessive individualism" to point out how in a society ruled by the market, social bonds are rendered as a network of exchange between proprietors.
10 Other data scholars have offered critical studies of data, illuminating its "constructedness" (Drucker), its materiality (Dourish, Blanchette), and its site specificity (Loukissas). See *Graphesis* (Drucker, 2014), *The Stuff of Bits* (Dourish, 2017), 'A Material History of Bits' (Blanchette, 2011), and *All Data Are Local* (Loukissas, 2019).

## References

Blanchette, J. (2011), 'A material history of bits', *Journal of the American Society for Information Science and Technology*, 62(6), pp. 1042–1057.
Brenner, N. (2017), 'Is tactical urbanism an alternative to neoliberal urbanism?', in N. Brenner (ed.), *Critique of Urbanization*. Basel: Bauwelt Fundamente Series, Birkhäuser Verlag, pp. 128–146.
Butler, J. (2005), *Giving an Account of Oneself*. New York: Fordham University Press.

Butler, J. (2010), 'Longing for recognition', in Kimberly Hutchings and Tuija Pulkkinen (eds.), *Hegel's Philosophy and Feminist Thought: Breaking Feminist Waves*. New York: Palgrave Macmillan, pp. 109–129.

Butler, J. (2015), *Notes Towards a Performative Theory of Assembly*. Cambridge, MA: Harvard University Press.

Canetti, E. (1962), *Crowds and Power*, trans. Carol Stewart. New York: The Viking Press, pp. 16–25.

Chomsky, N. (2012), *Occupy*. London: Penguin Books.

Deleuze, G. and Guattari, F. (1972), *Anti-Oedipus*, trans. Robert Hurley, Mark Seem and Helen R. Lane. London and New York: Continuum, 2004. Trans. of *L'Anti-Oedipe*. Paris: Les Editions de Minuit.

Deleuze, G. and Guattari, F. (1980), *A Thousand Plateaus: Capitalism and Schizophrenia*, trans. and foreword B. Massumi. Minneapolis: University of Minnesota Press, 1987. Trans. of *Mille plateaux*. Paris: Les Editions de Minuit.

Dourish, P. (2017), *The Stuff of Bits: An Essay on the Materialities of Information*. Cambridge, MA: MIT Press.

Drucker, J. (2014), *Graphesis: Visual Forms of Knowledge Production*. Cambridge, MA: Harvard University Press.

European Commission (2018), '2018 reform of EU data protection rules'. Available at: https://ec.europa.eu/commission/priorities/justice-and-fundamental-rights/data-protection/2018-reform-eu-data-protection-rules_en#abouttheregulationanddataprotection.

European Commission (2018), 'Data protection in the EU'. Available at: https://ec.europa.eu/info/law/law-topic/data-protection/data-protection-eu_en.

Feher, M. (2018), *Rated Agency. Investee Politics in a Speculative Age*. New York: Zone Books.

Foucault, M. (1977–78), *Security, Territory, Population: Lectures at the Collège de France, 1977-78*. Ed. M. Senellart, trans. G. Burchell. London: Palgrave Macmillan, 2007.

Hardt, M. and Negri, A. (2004), *Multitude: War and Democracy in the Age of Empire*. London: Penguin, p. 203.

Jameson, F. (1991), *Postmodernism: Or, The Cultural Logic of Late Capitalism*. Durham, NC: Duke University Press, p. 44.

Loukissas, Y.A. (2019), *All Data Are Local: Thinking Critically in a Data-Driven Society*. Cambridge, MA: MIT Press.

Macpherson, C.B. (1962), *The Political Theory of Possessive Individualism: Hobbes to Locke*. New York: Oxford University Press.

Morozov, E. (2012), *The Net Delusion: How Not to Liberate the World*. London: Penguin Books.

Musil, R. (1953), *The Man Without Qualities*, Vol. I. London: Secker & Warburg.

Ong, A. (1999), *Flexible Citizenship: The Cultural Logics of Transnationality*. Durham, NC: Duke University Press.

Ong, A. (2006), *Neoliberalism as Exception: Mutations in Citizenship and Sovereignty*. London and Durham, NC: Duke University Press.

Polanyi, K. (1947), 'Our obsolete market mentality: Civilization must find a new thought pattern', *Commentary*, 3, pp. 109–117.

Polanyi, K. (1968), *Primitive, Archaic and Modern Economies: Essays of Karl Polanyi*, ed. George Dalton. Garden City, NY: Doubleday Anchor.

REGULATION (EU) 2016/679 OF THE EUROPEAN PARLIAMENT AND OF THE COUNCIL of 27 April 2016, article (13), *Official Journal of the European Union*, 4.5.2016, L 119/3.

Somers, M. (2008), *Genealogies of Citizenship: Markets, Statelessness, and the Right to Have Rights*. Cambridge: Cambridge University Press.

Willig, R. (2012), 'Recognition and critique: An interview with Judith Butler', *Distinktion: Scandinavian Journal of Social Theory*, 13(1), pp. 139–144.

Wittig, M. (1985), 'The mark of gender', *Feminist Issues*, 5(2), pp. 76–89.

# Part I
# Politics

# 1 In praise of plasticity

## Underspecification, anarchism, machine learning

*Matthew Fuller*

## Plasticities

In neurology, plasticity is the ability of a brain or other system of nerves to adapt, change, grow, and find new forms at multiple scalar levels. It implies the ability to retain, reroute, or develop functions despite damage and for further learning to take place. Drawing on this usage, it is also a technological notion that has a history in adaptive technologies such as the design of power grids in order to manage uneven rates of supply and demand.

In the sense that I want to use it here, it implies the design, construction, or emergence of systematizations, process, and modes of reality-processing that emphasize:

- High degrees of systemic redundancy and acuity understood in terms of W.R. Ashby's concept of "requisite variety" (Ashby, 1964).
- Variation by configurations of responsiveness to internal and external conditions (without being merely autopoietic).
- Expressivity – the ability, through high degrees of granularity and cross-correlation between entities to generate or replicate complex features or processes.

The specific forms of plasticity or, more precisely, what constitutes the grammar of the plastic, which Stuart Kaufmann calls the "physics of semantics" (Kauffman, 2002) of specific formations of plasticity, are key to understanding the politics of computational technologies, since these are often about implementing and stabilizing such physics. The question of plasticity framed in these terms, of course, skirts quite closely to the question of what is natural, laminating it with what is optimal. Another problem to navigate is that of functionalism: descriptions of structures and dynamics should not be taken to imply that they actually fully work or that such a description is all there is to them.

## "Cases"

This chapter aims to examine aspects of logic and mathematics in computing that arrange qualities of plasticity and to address some of the constructivist approaches in Gordon Pask's cybernetics and machine learning and in the political disposition of anarchism that anticipates and works with such a condition in different ways. One suggestion put forward is that the quality of plasticity is arrived at from different conceptual and practical contexts. Furthermore, each grammar of plasticity has different, sometimes antithetical, political and aesthetic textures that characterize and differentiate it (where texture is understood in terms of the compositional array of speeds, granularities, idioms, grammars, and capacities for articulation that make up an expressive substance, however abstract they may be). A second consequence, then, is to try to articulate an understanding of forms of plasticity, of what is rendered mutable or immutable, as a way of understanding a more general reckoning of political, technical, and aesthetic compositions.

There is a certain speculative stupidity in bringing together these various "cases" of plasticity. The proposal here is not that there is any absolute equivalence between them, but that there are possible affinities that are suggestive. Cybernetics and machine learning are clearly related by a technical and philosophical genealogy explicitly concerned with forms of generality and with learning through interaction. Anarchism is significant in this context as an attempt to render learning, transformation, and an un-preformatting of political structure-in-process as part of a constitutive practice. The imperative to have the widest degree of redundancy or requisite variety in decision-making is a guiding force. Anarchism can be described, only partially, as an experimental political protocol that produces and is engendered by publics, one that emphasizes information processing as a form of collective intelligence. It is to this end that these cases can be brought together. Such comparative work always involves the articulation of a certain latitude of translation in which syntheses, differentiations, and distinctions must be made, but which in turn allows for a certain register of plasticity in itself.

One of the things that will be readily observed is that all three of the cases here concern the question of learning in different ways and understand learning as a form of undergoing, as a transformation of different sorts. It is their capacity for such transformation without "bottoming out" or entirely breaking, that perhaps characterizes something of their commonality. Learning is a form of transmogrification, of technical systems, of society and individuals, of relations between data that result from plasticity, but that also refine it.

## Plasticity vs. flexibility

To shift these three cases sideways slightly, as we know from art – the plastic arts – the term of formation of plasticity and the stakes it entails are played out in different "media", in each case with consequences. And to make another such shift, there are also multiple kinds of plasticity and different perspectival conditions in which certain arrangements are experienced as plastic, whilst they may not be so experienced from other such conditions, some of which are played out in different forms of economics, not all of which are congenial. One might assemble a short history of recent ways in which Western economies have imposed kinds of plasticity, each with different costs, and systems for the allocation of risk and cost, where the political capacity to render something plastic is an index of power. The 1970s achieved a plasticity in wages and prices via inflation; the 1980s saw an increase in state debt and cuts to social expenditure as means of rendering certain grammars of plasticity operative; and in the long present, austerity and the extension of private debt, coupled with an emerging phase of nationalisms to break up other kinds of fluidity, are part of the physics of semantics arrayed around the necessity to guarantee and to concentrate rates of profit. Such forms of plasticity are indeed better described as flexibility.

What entities are rendered plastic: what entities are said to exist, what is their degree of expressivity, and to what means or entities is this plasticity rendered? In such conditions, what looks like plasticity from one direction can be undergone as flexibility from another. An increasing majority of work has become like data: modular, low paid, and deskilled. Alternatively, such roles tend to the needs of systemic elements that are only required, as David Graeber notes, for the purposes of maintaining structures that have no direct social purpose (Graeber, 2018). Work contracts become as restrictive and unprotected as the terms and conditions of use for apps and websites. Under a general parametricism of contracts, jobs become simply platforms for self-employment. Working lives are reconstructed under vertically imposed grammars of flexibility that negate plasticity.[1]

Innovation too often means doing something via technology with less quality control, worse contracts, and more externalization of risk into the social. At the same time we are seeing the development of what Siva Vaidhyanathan calls "data imperialism", which sees anything pre-existing it (streets, books, languages, medical data) simply as raw material for private digitalization (2012). Such processes extend to the strip-mining of the social and the biological via social, health, and administrative data.

Along with these two tendencies, we are seeing the trashing of ecologies in order to stabilize rates of profit euphemized as growth. That is to say, this is a form of plasticity being written into the Earth by cartels, monopolies, and the violence of accumulation in the claustrophobic mania of capital at a moment when there is precious little left to accumulate from.

We are also undergoing a period in which publics are becoming incoherent to themselves, and old kinds of clarity are offered as a salve. Many societal problems are now so complex that there is no time to adequately compute them using the available institutional, organizational, or other decision-making resources. This is further complicated by the fact that they are made to fit into crude and large-scale systems of binaries, such as referenda and two-party elections that are mismatched either to the nuance or to the fundamental questions that are posed to them. Furthermore, when there are rarely apportioned opportunities to make a significant rather than superficial decision – that is to say, one with consequences – the temptation is to make the wrong choice, that of maximal systemic distress, simply to see what happens. One example of this is the UK holding the Brexit referendum based on a simple majority. There is insufficient granularity and traction of decision-making when compared to the amount of social and economic distress to which people are exposed.

The condition of crises makes things plastic – reformattable – in multiple ways. But it also invites a tendency to political cruelty and ostensive simplification. These factors, and others, make a political and aesthetic understanding of the grammars of plasticity compelling, but also suggest a need to differentiate them from the violence of flexibility.

## Pask: underspecification

In the pursuit of such an understanding, the first "case" of a form of plasticity I want to examine was delineated by Gordon Pask, a cybernetician whose aims included making maximally un-preprogrammed technologies (Pickering, 2010).[2] The particular term of interest here is "underspecification". This term is used to describe the avoidance of overdesign that might preclude the development or use of an object or system and thus forms a kind of plasticity out of a certain kind of reticence or humbleness in engineering. The architect and technologist Usman Haque describes the implications of underspecification in Pask's work as follows:

> If . . . a designed construct can choose what it senses, either by having ill-defined sensors or by dynamically determining its own perceptual categories, then it moves a step closer to true autonomy which would be required in an authentically interactive system.
>
> (Haque, 2007)

A technology would thus learn its uses by being receptive to its environment and could in turn develop a means of communicating with that environment as part of its general existence (Pask, 1976). At the same time, underspecification is an approach that focuses on what can be done, on being no more than adequate, non-totalizing, but having a more than functional capaciousness. An underspecified system is overtly finite, not precisely tailored to any single job, and its disposition with regard to potential relations is adaptive (Cariani, 1993). It thus works against mere functionalism by remaining predisposed to iteration and combination.

Further, if the plasticity of a system can be partially described by how much information it may hold, process, or embody and by the potential sets of relations between the states that together comprise that measure of information, underspecification emphasizes the latter as also being informational. Developing this, Pask's later writings on what he called "conversation theory" (1975) introduced a model of interaction in which reciprocities of relations that are asymmetrical in kind, rate, and reason can be incorporated into a dynamic model of co-composition. Consequently, his work on the penumbra of information that is lost by more apparently straightforward approaches to information systems suggested that "a control system could be built which evolved its own relevance criteria" (Pask, 1958). More broadly, under-specification has what can be called an ethical relation to time: things should be made such that their function can be reinvented, such that they can be coupled with other things and do not pre-empt the future. (Pask, 1969)[3]

This approach informed Pask's frequent involvement in architectural projects, such as Cedric Price and Joan Littlewood's Fun Palace designed for the Lea Valley in East London, a virtuoso elaboration of a plastic, interactive, and programmable architectural form.[4] More broadly, in urban planning, under-specification can be described in a number of ways: for instance, with reference to areas that are defined by the imperative for "minimum spatial definition, maximum social utilization" that anthropologist Franco la Cecla finds in the Sagrera district of Barcelona, implying a way of inhabiting spaces that are "not too encumbered either by the architecture or by the rules" (2012).

Under-specification is a useful technological thread to follow as a kind of anticipatory humbleness, but also as an ability to undergo change in the process of being worked out and worked on. The vocabulary is slightly different, the apparatus distinct, but we will also find related technological concerns in the development of neural networks, a technology that subtends certain aspects of machine learning.

Equally, I want to argue, we will also find some of these qualities in the self-understanding of anarchism as a confluence of political ideas and forms of activity. In this regard, anarchism can be understood as a political approach that emphasizes flows of information, not merely as a means of equitable distribution and democratic access, but also as a process of transformation. This has made it particularly attuned to present struggles over information. Anarchist approaches to information have often been complexly entangled with information politics more broadly in the age of the internet, sometimes, in spoken and unspoken ways, providing a key model for them and a driver of the development of networks, but also finding it difficult to respond to the consolidation of the large-scale monopolies that characterize much internet structure today. Rather than focusing on these specific concerns, however, the aim here is to discuss the development of a loose working concept of plasticity.

## Anarchism as an information politics

As a movement and disposition predicated on the abolition of all hierarchy, anarchism lends itself readily to being understood as an underspecified form of politics, one that is always minimal, requiring that politics must always be invented. This is so partly because the question of what constitutes hierarchy, what is necessarily and unnecessarily so, is a changing phenomenon. As Noam Chomsky remarks, "Anarchism, in my view, is an expression of the idea that the burden of proof is always on those who argue that authority and domination are necessary" (1996). Classically, this combination of political minimalism is aimed at the liberty of individual entities within the society, whether an individual or a collective of any size, ranging from a small group to a large federation, based upon equality. Mikhail Bakunin partners the striving for equality with the need for collective labor on the one hand and knowledge and learning on the other (1984, p. 53). As Bakunin suggests, "The people can only be happy and free when, organized from below by means of its own autonomous and completely free associations, without the supervision of any guardians, it will create its own life" (1984, p. 63). These qualities of equality and collectivity and the transformative necessity of learning are crucial to the characteristics of anarchism as an information politics.

Anarchism in this sense is a general unfolding of revolt and of a reorganization of life in ways that tend to work against processes and forms that can be characterized as authoritarian – that is, seeing hierarchy as a stable fact of life that only need be reorganized for justice to be properly arranged. The principles of refusing hierarchy and extending mutuality and solidarity proliferate into questions of gender, ecology, species, epistemology, and, in the work of Murray Bookchin (1971) and others, into the design and disposition of technologies.

In some of the early texts of what would become anarchism, and in particular anarchist communism, attention is paid to the circulation of information about political decisions and news, as well as new scientific, technical, and agricultural knowledge. Gerrard Winstanley's *The Law of Freedom in a Platform* (1652) is a remarkable proposition for a reform of the commonwealth after the English Revolution began to constrict under Cromwell. Here, Winstanley emphasizes the potential role of a postal service and the parish as a means of circulating and gathering news of progress on these fronts. Peter Kropotkin's *Fields, Factories and Workshops of Tomorrow* (1899), though published 250 years later, also makes clear that all new information and discoveries are to be shared. Like Winstanley, Kropotkin is attuned to the question of decision-making processes as a form of justice.

### Direct action

This question of the justice implicit in political decision – making runs through anarchist thought, providing a constant source of contestation about, for instance, the grounds on which a decision or a political description or account can be made. Privilege, even extending to characters such as William Morris, has always been an inspiration for denunciation or questioning – for instance, by Dan Chatterton, the hand-to-mouth publisher of tracts and the zine-like "Chatterton's Commune, the Atheist Communistic Scorcher" (Szczelkun, 1990; Whitehead, 1988) – since it entailed a lack of experiential and positional knowledge. This remains a core characteristic of anarchist movements, being both a valuable intersectional checking mechanism and also, at times, as Nietzsche noted in the 19th century, a means of conformism and a problem of normativity (1887), which Ursula Le Guin explores in her novel *The Dispossessed* (1974).[5]

Further, there is a strong tendency to produce systems of living and of decision-making that tend toward a preclusion of hierarchy and the maintenance of privilege, often involving the deliberated adoption of marginal geographic, economic, and social positions in order to do so.[6] Those excluded from modernist logics may also actively refuse them. And it is this focus on activity that also plays a significant role. Here the emphasis on direct action is key. Direct action works as a form of engaging directly with a problem and thus learning more about it, even perhaps overcoming it,[7] but it also works as a form of theory through doing and setting a "prefigurative" (C. Boggs, 1977) example without having the requirement – indeed, resisting any impulse – to posit such an example as an end point. Here, such approaches blend readily with imperatives of community activism of the kinds also discussed by Grace Lee Boggs (2011) and Colin Ward (1973), to name but two. At the same time, just as there is an opposition to representational politics, it also works as a form of nonrepresentational theory that works directly with the historical and material conditions it is presented with. As such, what the autonomia of the 1970s called the "archipelago of movements" (Goddard, 2018) are able to grapple with the substances of ideas, contradictions, crises, subjectivation and the difficulties and possibilities of organizing in a way that is appropriate to the problem being addressed. Direct action, organized around problems as they are collaboratively articulated by the people who face them, is thus key to anarchist forms of knowledge.

Indeed, at certain points, an ethics of direct action implies a suspicious relation to the way certain kinds of act, such as speech, lend themselves to evasive representations. A crystalline example is Gerrard Winstanley's statement, in the urgent pamphlet of 1649, *A Watch-Word to the City of London and the Armie*, "That words and writings were all nothing, and must die, for action is the life of all, and if thou dost not act, thou dost nothing". In an era dominated by climate damage and political systems that are incapable of dealing with the problems that they have co-constructed, such an imperative returns with full force. Nevertheless, such an imperative runs the risk of implying an uncomplicated relationship to the truth.

This kind of *thinking through action* renders anarchism, in some respects, close to various currents in the arts[8] or to cultural currents in which rebellion is worked on as a form of embodied knowledge. As a result, it can also inherit varying difficulties and presumptions. Perhaps curiously, though, there is also a certain commonality here with theorists such as Foucault who refuse to identify or to work with the accretions of an ideological position such as anarchism per se, rather preferring to let the ideas or actions, and actions within ideas, *speak for themselves*, or to be understood as nuanced and multiplexly contingent rather than readily available and derivable from a set of universal principles.

## Learning as transformation

Chomsky also makes the argument that anarchism is a particular approach to politics that is formulated as a process of learning and experiment. The currently established forms of politics redirect peoples' intelligence towards non-issues, relatively harmless grounds for its elaboration, unless, due to some glitch, of which there are plenty, some traction is given to the extent that a problem can be made. The early anarchist writer William Godwin emphasized education as a key factor in politics. Education and the capacity for thought became, in his work, a threshold around which a free politics could be formed or could not be. Learning, in turn, acts as a meta-categorical process in which direct action and struggle become the crucial modes. Society, movements, and individuals learn by engaging directly with problems that may be highly concrete or more general, such as the nature of justice and equality. Consequently, the correct form of organization adequate to a problem, one that does not overdetermine it or make the organization into something that unnecessarily outlasts the problem and takes on a life of its own, remains an ongoing question.

This approach is echoed by Rudolf Rocker, who says,

> I am an anarchist not because I believe anarchism is the final goal, but because I believe that there is no such thing as a final goal. Freedom will lead us to a continually wider and expanding understanding and to new forms of social life.
>
> (Rocker, 2005, p. 111)

This open-ended pragmatism is partially paralleled by certain aspects of "reformist" politics (for instance those of John Maynard Keynes in his emphasis on politics as an art of the provisional) (Mann, 2017) and the molecular politics described by Guattari and others, which rely for their inventiveness on the capacity of people to continually work intelligence into their conditions and, as such, rework them, but it also entails questions around instituting, or the creation of organizations, which in turn has its own aesthetic dimension, albeit one that is also functional and political.[9]

One of the key questions becomes that of whether there is sufficient time for the information processing of the collective to occur in relation to the specific problem with which it is faced or even to constitute itself as such. The search for an optimal or appropriate decision and action becomes a formative constraint. This gives rise to organizational forms such as the assembly, the worker's council or soviet, affinity groups or small collectives, forms of federation using delegates typical of anarcho-syndicalism, and individualism (Leval, 1975).[10] It also gives rise to many of the primary critiques of anarchist methods, in that structures such as party formations are seen to be better at parsing information and arriving at decisions within shorter periods of time. The traditional response is that these deprive participants of liberty and the chance to learn – Lenin described anarchism and left-wing communism as infantile disorders. However, the condition of the infant is one that implies learning and refoundation. As Jack Halberstam remarks, "If kids were not anarchistic then we would not need to train them" (2014). What is suggested here is that anarchism is a deliberately underspecified form of politics, one with great implicative latitude. Indeed, further to the catalogue of forms listed earlier, one can observe with Lucy Parsons that the "reinvention of daily life means marching off the edge of our maps" (2003).

Here, I want to suggest that the emphasis on learning through struggle and direct action as a form of learning coupled with the imperative to find appropriate forms of organizing or instituting such learning, whilst also maintaining the flexibility and openness that enables a capacity to move beyond a problem or a settled condition, articulates a dual condition in which anarchist forms of plasticity emerge. There is a double imperative that acts to instigate learning through engagement with problems and an egalitarian attention to the structures by which such learning is made, which together create a method of working that, when undertaken without dogmatism, creates the capacity for the kind of freedom that Rocker proposes.

The neurology of plasticity from Vygotsky onward describes learning as transformation. This is not something that simply works for organisms but also organizations. It is an approach to information processing and information production that, contra Shannon (1948), does not just imply, but requires, transformation. Such an understanding of transformation implies an art to the composition of learning, which is again to be worked on by the double imperative to work directly on problems and to maintain an egalitarian inquiry into the means of working.

It will be relatively swiftly recognized that such a pair of working methods bears some relation to much of the pragmatic working of technical teams in current software development, scientific research, and other relatively advanced forms of knowledge organization. And there is a rich set of potentially diverging and interwoven pathways that arise here (Stengers, 2018). For instance, a social formation builds a hospital so as to have the capacity to respond to illnesses and promote health. Over time, in order to improve such work, there is a requirement that the organization itself grow. In turn, as the extent of relevant knowledge grows, there is a tendency to partial specialization of equipment, people, skills, and teams that potentially works against equality. The more directly and precisely such work and learning is brought to bear on problems entailing learning, the more it is prone to difficulties in spreading information. Here, the interplay between problem and egalitarianism, whilst actively doing the work of medicine in the timeframe of peoples' actual lives, creates potential conditions for a paradox. How is the collective to maintain this developmental trajectory without producing a second-order structure (perhaps verbose meetings of the hospital soviet or, worse, a distinct managerial class) that feeds off and slows down or impedes the aims of the hospital? Dealing with the information that arises in such circumstances simply through its own impetus or growth entailed in dealing with a problem creates a potential for separation that may undermine egalitarian possibilities, which, in turn, have to be incorporated by other means.

Alternatively, the question of knowledge as direct action, as working on a problem, helps to fend off the idea that an idealized version of some particular subject – for instance, the proletariat – will undergo an instance of transubstantiation at the right moment that will allow it to "know" what it immanently knows. Moreover, it articulates the way in which, for instance, those who are most intimately knowledgeable about a social problem are often those who suffer or undergo it, and are thus best able to lead or determine ways of going beyond it – as can be readily seen in feminism, movements opposing racism, or in the struggles for indigenous rights. In the face of knowledge as direct action, as involvement, one has, hopefully, to maintain the task of not being annihilated by the problem and those that seek to maintain it, as in the cases of resistance to fascism, tsarism, etc. or to find means of reckoning with that annihilation in dark times.

Knowledge as direct action also involves experimental practices: those of art, as has been mentioned, but also practices more broadly relating to the formation of knowledge. Rather than, for instance, assuming that a solely human collective is able to resolve a problem, we might consider the possibility that a solution could involve non-human elements: mathematical entities, a river, a certain type of medication, and so on. Such elements might provide the problem of knowing with sufficient grist – that is to say, difficulty – to enable a capacity for it to be worked on. A problem becoming an unspoken member of a collective and thereby operating as a trauma, the elephant in the room, is one way this might happen. However, its becoming an explicit participant may be one way in which the imperatives of egalitarianism and direct action open themselves up to question.

## Machine learning

The immense bequest of both flexibility *and* plasticity that computing inherited from the universal Turing machine and the earlier mathematical logic it drew on creates a problem for understanding its impact. Computing effects different fields of culture, politics, knowledge, and so on variably, because they, and the elements they contain, are interpolated differently by diverse aspects of computational and networked structures and because they are, in turn, taken up by different economic and social formations. In short, the saturation of contemporary life with computational forms renders the comparative work of distinction tricky. Given this, it is interesting to look at machine learning as a technology of plasticity, one that is sufficiently nuanced to carry and sustain such diversity whilst shifting its grounds into a condition with its own particularities. It is these qualities in relation to the question of plasticity that allow for both such a diversity of manifestation and a more general re-articulation through the very particularities of such generality that are of interest here.

Machine learning is a broad field comprising aspects of artificial intelligence, Bayesian probability, information theory, control theory, analyses of computational complexity, cognitive science, statistics, and other areas. Indeed, it can be seen as a way of working around some of the relatively intractable problems in each of these fields by introducing work-arounds via the techniques inherited from other fields. Machine learning focuses on the development of software, and some hardware, that allow for inferences to be made about data. Such inferences might include, or lead to, pattern recognition, prediction, analysis, and so on. The term *learning* is applicable because over time, and with exposure to more data, the programs concerned are trained to adapt to the data, thereby allowing for the fine-tuning of these inferences.

Machine learning answers the vast nameless obscurity of contemporary life with a vast nameless obscurity of its own. If discourse is a murmur, then machine learning aims to map a murmuration of murmurs. The murmurs of people on networks; the background noises of homes and offices; the decisions and orders; the gropings for some kind of insight; the dull repetitive watching that must be done in order to participate, to send emails, to shoot opponents, to shop, to like, to depict – all the events that have not quite yet articulated themselves into what is deemed to be culture proper, a kind of effluent with no meaning as such except in its conjunction with other such things – all this can be sifted, reworked and watched for long enough such that some kind of glimmer is found within it. The vast nameless obscurity records and sifts, analyzes, predicts, interprets, finds patterns and correlations. It congeals something sufficient for other work to be done.

But this is merely a romantic reading. Machine learning is the latest iteration of a set of techniques initiated in the 1950s, parallel to the experiments of Pask and others, which aim to create something logically malleable enough to take an impression of the world and to assign values to that impression (Anderson and Rosenfeld, 1998). As a historical entity, it has had its moments of being an outcast (as for instance in the "AI Winter"), and, as an entity that tries to mobilize itself within capitalism, it has also been rebranded, rejigged, and given a few jolts of stimulus. One of these has been the massive increase in the capacity of computing; another has been the avalanche of new kinds of data, often in highly unstructured forms, to which, compared to other approaches based on more static formations, along with new forms of storage, database design, and programming language, it is more finely attuned (Anderson and Rosenfeld, 1998). Machine learning is a technology predicated on the capacity to map phenomena with high levels of granular detail and to use the accretion and the analysis of such mappings to generate new data. As such, a crucial form of the plasticity it embodies is described by its capacities of expression.

## Expressivity

The expressivity of a configuration is determined by:

- The degrees of granularity of analysis (what constitutes a significant difference, and what scale of weighting in value is used to mark such differences in training and in actual use).
- The degrees of freedom or interpretation allocated to each of those granular entities. That is to say, within what rules of association with other such entities, such as their logical "neighbors", do the granular entities operate?

Together, the granularity of these entities and the rule sets and structures that articulate them in relation to each other produce their texture. The particular texture of expression that is established by a system is a key part of its function as a technical, social, cultural, and scientific operator.

The plasticity of a system is textured by the extent of the granularity in such mappings as they are established in the internal representations of the program or system. As computer scientist Tom Mitchell puts it in his early book on this field, "The more expressive the representation, the more training data the program will require in order to choose among the alternative hypotheses it can represent"(Mitchell, 1997, p. 8). That is to say, the more dimensions a problem has, the more expressive the representation required to map it, the more data is required to make something like a trained choice. In such a condition, "learning a feature is equivalent to searching for a transformation that stabilizes it" (Paul and Venkatasubramanian, 2015, p. 2). Furthermore, each of the kinds of structure used in machine learning, such as linear functions, logical descriptions, decision trees, artificial neural networks, and many others, all have their idiomatic expressive characteristics, the particular *texture* of plasticity that they afford. Each has the propensity to stabilize different sets of features with more acuity, something that is being worked out as the array of techniques is elaborated in practice (Mackenzie, 2017). As Mitchell suggests, however, expressivity is resource intensive, and indeed, it is an old problem; in 1814 Laplace (1902), for instance, famously ruminated on the question of how many atoms in the universe it takes to express the position of all atoms in the universe. This remains a question, but the language by which it is articulated has changed – now we talk about it in terms of NP computation (nondeterministic polynomial – a calculation of the likelihood of a calculation being solvable within a given time and set of computational resources). Access to computational resources becomes a question of access to the means of plasticity in these terms. There are a number of consequences.

Firstly, along with the question of the texture of plasticity afforded by such systems, the political economy of plasticity becomes a bittersweet reminder of the distribution of other kinds of capacity. The concentrations of computing resources produce gravity wells into which the plasticity of machine learning is itself drawn, along with the concomitant deformations of the conditions of possibility that they imply. Secondly and equally, the wider framing of the enterprise that works with the machine-learning project shapes its capacity. The machines that train the machines to be trained trainers have, in turn, their retainers: that is, their various short or long tethers to the creation of profit or control (the algebraic emphasis on each shifting according to which version of the internet pertains in the particular state-form concerned), rendering their degree of relation to jargon words such as *disruption* and *innovation* and, indeed, their relation to "disinterested" curiosity-driven research rather moot.[11] Thirdly, the need and the capacity to learn have transformed the condition of computing in many respects. Because of the present differentials in the capacity of corporate versus other organizations to centralize and analyze data, hire researchers, and "convene" problem sets, as well as to integrate machine learning into complicated products such as cars, it has done less transformative work for the wider matrices in which computing is embedded. A question hovers on the horizon, however, and that is whether the centralization of power aggregated by these companies necessarily entails a significant risk once they become sufficiently detached from the grounds upon which they were gestated.

Complicating, but also vindicating, this critical line of inquiry is the simple fact that machine learning projects as a set of interesting techniques are possible to actualize on multiple scales, including those with high degrees of independence and low levels of resources. The expressivity of machine learning thus has a degree of autonomy from its historical conditions but is also increasingly woven into them. The texture of that weave is also significant and is a crucial factor in understanding its plasticity.

## Textures of computing

Data may be being dynamically produced in relation to a massive diversity of flows of social media, life streams, medical administrative and diagnostic data, archaeological data, genomics, sensors, models establishing climate damage, and so on, but it is also interpolated through things such as arrays, lists, matrices, indices, file systems, and data formats and integrated into larger database systems. More recently, tensors, which in the machine learning context are elaborated forms of array, allow for data to be manipulated and worked as complexly interwoven fabrics of algebraic relations (Abadi et al., 2015). All of these are what Adrian Mackenzie calls the general "connective tissue" (Mackenzie, 2017, p. 47), provided by standard formulas and equations embedded in software and tangible in the calculations carried out by it. These material formations have consequences in terms of further variations such as processing speed and the degree to which an entity may be analytically isolated and the combinations amongst which it will be matched.[12] Part of this texturing is further reformulated by storing data in hyperdimensional arrays in the newer forms of database system that allow unstructured data. These reduce their liability to be "reformatted", adopting the more general condition in which the technologies work around the limitations of some of the preceding abstraction layers. But there is also a concatenation of different kinds of increasingly plastic forms being elaborated as the heterogeneity of data types, and the increasing dimensionality of the data, drive the form of the data structures employed to handle it.

The texture of computing is thus often highly mutable at certain scales, and hence its power; but it also has certain degrees of intractability that require the workings of further layers of analysis, interpolation, and reworking. Such scales might run from the underlying mathematical domains of number theory and calculability, to forms of logic, to the articulation of sets, through to languages, file formats, data structures, and so on. The question is further complicated by the way in which social forms are recapitulated, complexified, or entrenched as they are digitalized. There is, for instance, work on the texture of computing that aligns and channels plasticity to flexibility at different scales, and the presiding logics of these conditions in turn have consequences in the numerous fields to which the technologies are applied. Indeed, this conflation of plasticity and flexibility is one of many compounds in which inequalities of differing kinds can be entrenched and intensified by being passed off as more plastic.

In a culture that is increasingly digital, the means by which a machine-learning configuration explores the problem-space that is posed to it is already pre-textured by the formats in which the data is stored and active. That is, it may not "get to" the problem concerned at all, but instead engage with multiple layers of mediation of this problem, each with its own degree of slipperiness and intransitivity. As well as providing variegated capacity, these textures of computing, in the wider ensembles and ecologies of which they are a part, require work to render tractable the blockages, difficulties, and crashes that they also are subject to amidst the smooth flows and analyses of data. This work, which entails tweaking procedures, checking operations against the data they yield, and revising the scope and extent of data that is gathered, is, as Mackenzie's *Machine Learners* illustrates in great detail, part of the pragmatics of machine learning as it currently stands and of its expressive potential. This is not to place any false hope in the idea of the human in the loop, but merely to recognize that the vision of all phenomena becoming a data-effusing barium meal making its intricately traceable passage through an efficient stomach of numbers may be subject to certain hiccups. The scale and consistency of such spasms, alongside the constitution of these numerical organs, should be perpetually held up against the question of what kinds of plasticity machine learning establishes. At the same time, the new grounds for experimentation that it offers and the wider kinds of plasticity it may support should be tested.

## Correlations?

It is tempting to see possible correlations between the three cases – the presence not of isomorphisms per se but of affinities that might allow for some kind of mutual recognition and reworking. The question of direct and iterative engagement with a data set as the translation of a problem and allowing the potential loss of control that learning implies have affinities with the idea of direct action and learning through struggle. The political and technical principle of elements being arranged in a way that predisposes the traction of all elements in a polity on a mutual outcome suggests a limited correspondence with the architecture of a neural network, as, in turn, does the principle that information and decision-making are best not bottle-necked by a central node such as a state or that the wealth produced by a society is not best allocated by a particular social class, gender, and so on. Equally, as has been shown, Pask's idea of underspecification has a familial resemblance to the tendentially open structures of machine learning, but also to the emphasis on a minimal political form in anarchism.

It is in their textures – in more or less abstract, more or less concrete terms – that they may partly align or differentiate. Drawing out such affinities must in turn be a matter of an experimental pragmatics that shifts and works amidst a more substantial ground.

## Subtending plasticity

Analyzing the formations of different kinds of plasticity at different scales, including those of politics and technologies, and articulating such plasticity in relationship to the capacity to transform and to learn, entail recognizing not only plasticity but also obduracy, repetition, patterning, interweaving, systematization, symbiosis, and throngs of other kinds of formation as occurring in composition with myriad other dynamics of differing degrees of abstraction and concretization in mutual and discrete ways. I will finish with some notes on these in relation to the question of how plasticity interacts with the condition of individuation.

Once the hegemony of digital computing became established from the 1960s on, Pask's work moved more in this new direction, but it should be noted that in the 1950s, Pask's control systems were designed to "grow" their own sensors, to look for things in the world that might satisfy their "relevance criteria", things that would constitute an event/entity of significance. These were computers made of electro-chemical soups. One thing that is interesting about these experiments is that they took on the question of an open world in which computational entities might self-design in response to the processes of the world. That is to say, the question of plasticity is recursive – one needs a highly expressive medium in which to grow entities and processes that are themselves plastic enough to respond to or to interact with the world. Such a medium should also be stable enough to stay sufficiently consistent for this process to occur fulsomely or be capable itself of transformations that operate at another scale and feed back into the initial conditions.

In this, the question of plasticity meets that of *individuation*. The numerous grounds and conditions in and of which grammars of plasticity iteratively assemble a medium in which individuation takes place and that both recursively shape. No absolute cartography of individuation is conceivable, but there is an interesting relationship between plasticity and individuation that concerns all the cases here in their integral linkage of learning and transformation. In this, they articulate and construct specific scales and textures of working, and of the capacity to work, with all the difficulties that each implies. But in their own transformation, and in their own individuation, they also attempt to tease out something about the nature of becoming in and of itself.

Gilles Deleuze remarks that "Individuation as such, as it operates beneath all forms, is inseparable from a pure ground that it brings to the surface and trails with it" (1968). Each form of individuation here brings its own capacity for expressing and thickening such trailing and bringing to the surface. This is the process of chaosmosis: a version of which Deleuze sees operating in Leibniz's *Theodicy*, where the composition of the world is brought into being by God.

At a more mundane level, one that is indeed pragmatic in its relation to these matters but that, I would argue, in all three of these cases has both explicit and implicit cognizance of this relation to the protean qualities of becoming, as they are gestured toward, mapped, drawn out, textured, modeled, and instantiated, this question of plasticity reiterates the question of chaosmosis as what might be called a design problem. It is hoped that this chapter's comparative approach encourages some glimpses of this chaosmosis in motion in relation to the cases it reflects on as each in different ways attempts to find some capacity to work in some kind of knowing or palpable relation to it.

## Acknowledgments

With thanks to Warren Sack and the Cultural Studies Seminar at UCSC; to Yoshitaka Mouri, Ai Kano, and all others at the Tokyo University of the Arts Graduate School of Global Arts and the Postmedia Research Network, Japan; and to Peter Mörtenböck and Helge Mooshammer for convening this volume.

## Notes

1 This in turn has interesting effects where, as was seen in the strikes by Deliveroo riders in February and March 2019, some of the laws limiting strikes

cannot be applied to the "self-employed" because the design of these laws dates back to the era of mass workers. See https://libcom.org/news/deliveroo-couriers-strike-against-poverty-pay-manchester-26th-feb-23022019.

2 For an account of Pask's work, see Andrew Pickering, *The Cybernetic Brain*.

3 See also Fuller (2017).

4 The development of forms of plasticity in architecture tends to privilege the moment of design rather than of use in some respects. A notable contribution to another genealogy can be found in the work of Oskar Hansen.

5 There is of course a section of the anarchist literature characterized by bitter and boring wrangling over what is and is not in a permissible canon, and by policing operations devoid of curiosity or empathy around the borders are carried out.

6 See, for further on this aspect, books such as Stefano Harney and Fred Moten, 2013, *The Undercommons: Fugitive Planning and Black Study*, Wivenhoe: Minor Compositions; James Koehnline and Ron Sakolsky, eds., 1993, *Gone to Croatan: the Origins of North America Drop Out Culture*, Brooklyn: Autonomedia; Marcus Rediker and Peter Linebaugh, 2001, *The Many-Headed Hydra: Sailors, Slaves, Commoners, and the Hidden History of the Revolutionary Atlantic*, London: Verso; James C. Scott, 2011, *The Art of Not Being Governed: An Anarchist History of Upland Southeast Asia*, New Haven: Yale University Press.

7 Movements as diverse as the anti-nuclear movement, AIDS activism, access to medicine, and anti-gentrification movements have all historically generated high levels of expertise that change the field in which they are active.

8 A strong example of this can be found in the interview with Jacqueline de Jong about the function of the material gathered in the publication she edited, *The Situationist Times*, where she argues against explanation, rather pointing to the magazine's role of simply showing, with readers making their own connections. (See Institute for Computational Vandalism, "Situological Applications: Digitizing the Situationist Times", in Ellef Prestaeter, ed., 2019, *These Are Situationist Times*, Oslo: Torpedo Books, pp 233–245.)

9 See, for an elaboration of such a discussion, Goffey, A., "Guattari and Transversality", *Radical Philosophy* 195 (Jan/Feb 2016) pp 38–47.

10 See also Skirda (2002), Stirner (1844), and (Freeman (1970).

11 See, for one of many such instances, the highly publicized instigation of a "for-profit" branch of the OpenAI initiative in March 2019. That the billionaire funders of this initiative imagine that researchers are primarily motivated by money perhaps indicates the presence of a confirmation bias, but the wider trend of those trained in the physical sciences moving to finance and of AI research moving from universities to businesses is indicative.

12 Processing speed is partly articulated through the number of cycles of calculations and related processes, each algorithm, its associated data structures, and the various abstraction layers that constitute the computing platform, not to mention the quality of the data itself. The field of algorithm analysis works on this question. See, for instance, Donald Knuth, *The Art of Computing Programming*, Reading: Addison-Wesley, ongoing.

# References

Abadi, M., et al. (2015), 'TensorFlow: Large-scale machine learning on heterogeneous distributed systems', arXiv:1603.04467.

Anderson, J.A. and Rosenfeld, E. (1998), *Talking Nets: An Oral History of Neural Networks*. Cambridge, MA: MIT Press.

Ashby, W. (1964), *Introduction to Cybernetics*. London: Methuen.

Bakunin, M. (1984), *Marxism, Freedom and the State*. London: Freedom Press.

Boggs, C. (1977), 'Marxism, prefigurative communism, and the problem of workers' control', *Radical America*, 11(November), p. 100.

Boggs, G.L. with Kurashige, S. (2011), *The Next American Revolution: Sustainable Activism for the Twenty-First Century*. Berkeley: University of California Press.

Bookchin, M. (1971), *Post-Scarcity Anarchism*. New York: Ramparts Press.

Cariani, P. (1993), 'To evolve an ear: Epistemological implications of Gordon Pask's electrochemical devices', *Systems Research*, 10(3), pp. 19–33.

Cecla, F.L. (2012), *Against Architecture*. Oakland: PM Press.

Chomsky, N. (1996), *On Anarchism* [Interview], 23 December 1996.

Deleuze, G. (1968), *Difference and Repetition*. London: Athlone.

Freeman, J. (1970), *The Tyranny of Structurlessness: The Tyranny of Tyranny*. Beulah: s.n.

Fuller, M. (2017), 'Underspecified dreams of parts and wholes', in *5 Designing Media Ecology*. Tokyo: Tokyo University of the Arts.

Goddard, M. (2018), *Guerrilla Networks: An Anarchaeology of 1970s Radical Media Ecologies*. Amsterdam: University of Amsterdam Press.

Graeber, D. (2018), *Bullshit Jobs*. London: Allen Lane.

Guin, U.K.L. (1974), *The Dispossessed*. New York City: Harper & Row.

Halberstam, J. (2014), *The Wild: The Aesthetics of Queer Anarchy*. London: Lecture at Goldsmiths, University of London.

Haque, U. (2007), 'The architectural relevance of Gordon Pask', *Architectural Design*, 77, pp. 54–61.

Kauffman, S.A. (2002), *Investigations*. Oxford: Oxford University Press.

Kropotkin, P. (1899), *Fields, Factories and Workshops*. London: Houghton Mifflin Harcourt.

Laplace, P.S. (1902), *A Philosophical Essay on Probabilities*. London: Chapman & Hall.

Leval, G. (1975), *Collectives in the Spanish Revolution*. London: Freedom Press.

Mackenzie, A. (2017), *Machine Learners: Archaeology of Data Practice*. Cambridge, MA: MIT Press.

Mann, G. (2017), *In the Long Run We Are All Dead*. London: Verso.

Mitchell, T.M. (1997), *Machine Learning*. New York: McGraw Hill.

Nietzsche, F. (1887), *On the Genealogy of Morality*. Cambridge: Hackett Publishing Company Inc.

Parsons, L. (2003), *Freedom, Equality and Solidarity: Writings and Speeches, 1878–1937*. Chicago: Charles H. Kerr Publishing Company.

Pask, G. (1958), *The Growth Process Inside of Cybernetic Machine*. Namur, Belgium: s.n., pp. 765–794.

Pask, G. (1969), 'The architectural relevance of cybernetics', *Architectural Design*, s.l.: s.n., pp. 494–496.

Pask, G. (1975), *Conversation, Cognition and Learning*. New York: Elsevier.

Pask, G. (1976), 'Introduction to aspects of machine intelligence', in N. Negroponte (ed.), *Soft Architecture Machines*. Cambridge, MA: MIT Press.

Paul, A. and Venkatasubramanian, S. (2015), 'Why does deep learning work? – A perspective from group theory', arXiv:1412.6621.

Pickering, A. (2010), *The Cybernetic Brain*. Chicago: University of Chicago Press.

Rocker, R. (2005), *The London Years*. San Francisco: AK Press.

Shannon, C.E. (1948), 'A mathematical theory of communication', *Bell System Technical Journal*, 27(3), pp. 379–423.

Skirda, A. (2002), *Facing the Enemy: A History of Anarchist Organisation from Proudhon to May 1968*. Edinburgh: AK Press.

Stengers, I. (2018), *Another Science Is Possible: A Manifesto for Slow Science*. Cambridge: Polity.

Stirner, M. (1844), *The Ego and Its Own*. s.l.: s.n.

Szczelkun, S. (1990), *Class Myths and Culture*. London: Working Press.

Vaidhyanathan, S. (2012), *The Googlization of Everything (And Why We Should Worry)*. Berkeley: University of California Press.

Ward, C. (1973), *Anarchy in Action*. London: Freedom Press.

Whitehead, A. (1988), 'Dan Chatterton and his "aesthetic communistic scorcher"', *History Workshop Journal*, 25.

Winstanely, G. (1652), *The Law of Freedom in a Platform*. London: s.n.

# 2 Data capitalism, sociogenic prediction, and recursive indeterminacies

*Luciana Parisi and Ezekiel Dixon-Román*

## Introduction

The planetary conquest of data capitalism coincides with the impossibility of thinking beyond the horizon of datafication of the world, whereby data have fused the world with nature. The *becoming data* of the environment is directing perceptions and conceptions of a world in a way that mirrors the self-sufficiency of a system that needs no mediation, no theory, no thought. Data are us, we are told: the gap between capital and the real has shrunk to the infinitesimal point of becoming an immanent state of identification based on variables of variables.

From high-frequency trading to Netflix and Amazon recommendation algorithms, from RankBrain search algorithm to Uber and AirBnB self-profiling platforms to micro-targeted dating services, data capitalism has to be placed within the epistemological reconfiguration of symbolic and deductive models of computation into heuristic algorithms that correlate data and determine metadata through a general system of inductive thinking.

Data capitalism, however, does not see machines as fixed systems of accumulation: that is, machines as a guarantor of the whole engine of capital reproduction. Fixed capital no longer runs according to a symbolic logic of deduction, whereby the machine ensures that outputs meet inputs, that results match premises, and that means of production become accelerators of surplus value. Capital accumulation relies on the predictive intelligence of machines, insofar as fixed capital has enfolded the temporal potentiation of value in the computational processing of variations. At the core of data capitalism, therefore, is a new mode of machinic production that preserves within itself the future value of data. It is here that data never matches its face value, but it is stretched beyond its actuation only to pre-empt its future becoming according to the pre-set paradigms of capital reproduction. In other words, data accumulation has become granted by the calculation of probabilities that capture the varying variations of value for the predictive extraction of surplus value. Predictive intelligence therefore takes data as a source of continuous valorization insofar as it deploys a mode of calculation of probabilities based on the enumeration of proofs;

that is, the automation of data retrieval generates a list of variations in relation to a given set. Importantly, it is this inductive mode of finding proof through data retrieval that has demarcated a shift in models of predictive intelligence from being determined by predefined sets into becoming rather dependent on the heuristic training of data. For data capitalism precisely deploys machines of prediction based on trial and error to ensure that more data is available to the circuit of reproduction of value. From this standpoint, the shift to heuristic enumeration of proof – whereby data is trained through a dynamic function of trial and error – has not only transformed the mode of accumulation of value in fixed capital, but has also eventuated strategies of governmental control that rely on what functions of predictive intelligence allow.

Data capitalism takes the capacities of computational machines to carry out heuristic estimations of data in order to anticipate responses and direct behaviors toward constantly rehearsed scenarios that reinstate the self-posing of capital as ontology. Brian Massumi calls this heuristic regeneration of control *Ontopower* (2015). This includes both processing, or the functions of a system, and process, or the temporal qualities of a system. In particular, ontopower overlaps sovereign, disciplinary, and control technologies of capture that manifest in the aesthetic or visceral pre-emption of possible responses, whereby variations are measured upon sets of data as much as these sets of heuristic estimations become adaptable to changes.

Heuristics as a mode of prediction is tailored not to anticipate correct use or response, but mainly to activate a form of control that ensures that more data is captured within the reproductive circuit of capital. In particular, the more prediction shows that there is no linear causality between input and output, the more the science of statistics has come to include an indeterminate set of data into automated procedures. The shift from data modeling to algorithmic modeling here is paramount. However, before delving into the epistemological expansion of statistical prediction from given sets of probabilities to the generative functions of algorithmic search, we will discuss first the political and cultural implications of ontopower as describing the becoming or the transformation of sovereignty in the context of planetary computation.

## The black box and the sociogenic

One important argument within this context is how these predictive systems of control that constitute the backbone of data capitalism impart a specific form of decisionism on data. Here, the replacement of the law with computational sovereignty implies that the algorithm operates according to objective, mindless, and causeless principles (that only rely on the empiricism or the evidence of data) that instead continue to perpetuate discriminatory knowledge according to the monolithic ontology of man. Here, ontopower entails a potentiation of value from and through machines in order to grant a recursive reconfiguration of being, whose transparency principle[1] continues to haunt the machine.

From this standpoint, what is claimed to be opaque in the black box of machine learning algorithms cannot be disentangled from the normative apparatus that reproduces the transparency of the self-determining subject. The heuristics of data results now include not simply statistics of probabilities based on a given data set but, more importantly, set in motion a mode of predictive learning from infinitesimal variations; it has been argued that at the level of algorithmic design, it is possible to counterattack the perpetuation of biases with the design of equality within coding. If the algorithmic design of machine vision today employed in self-driving cars as well as in airport security cameras obliterate black features as much as non-Caucasian skin color, it is because what machines learn is the specific point of view of the "changing same", which self-determines anything else as other.

Far beyond the algorithmic misrecognition of skin color, the machine learning of the flesh inherits Western histories of man that enter the constitution of new assemblages in a system of socio-political relations. As first coined by Fanon (1952/1967), the sociogenic principle is a concept that Sylvia Wynter (2001, 2007) further developed as a way to account for how the socio-political becomes flesh. For Wynter, the sociogenic principle is an ontological account of how the socio-political assemblages of man and the logic of symbolic "difference" become programmed in the body according to ontogenic formation of identity that has branded the flesh. This socio-political assemblage of man, what Wynter also calls Western man, has gone through a process of auto-determinations based on the cosmogonies of human origin. She argues that the current iteration of cosmogony corresponds to a bio-humanist homo economicus, as informed by the economic theories of Adam Smith. Here the correlation between biological and economic survival, through the forces of selection and optimization of survival, defines the epistemological explanation of who is and who is not successful as an individual belonging to a species. It is this correlation that consolidates the formation of the sociogenic code and ensures the reproduction of the racialization of the world. This also corresponds to what could be called the socio-political constitution of man, as a fictive (and yet dominant) genealogy that tells the story of being human. For Wynter understands the reproduction of racialization in terms of autopoetic and self-regulatory practices that are imprinted within the flesh and, as a result, enable the ontogenic self-replication of this originary myth. By drawing from neurobiology, Wynter explains how symbolic "difference" materializes as ontologies via neurochemical processes that produce a racialized e/affect, making the materiality of "difference" seem natural and thus granting a monolithic explanation of the human. However, following from the discussion in the previous section, it is important to suggest that the autopoetic institution of the sociogenic code permeates not just human ontologies but also more-than-human ontologies, including the socio-technical assemblages of data and algorithms (Dixon-Román, 2016).

The sociogenic coding of the other as the negative marker, it is argued, is necessary to the recursive loops of the colonial enterprise, whereby the naturalization of the dyadic structure of equivalence between man and the world ensures that all remains the same under the Western sun. From this standpoint, it seems insufficient to claim that the transparency of the self-determining subject must be unveiled by demanding more transparency from the system and, for instance, asking to recode machine learning programs in the name of an equality of representation. The demand for enlarging the normalized category of the human to include excluded differences and shed light on the blindness of the machine does not seamlessly ensure a political overturning of the dyadic pattern of self-recognition.

It is already evident therefore, that if ANN (artificial neural networks) will be trained to recognize non-Caucasian features and skin colors, it will do so only by learning to extend the sociogenic commitment to the evolutionary ground of the biological man into the smooth machines of a technical strata. In other words, within the cybernetic regime of immediate communication, there is no possibility of defying what Sylvia Wynter calls the autopoetic self-determination of Man, predicated upon the negative side of the color line (Wynter, 12). The predictive intelligence of machines here becomes a socio-technical assemblage that contains within itself the seeds of an ontological re-origination of a "speciated genre or Mask of being human" (Wynter, 13).

From another standpoint, however, one could ask how to refuse the transparency thesis of the computational network of communication. Which practices of refusal can be put in place in order not to fall back in the autopoetic re-origination of sameness under the guise of data evidence or mindless objectivity? To unpack the implications of what a refusal of transparency could be, in the context of a computational explanation of the natural order of consciousness recurring in the mindless operations of the machine, it may be useful here to turn to the collective Tiqqun's argument against the cybernetic apparatus of governance (2001).

As a political program that originates from the liberal view of the individualized human subject, cybernetics, it is argued, enfolds biological, physical, and social behaviors into information systems. It grounds this liberal view into sets of recombinant dividuals steered toward certain actions so as to benefit the system upon which they depend. As a science of prediction, cybernetics incorporates and transcends liberalism by transforming the social field of relationships into a laboratory of trial and error, testing all possible results according to an "experimentation protocol" (2001). This is possible because cybernetics replaces the model of governance based on law with a mechanism of information retrieval and transmission subtending a sea of data that directly gives truth. For Tiqqun, the cybernetics bonding of machines to the social results from extending the war of communicability amongst superpowers into a total war against all that is living (2001). By implementing heuristic principles that would grant the statistical calculation of probabilities, the cybernetic subsumption of social variations now takes the uncertainties (of living and life) as variations that become central to the algorithmic modeling of everyday scenarios. This predictive steering of uncertainties through the computational function of algorithms is said to give the illusion of a united social body that shares a profound faith "in the genius of humanity" (2001). In other words, as cybernetic networks impose on the social body an infrastructure of seamless communication based on the equivalence of connections, the heuristic medium of governance withdraws into the background, out of sight in the recursive colonialism of the transparent subject.

To refuse this planetary colonization at the core of data capitalism, the collective Tiqqun argues for is a return to tactics of opaqueness – or what they call a fog-like micropolitics – that can rather experiment with the dimensions of the impersonal, the indifferent, and the invisible (2001). As opposed to the comforting self-mirroring subject of social media, these are practices of non-existence, refusing to participate in recursive data networks. This calls for a radical break from the cybernetic spell of immediate communication so that faceless, unconnected, unclear subjectivities can divorce from the predictive analytics of computable, classifiable, and forever interchangeable data.

Nevertheless, if, as mentioned earlier, the transparency of data capitalism cannot be overturned by the claim of and for a clarity of code, one may also call into doubt how opacity can activate a radical refusal of sociogenic principles. To put it in another way, can this form of existential opaqueness (of a human opaqueness hiding within itself a transparent subject) escape the continuous demand of identification that is precisely set to search for what is not yet known? To what extent can these practices of refusal, of collective anonymity, disentangle from the autopoetic replicator of the code of man?

## Sociogenic modeling

How to understand the continuation of the sociogenic principle in data capitalism? If the transparency of the self-determining system of identification persists in the category of data, no matter how many variations it can include and, similarly, if it cannot be defied by simply withdrawing into the opaque zone of misrecognition, does it follow that predictive intelligence is here entrapped into the circuit of representation, without any possibility to expand the techno-scientific horizon beyond the sociogenic principle of man? How might it be possible to defy the paradigm of data capital?

What is needed here is perhaps not simply a proposition to reveal the relentless reproduction of the transparency thesis and its demands for either more inclusion in the circuit of the changing sameness or for more opaqueness in order to remain invisible in the normative dyad. While these forms of critique have re-activated debates about the persistence of the colonial modern project in and through today's computational sovereignty and the wider complex ontology of power, a closer analysis of predictive intelligence can offer insights about how to challenge data capitalism's epistemological project. In other words, if, as we are now going to discuss, the science of statistics has identified fundamental shifts in the operations of predictive intelligence from the use of a data model to that of an algorithmic model, these shifts are also indicative of an epistemological transformation in modalities of know-hows: that is, of methods or procedures that aim to abstract indeterminacies in predictive functions.

In what follows, we will trace the transformations of these know-hows – that is, of methods or procedures of learning – to predict unknowns in the context of the science of statistics. In particular, the paradigm of statistical prediction can help clarify how the shift from data to algorithmic modeling can be discussed in the context of the transparency principles. In particular, the statistical procedures of re-estimation can explain how predictive intelligence comes to depend on the incomputable and to extend and intensify the sociogenic forms of identification through data interpellation. It is in the predictive function of re-estimation that data returns as already given in the socio-cultural structure of identification, whereby transparency and opacity are played against each other to maintain a system of equivalence of values. In this instance, the human-machine equivalence is maintained in an extended structure of fixed capital, where value accumulation is increased, accelerated, and diversified according to the statistical systems of prediction. We will now turn to statistical modeling to unpack the specific processing that ensures the predicament of automated modes of racialization.

Our contention is not only that sociogenic principles are differently articulated in modalities of estimation that have shifted from data to algorithmic modeling but, more importantly, that these recursive procedures also demonstrate the tendencies of predictive intelligence to enter a space of futurity. In what follows, the analysis of the shift from data modeling to algorithmic modeling will help us configure this space in the estimated functions that run between the multi-layered network of algorithms, the recursive processing of data, and the prediction of uncertainty in machine-learning systems. To what extent, one can ask, are strategies of pre-emption and sovereign computation activated in the estimation procedures of predictive policing? How does prediction here enter the space of the future to constantly eliminate the incomputable from given results? How can learning systems of prediction continue to grant a politics of certainty (i.e., of biased results)?

## Sociogenic prediction

If the transparency thesis enabled the formation of the sociogenic principle in science and technology, then does the sociogenic principle haunt the becoming recursive of predictive intelligence?

In Leo Breiman's 2001 article "Statistical Modeling: The Two Cultures", the late statistician argued that two cultures have emerged in statistics: one based on data modeling and the other algorithmic modeling. For Breiman, the main distinction that is made between the two approaches is how they treat the black box of nature in the model. However, we conceptualize a third approach of computational modeling that is distinct from both data and algorithmic modeling in how they account for error and the incomputable. We explain further later in this chapter.

Data modeling is the approach that is most familiar to statistics and the social and behavioral sciences. Breiman characterizes data modeling by the fitting of parametric statistical models (e.g., logistic or linear regression) to a sample of data of the population. This means that these models make particular assumptions (e.g., linearity, homoscedasticity, normality of model residuals, or large sample size for asymptotic distributions) in order to produce statistically unbiased estimates. The statistical model or function is a known specified model that also makes particular assumptions about what predictors are associated with the response and how they are associated. The models are then evaluated based on an analysis of the model error, residual variance, and goodness-of-fit (e.g., $R^2$). The best fit model to the data is then used for prediction.

As an example, data modeling might be used in the context of predicting the risk of someone committing a violent offense in the context of predictive policing. Here, if it is assumed that there are three categories of risk (i.e., high risk, low risk, and no risk), then an analyst would likely use an ordinal logistic regression. The ordinal logistic regression would necessitate a large sample size in order to meet the asymptotic properties of maximum likelihood estimation and would try to find the most parsimonious model (i.e., number of predictors) to fit to the data. The predictors and their functional relationship to the response variable is specified by the analyst. As with any model, once the ordinal logistic regression has been parameterized from existing data, its life of prediction is limited. Eventually, the predictions from this model will increasingly produce greater prediction error and, as a result, more false positives and/or false negatives. At this point, the ordinal logistic regression will need to be re-estimated by fitting to the sample with up-to-date data. Here, the sociogenic has multiple pathways on algorithmic institution. The choices made by the analyst (e.g., how is the response variable (i.e., risk) operationalized, what predictors are used, how are the predictors operationalized, what is their specified functional relationship, and what and who comprise the sample for parameterizing the model) are all discursive formations with socio-political significance. For instance, why operationalize the predicted outcome as risk of committing a violent offense instead of the economic impact to society or threats to democracy?

Another pathway is via the choice of the model itself. It turns out that the early developments of the logistic function were by the demographer and eugenicist Raymond Pearl, who pioneered the use of the logistic function for comparative population growth research. Thus, the ordinal logistic regression seeks to predict an ontology that assumes a transparent subject that is influenced by a Darwinian eugenic model of selection/dyselection. Finally, the data is an assemblage that is imbued with forces of socio-political relations and thus sociogenically institutes the parameterization of the model and, as a result, its predictions. These predictions ultimately shape the feedback loop that becomes part of the re-estimation of the model. It turns out this is an issue that remains unresolved with algorithmic modeling.

If data modeling is based on a known specified parametric model that is fit to the data, then algorithmic modeling is based on an unknown model (i.e., black box) that is determined by the data. Algorithmic modeling is understood to include nonparametric, non-linear models (e.g., Support Vector Machines, Random Forest, or Neural Nets) that are designed to optimize predictive accuracy; thus, the algorithm is determined by the data, which is not a priori to data processing. This inductive approach trains the algorithm on a set of training data and then cross-validates the model with a separate set of unknown existing data. In theory, the only assumption these models make is that the data is drawn from an independent and identically distributed unknown multivariate distribution. Models are evaluated not based on how well the model fits to the data but rather on the model prediction's accuracy and, consequently, an analysis of the error in prediction. In contradistinction to data modeling, the model from algorithmic modeling is uninterpretable and thus unknown in advance. Apart from Breiman, our characterization of algorithmic modeling is based on nonautomated processes of model updating. Our contention is that Breiman's conception of algorithmic modeling is not enough to account for the more profound historical transformation of automation itself, what we characterize as computational modeling here.

Applying this predictive policing example to algorithmic modeling results in other patterns of sociogenic violence, under the algorithmic modeling paradigm, the analyst may train several different supervised machine learning algorithms and test which one produces greater predictive accuracy with a known existing data set. The response variable is still operationalized by the analyst, but the algorithm examines for patterns of association with the response variable in the training data. These models have much more computational power, are more flexible, and able to process as many predictors as possible. In contradistinction to data models, noise (i.e., error) is information and needed for these models; the more noise the better they perform; and, finally, they are only concerned with overfitting the model to the training data. Overfitting results in a less than optimal model for future predictions; thus, some prediction error is necessary. In our characterization of algorithmic modeling, the model is not specified to automate re-estimation. The algorithm is trained, calibrated, and deployed as a fixed model and re-estimated by a data scientist on a specified regular basis. With this paradigm of prediction, the sociogenic institution of the algorithm is by way of how the response variable is defined and measured (i.e., operationalized), algorithm programming decisions of cost ratio of false negatives to false positives, the determined patterns learned from the data assemblages, and the performative enactments from feedback loops. Under algorithmic modeling, both data assemblages and feedback loops may be more determinative than was the case with data modeling, as the learning of the algorithm is determined from patterns in the data. These are patterns of policing behaviors that are already constituted by the sociogenic principle. Thus, as statistician Kristian Lum (2016) argues, "What the machine learns about, in fact, is patterns not about crime, per se, but about how police record crime", and those recorded patterns of crime are often part of the iterative performative work that make temporal, spatial, and material demarcations, marking the flesh with socio-political violence.

While algorithmic modeling is determined by the data and designed to make more accurate predictions than data modeling, the process of handling indeterminacy or the incomputable is distinct from what we are calling computational modeling. While the type of algorithms used in computational modeling does not necessarily differ from those used in algorithmic modeling, there is a minor difference in deployment that we argue has substantial implications for algorithmic reason and the sociogenic. When the process of algorithmic re-estimation (i.e., learning) is automated, it introduces time or temporality into the algorithmic procedure of re-estimation. Temporality is at the core of an automated prediction model that must account for the non-linear and recursive loops between inputs and outputs. The limit of the finite algorithmic model to account for infinities already sets up the conditions for a reflexive function in the algorithm. The automation of this process enables the prehension of incomputables and forms of thought that are immanent to the algorithm (Parisi, 2013). While the nonautomated process of model re-estimation accounts for the incomputable, it does it in a way that is simply adding new data to the existing training data to estimate the algorithmic model. Instead, with computational modeling, this is an ongoing iterable process that continues to build the model based on algorithmic randomness without returning to the original condition.

Employing computational modeling to the predictive policing example will point to similar pathways concerning sociogenic violence, but with a force of alterity. Similar to algorithmic modeling, the analyst of a computational model will train several different supervised machine learning algorithms and test which one produces greater predictive accuracy with an existing data set to cross-validate. The operationalization of the response variable does not change, and the algorithm continues to examine for patterns of association with the response variable in the training data as well as new data. Again, noise is not just needed information but in fact a necessary source for predicting the unknown, as the model of re-estimation coincides with the automated processing of non-linear time and indeterminacies. The sociogenic in-formations of the algorithm via the computational modeling paradigm of prediction is similar through the operationalizing of the response variable: algorithm programming decisions of cost ratio of false negatives to false positives, the determined patterns learned from the data assemblages, and the performative enactments from feedback loops. Under computational modeling, data assemblages and feedback loops are most determinative, as the automated learning of the algorithm is determined from patterns in the data and the incomputable (discussed further later in the chapter). Thus, while algorithmic modeling engages in performative acts of prediction based on a model that was calibrated at one point in time, computational modeling, via the work of the analyst, will continue to automatically recalibrate estimation parameters based on the processing of new data. This means that the sociogenic constitution of the algorithm is likely to shift or reconfigure as patterns of policing and public behaviors change. While the sociogenic may have similar pathways for algorithmic constitution, it is the incomputable and its prehension over time that creates conditions for alternative configurations of algorithmic thought (Parisi, 2013).

The computational model directly deals with the incomputable – with incompressible volumes of data that grow across and between recursive feedback of the ANN. Here, predictive intelligence is determined neither by a given data set nor by passive learning from data. Prediction here coincides with algorithms that actively learn from processing data. What is learned is not the meaning of data (i.e., whether or not data correspond to a given meaning), but the inferring of meaning from correlating data according to specific searches. In particular, what is actively learned is what is not already prescribed in the data set or in the sea of data. It is the recursivity of many levels of feedback that exposes predictive intelligence to error – here corresponding to incomputables. The processing of incomputables has transformed predictive intelligence into a mode of thinking about what is not yet known and thus advancing hypotheses about what could be known (Parisi, 2014). Learning in computational modeling becomes a mode of predicting what has not been compressed: a mode of mediating randomness.

Within computational systems of prediction, randomness can also be understood in terms of the problem of the incomputable. If a program is left to run according to precise algorithmic instructions based on the evolutionary drive of growth, change, adaptation, and fitness, then the computational limit arrives as a space of incomputable probabilities. Generative algorithms, for instance, do not simply lead to new orders of complexity (in which one level of complexity builds on the previous one – e.g., by transforming entropic energy into useful information), but instead encounters a wall of data that cannot be synthesized in smaller quantities. This wall of incompressible data instead overruns the program and thus neutralizes or reveals the incompleteness of the axioms on which the program was based in the first place.

These incomputable probabilities are discrete states of non-denumerable infinities. Algorithmic information theorist Gregory Chaitin calls these infinities Omega (2005). The latter corresponds to the halting probability of a universal free-prefix self-delimiting Turing machine. Omega is a constant that is computably enumerable, since it defines the limit of a computable, increasing, converging sequence of rational numbers. Nevertheless, it is also algorithmically random: its binary expansion is an algorithmic random sequence, which is incomputable (Parisi, 2013).

Hence computational modeling is used not simply to build profiles based on pre-fixed sets of algorithms, but to exploit the self-delimiting power of computation, defined by its (in)capacity to decide when a program should stop. By transforming non-denumerable infinities into random discrete sets or Omega probabilities, computational modeling manifests random actualities. These actualities are part of the operative functions imbued with infinite amounts of data, with a future activation that cannot be compressed into a complete procedure. In other words, according to Chaitin, these discrete states are themselves composed of infinite real numbers that cannot be contained in discrete axioms (2005). This means that the incompleteness of computational models cannot simply be explained away by the paradigmatic substitution of deductive axiomatics with inductive learning. On the contrary, one must explain the incompleteness of computation by addressing the temporal and heuristic process of automation in algorithmic processing.

When automated procedures become temporal operators of variations and heuristic searchers of results, automation itself – that is, the computational procedure – becomes open to the indeterminacy of its own function. In particular, algorithmic iterations, it has been argued, have become opened to the circular looping of time. If we are to draw on more challenging conceptions of automation, inspired, for instance, to Gilbert Simondon's general theorization of the modes of existence of technical objects, our argument for a dynamic view of automation can suggest that temporal processing in automation radically challenges the reproduction of the sociogenic principle in systems of prediction. For Simondon insisted that machine design includes a principle of indetermination, which is to be added to the space of indeterminacy in the human-machine relation. In particular, as Yuk Hui as recently suggested, there is a possibility of approaching this question of the inorganic time of the machine in terms of recursivity (2016). It is precisely this link between the inorganic time and the inorganic thought of the machine that can allow us to discuss machine thinking either away from an optimization of mechanical functions or simply as an extension of the soul of man.

In particular, Hui takes Simondon's proposition of a non-Cartesian form of cognition to challenge the assumption that thinking follows a linear chain of causes and effects: namely, where reasoning is confined to a procedure for transporting evidence from one point to another without having any active function to rather change the course of things (2019). According to Hui, Simondon refuses Descartes rationalism by demonstrating that the cybernetic principle of feedback adds a new temporal structure to thinking that is described in terms of a spiral (2019). As Hui further explains, according to Simondon, cybernetics replaces the telos of thought with a self-regulatory process (2019). In particular, insofar as the recursivity of feedback makes the cybernetic system possible, it also impedes the system to become systematic, complete, and simply a reproductive whole. However, since human relations are abstracted and re-integrated into the temporality of machines, which, as we have suggested so far, constitute the engine algorithmic governmentality, the question of temporality – and thus of recursive temporality in nonorganic machines – is still in need of further exploration. For instance, Hui suggests that one may need to start re-addressing this savoir technique – technical knowledge – as part of today's system of knowledge production (2019). Similarly, Simondon's insistence on the margin of indeterminacy of technical machines admits a metaphysical dimension to cybernetics – and thus a non-linear mode of existence (without ultimate finality) of the technical object that constitutes a system, but also precludes its systematic telos.

For Hui, margins of indeterminacy describe not only the recursive temporalities of machines, but, more importantly, a recursive thinking in machines (2019). This remark suggest that the technical machine is not simply a mirror of the normative apparatus of knowledge reproduction. By following Hui's argument, we can suggest that automation can include both contingency and chance within itself, because the temporality of the technical object or cybernetic machines precisely admits that errors, incident, failure are part of the causal process of machine learning: namely, contingencies do not interrupt the cause but precisely expose the workings of non-linear causality. Similarly, the analysis of computational mediated knowledge also must admit to thinking and knowing as being autonomous from an organic ground. Far from simply extending the bioeconomy of man in machines, automated systems can rather be taken to act against the anthropomorphic biases of modeling for which a machine is merely a tool of reproduction. Instead, we have suggested that the systematic view of the world implies the possibility of rethinking the human through the horizon of the inhuman and as unbounded from the biological rule: that is, from the biocentric epistemology that grants the prosthetic extension of the sociogenic principles in machines.

Nevertheless, and this may be a question we can return to later, it is still possible to ask here: can computational modeling, and in particular ANN and machine-learning systems such as deep learning, push the heuristic methods so far as to include wider margins of indeterminacy, ultimately overturning sociogenic programming all together? To put it in another way, if machines can incorporate contingencies in their heuristic method of know-hows, does it mean that learning systems of artificial intelligence, at the core of data capitalism today, have absorbed within themselves the horizon of the unthought, of thinking beyond what we already know? If so, it will follow that the epistemological shift to computational modeling eradicates all possibility of a thought and a knowledge beyond the sociogenic principles; namely, the biocentric ground of recognition is always extended and never overturned in and through systems of predictive intelligence. This view, however, seems naive because it fully discounts Simondon's insight into the histories of cultural transformations originating with and through technical objects as insisting that margins of indeterminacy are there to dissolve any fixed opposition between axioms and contingencies, or law and chance.[2] Instead, following this critique of technicity, it is rather crucial to maintain the argument that indetermination in information systems comes first.

One way to undermine the totalizing tendency of cybernetics is to continue the critical inquiry about the relation between the function of recursivity and the computational processing of randomness (i.e., incomputables) in automated systems. If, as we have seen, recursive feedback is at the core of the re-estimation model used in statistics to predict outcomes on the basis of a given data set or of a training data set, then it is important to further re-envision how recursivity works through infinities: that is, how what cannot be known in advance becomes a problem of compression or patterning of infinities. From this standpoint, one can argue that the science of statistics can be taken as a techno-scientific instance of epistemological reconfigurations of the problem of the incomputable in the formation of feedback systems of predictive intelligence.

What we are arguing, therefore, is that assumptions of technological determinism that we find in debates about the reproduction of biases in systems of predictive intelligence have nothing to do with the technical machine, but are rather the result of a continuous re-territorialization of the techno-social possibilities of reinventing epistemological paradigms outside the framework of colonial capital. From this standpoint, data capitalism takes recursive accumulation in statistics to preserve human capital in machines so that feedback procedures of estimation remain anchored to the reproduction of social relations, embedded in the material-historical determination of man. In other words, what is deterministic in statistical procedures of estimation is not the cybernetic principles of feedback or computational patterning but, above all, the matrix of representation, where the sociogenic principles are amplified and distributed through the image of the automata that must maintain an objective efficiency – simply coinciding with an apparatus of enumeration of what is already there.

## Coda on the incomputable paradigm

We have discussed models of predictive intelligence as demarcating an epistemological shift toward data capitalism and a transformation of fixed capital – and of automated systems into systems of recursive feedbacks. This shift, we have argued, entails more importantly a governmental reconfiguration of the telos of Western metaphysics that has come to constitute the socio-technical assemblages of the more-than-human agents of command and control. Within this framework, we have discussed dynamic modes of technicity that insist on a principle of indeterminacy internal to the system of feedback. We have suggested that data capitalism extends the sociogenic principles of racialization of the world through heuristic modalities of prediction, defined by the inclusion of contingencies in algorithmic and computational models of prediction. Here, the sociogenic principle has entered the recursive qualities of the technical machine and constituted larger assemblages of racialization in as much as unknown probabilities have become part and parcel of an immediate system of recognition. This latter takes over all the spectrum of infinities in order to pre-emptively decide the outcomes. Ontopower, we have suggested, naturalizes both process and processing to the extent that its manner of governance is not simply above the law, but has turned the law into an adaptive techno-social assemblage that responds to contingencies. In particular, we have suggested that the centrality of the incomputable in post-Turing systems of prediction, defies the ready-made assumptions that computational modeling always already reproduces truths and facts.

We have suggested that the current critique of automated prediction risks a naive jump to the conclusion that incomputables are either outside onto-power or that the technical dimension of indeterminacy is already part of a fast advancing hegemonic block – a planetary sovereignty, where pro-grammed decisionism ensures the inheritance of the sociogenic metaphys-ics of man. From this standpoint, incomputables correspond to infinities as sublimated forces (glitches, breakdowns, errors, failures) that always already exceed the system even if they become captured, co-opted or incorporated. Our insistence on recursivity instead is an effort to argue that since the system is incomplete in the first instance, it has no given inside or outside. Instead, these are only constituted in the mediating functions of recursivity as these become increasingly layered and acquire new dimensions of com-plexity in the ANN of computational modeling.

It is worth considering instead that with the formation of a computa-tional model, as we have suggested so far, the self-regulatory systems of predictions take what were statistically understood as errors as part of the spectrum of variation. Here, incomputables are neither inside nor outside the computational model, but are rather the conditions for a recursive pro-cessing to determine results according to a mode of experimentation that extends heuristics into the realm of indeterminacy in the compression of infinities. From this standpoint, incomputables are not simply open to be co-opted because they already constitute or structure the system to define a new order of cosmogony that admits to the indeterminacy of knowledge that results from computational know-hows. This proposition is only one possibility for continuing to question – debunk and construct anew – the implications of techno-scientific epistemology in matters of governance. This inquiry into paradigms of automated modeling, therefore, must address the limits of techno-scientific epistemology whereby the technical machine remains a tool for capital extraction and reproduction and continues to grant the space of analytic explanation of the sociogenic principles. At the same time, however, this inquiry must also account for the epistemological origination of the paradigm of the incomputable whereby temporalities in information processing are already unleashing cultural transformations that rely upon indeterminacy in recursive systems of prediction and that demand new accounts of what a machine can do, know, and activate against the ontopower of data capital.

## Notes

1 Here, we refer to Denise Ferreira da Silva's (2007) articulation of Hegel's transparency thesis. Da Silva locates the consolidation of the racializing ghost of modernism at the feet of Hegel's transcendental poesis and, in particular, its transparency thesis. Transcendental poesis, she argues, is the result of the coming together and consolidation of Immanuel Kant's transcendental explanation of the subject and Johann Gottfried von Herder's historical ground for the subject. This is the modern consolidation of the subject as embedded in historical changes and at once as a rational and transparent being. Thus, as da Silva claims, Hegel rather introduces through the backdoor, a central transparency thesis of natural human difference into the liberal subject of modernism. This sets the context for the later analytics of raciality of the sciences, based on the comparative analysis establishing the scientific grounds for human difference.
2 For Simondon, a cybernetic system can be considered as an open machine as its margins of indetermination are manifested in its recursive structures and causality.

## References

Breiman, L. (2001), 'Statistical modeling: The two cultures', *Statistical Science*, 16(3).
Chaitin, G. (2005), *Meta Math! The Quest for Omega*. New York: Vintage.
Da Silva, D.F. (2007), *Toward a Global Idea of Race*. Minneapolis: University of Minnesota Press.
Dixon-Román, E. (2016), Algo-Ritmo: More-Than-Human Performative Acts and the Racializing Assemblages of Algorithmic Architectures. *Cultural Studies-Critical Methodologies* 16(5): 482–490.
Dixon-Román, E., Ama Nyame-Mensah and Allison R. Russell (21st October 2019), "Algorithmic Legal Reasonng as Racializing Assemblages." *Computational Culture* 7. Available at: http://computationalculture.net/algorithmic-legal-reasoning-as-racializing-assemblages/.
Fanon, F. (1967), *Black Skin, White Masks*. New York: Grove Press.
Hui, Y. (2016), *On the Existence of Digital Objects*. Minneapolis: University of Minnesota Press.
Hui, Y. (2019), *Recursivity and Contingency*. London: Rowman & Littlefield International.
Lum, K. (2016), 'Predictive policing reinforces police bias', *Human Rights Data Analysis Group*. Available at: https://hrdag.org/2016/10/10/predictive-policing-reinforces-police-bias/.
Massumi, B. (2015), *Ontopower: Wars, Powers, and the State of Perception*. Durham, NC: Duke University Press.
Parisi, L. (2013), *Contagious Architecture: Computation, Aesthetics, and Space*. Cambridge, MA: MIT Press.
Parisi, L. (2014), 'Affect and automation', in M.L. Angerer (ed.), *The Timing of Affect*. Zurich: Diaphanes (in German), Chicago: University of Chicago Press (in English).
Wynter, S. (2001), 'Towards the sociogenic principle: Fanon, identity, the puzzle of conscious experience, and what it is like to be black', in A. Gomez-Moriana and M. Duran-Cogan (eds.), *National Identities and Sociopolitical Changes in Latin America*. New York: Routledge.
Wynter, S. (2007), 'Human being as noun? Or being human as praxis? Towards the autopoetic turn/overturn: A manifesto'. Available at: https://s3.amazonaws.com/arena-attachments/1516556/69a8a25c597f33bf66af6cdf411d58c2.pdf

# 3   *Emotariat* accelerationism and the republic of data[1]

## Ignacio Valero

## Introduction

> Thereafter rose Desire in the beginning, Desire the primal seed and germ of Spirit, Sages who searched their heart's thought discovered the existent's kinship in the non-existent.
>
> > (Griffith, translator, *The Hymns of the Rig Veda*, 1896/2019)

> In the beginning of Things, black-winged Night/Into the bosom of Erebos dark and deep Laid a wind-born egg, and, as the seasons rolled,/Forth sprang Love. . . . Love the Delight.
>
> > (Aristophanes, 414 BCE)

> Constant revolutionizing of production, uninterrupted disturbance of all social conditions, *everlasting uncertainty and agitation* distinguish the bourgeois epoch from all earlier ones. All fixed, fast-frozen relations, with their train of ancient and venerable prejudices and opinions, are swept away; all new formed ones become antiquated before they can ossify. *All that is solid melts into air*, all that is holy is profaned, and man is at last compelled to face with sober sense his real conditions of life and his relations with his kind.
>
> > (Marx, *Communist Manifesto*, 1848, emphasis added)

> The bourgeoisie, wherever it has got the upper hand, has put an end to all feudal, patriarchal and idyllic relations. It has pitilessly torn asunder the motley feudal ties that bound man to his "natural superiors", and has left remaining no other nexus between man and man than naked self-interest, callous "cash payment". It has drowned the most heavenly ecstasies of religious fervor, of chivalrous enthusiasm, of philistine sentimentalism, in the icy water of egotistical *calculation*. It has resolved personal worth into exchange value, and in place of the numberless indefeasible chartered freedoms, has set up that single, unconscionable freedom.
>
> > (Marx, *The Fragment of Machines*, 1858)

Our world lives under an urgent rush and "zapping", obsessed by movement and action. Everything must change and move along unceasingly: men, machines, information, ideas and ideals. Our modern societies have created a perpetual motion religion, which does not even spare politics, knowledge or people.

(P. Sloterdijk, 1989, 2000 author's translation)

The soul is the *clinamen* of the body. It is how it falls, and what makes it fall with other bodies. The soul is its gravity. This tendency for certain bodies to fall in with others is what constitutes a world . . . a rhythm, a certain way of vibrating, a resonance. . . . The soul is not simply the seat of intellectual operations, but the affective and libidinal forces that weave together a world: attentiveness, the ability to address, care for, and appeal to others. The contemporary subject of cognitive capitalism . . . the cognitariat, but perhaps there are other names. . . . Capitalism is the mobilization of a pathos and the organization of a mood; its subject, a field of desire, a point of inflexion for an impersonal affect that circulates like a rumor.

(Berardi, 2009a)

Freedom will prove to have been merely an interlude. Freedom is felt when passing from one way of living to another – until this too turns out to be a form of coercion. Then, liberation gives way to renewed subjugation. Such is the destiny of the *subject*; literally, the 'one who has been cast down'. Today we do not deem ourselves subjugated *subjects*, but rather *projects*: always refashioning and reinventing ourselves. . . . [T]he *I* is now subjugating itself to internal limitations and self-constraints, which are taking the form of compulsive achievement and optimization. . . . The freedom of *Can* generates even more coercion than the disciplinarian *Should*. . . . Psychic maladies such as depression and burnout express a profound crisis of freedom. They represent pathological signs that freedom is now switching over into manifold forms of compulsion. Although the achievement subject deems itself free, it is a slave. . . . As the entrepreneur of its own self, the neoliberal subject has no capacity for relationships with others that might be *free of purpose*. . . . "Freedom" and "Friendship" have the same root . . . *relationship*.

(Han, 2017b)

China's rise may be Exhibit A for neoliberal accelerationism, good when many mouths watered at the prospect of quick access to a vast Chinese market, but ultimately dried out when they did not get what they wanted. Since colonial times, "free trade" has been the *cris de guerre* of imperial powers who have had the naval power to back up their claims for "freedom of the seas" and have thus imposed onerous unequal terms of trade to the weaker parties. It was a zero-sum game of Western imperial interventions carrying their "White Man's Burden" to the rest of the world. During the 20th century, "import substitution" in Latin America was a key policy that tried to extricate itself from unequal exchange, cheap raw materials and costly finished products and develop more intra-region science, technology and trade. But it never took off because the populations were fragmented, politically divided, and never had the bargaining power to ask for better terms.[2] Nobody cried "unfair" then, or when multinationals rushed to the Global

South in search of super-profits, as Raj Patel and Jason W. Moore show in *A History of the World in Seven Cheap Things*: nature, money, work, care, food, energy, lives (Moore, 2018). This unequal exchange comprises an ugly and unfair history reflected today in massive social inequality, runaway climate change, and a generalized angst about the future of our Earth.

It is true also that the vast changes created by the neoliberal knowledge economy have represented an important increase in productivity, but its biggest gains have been largely appropriated by a minuscule minority, even more acutely since the 2008 Great Recession (Nova, 2019).[3] But we now seem to be coming down from this high of "cheap things" and realize that this mindless, banal, but potentially deadly acceleration is leading us into a cosmic ditch. Can we overcome Lyotard's *Libidinal Economy* aporia? His proposal of "an energetics that not only voluntarily risks anarchic irrationalism, but issues in a scandalous advocacy of the industrial proletariat's *enjoyment* of their machinic dissection at the hands of capital; . . . [and] dares us to 'admit it'. . . . [T]he deracinating affect of capitalism, also, is a source of *jouissance*, a mobilization of desire" (Mackay, 2014).

This mobilization of affect can lead to a bifurcation to 1) an alienated *emotariat* or emotional proletariat or to 2) an emergent communicative and democratic future, "whose 'sociality' and 'conviviality' is based upon an 'aesthetics of living'" (Overing, 2000), ideally, an "art of living and making (in) common(s)", an *EcoDomics* (Valero, 2015).

I would thus briefly engage in a transversal genealogical exploration to try to understand why this *emotariat* burnout has become so entrenched. It would be necessary to call on an array of epistemological and empirical observations depicting a rhizomatic assemblage of "particles and waves", a kind of micro-macro ecosystem acting as a Platonic/Derridean *pharmakon*, healing and poisoning us at the same time (Stiegler, 2010).[4] In keeping with the nature of a "rhizomic assemblage", I employ an experimental structure structured around epigraphs at the beginning of each section. This structure encourages fluid reflection, as in a short chapter like this, it would be impossible even to superficially cover some of the main questions, as the sheer amount of information and expertise required for this undertaking goes beyond the knowledge of one single individual. Nevertheless, some highlights and connective tissues will be attempted, regarding the health of our socius, polis, and psyche with their semiotic and material subjection to an accelerated accumulation of capital, where the undemocratic and ever-expanding data "server farms" supporting "the Cloud", are an apt real and metaphorical expression of a neofeudal form of social, individual, and ecological alienation and servitude.

## Emotariat accelerationism, burnout, and grief – empirical overview

Stress and mental health concerns are not unique to our generation. But this is a generation expected to be connected and responsive all the time, entering a workforce where there is hardly a beginning or an end to the day. This is a generation for whom teenage insecurities are subjected to an onslaught of image-conscious, carefully curated social media platforms. When we talk about burnout, we are not just talking about money and jobs; we are talking about the fractured lives we live and the toil it takes. It's no wonder this generation is increasingly turning to drugs as a means to escape and unplug. . . . But when and how do drugs go beyond simple stress relievers and become fill-ins . . . for the things we have lost in our lifestyles? Do drugs and drug trends overlap with a rise in stress? Have our brains been rewired because of various inputs from society, and how do people try to unravel?

(Jones, 2018)

We have the uneasy feeling that our influence over the rest of the world is coming at a great cost: loss of the world's diversity and complexity. For all our self-incrimination . . . our most troubling impact on other cultures (is) how we are flattening the landscape of the human psyche itself. We are engaged in the grand project of Americanizing the world's understanding of the human mind.

(Watters, 2010, p. 1)

Western mental health discourse introduces core components of Western culture, including a theory of human nature, a definition of personhood, a sense of time and memory, and a sense of moral authority. None of this is universal.

(Summerfield, quoted in Watters, 2010, p. 65)

Mental health at the heart of the climate crisis. Life on Thin Ice: Greenland's melting has been adopted by the world as its own problem. But for the islanders grieving their dissolving world, the crisis is personal, and dangerous. "Ecological grief": Greenland residents traumatized by climate emergency.

(McDougall, 2019)

*"Trumps Scraps Trip to Denmark, as Greenland is Not for Sale"*. . . . This week, Mr. Trump confirmed reports about his long-held interest in buying Greenland from Denmark, a land deal he has become interested in because of the country's natural resources, like coal and uranium. "Well, a lot of things can be done", Mr. Trump said on Sunday. "Essentially, it's a large real estate deal".

(Karni, 2019)

In the first part of this chapter, I suggest that the "deracinating *affect* of capitalism" is linked to *emotariat* accelerationism, burnout, and grief, on several empirical and psychological registers. In Ethan Watters's *Crazy Like Us*, the mega-marketing of depression in Japan, the rise of anorexia in Hong Kong, the tsunami-related PTSD spike in Sri Lanka, and the changing concepts of schizophrenia in Zanzibar seem to share a strong connection with the neoliberal project of accelerated emotional capitalism, the rise of the control society and populism, the massive wealth gap greatly accentuated by the 2008 Great Recession, climate change,[5] and the "globalization of the American psyche".

This "American" approach to the psyche seems to also reflect a recurrence of the "Platonic break", that age-old body-soul dualism and tension inaugurated at the transition from an oral to a written culture. In this context, Hippocratic medicine became a *muta ars*, an art without words, emphasizing diet, drugs, and surgery, while the *therapeía* of the psyche, split from somatic embodiment, was left to the "therapy of the word" of philosophers, as Dr. Laín Entralgo argues:

> [T]he Greek physicians of the fourth century BC rejected as quackery the magical verbal therapy common to all early cultures, and relied on management of the *physis*, although at this same time the philosophers were rationalizing the word and mapping out the forms of verbal psychotherapy. Since the Greek physicians were unable to integrate the new knowledge into "naturalistic" medicine, they ignored verbal psychotherapy in their scientific medicine. When they did employ the word, it was in a magical and superstitious context.
>
> (Entralgo, 1958, 1970)

This Platonic-Hippocratic dualistic loop is still operative, and it may partly explain the contemporary overreliance on pharmaceuticals and Big Pharma.[6]

But, as suggested earlier, this "crisis of the soul" is both semiotic and material, expressed among other things in the fetishism of speed, change, and efficiency, as Sloterdijk, Foucault, Virilio, Han, Berardi, and others have observed. A recent online issue of *VICE* magazine was dedicated fully to the question of "burnout", as other recent articles of the American mainstream press.

> This is a generation expected to be connected and responsive all the time, entering a workforce where there is hardly a beginning or end to the day. . . . When we talk about burnout, we are not just talking about money and jobs; we are talking about the fractured lives we live and the toil it takes.
>
> (Jones, 2018)

> We are all burnout and trying to escape it: Poor mental health is not unique to one generation. But Gen Y and Gen Z are connected and responsive 24/7. It's no wonder they are increasingly turning to drugs as an antidote to our digital dystopia.
>
> (Daily, 2018)

Case and Deaton speak of "deaths of despair" to refer to the increased US mortality since the 2008 Great Recession. They demonstrate that

> the increases in deaths of despair are accompanied by a measurable deterioration in economic and social wellbeing, which has become more pronounced for each successive birth cohort. Marriage rates and labor

force participation rates fall between successive birth cohorts, while reports of physical pain, and poor health and mental health rise . . . document[ing] an accumulation of pain, distress, and social dysfunction in the lives of working class whites that took hold as the blue-collar economic heyday of the early 1970s ended, and continued through the 2008 financial crisis and the subsequent slow recovery.

(Deaton, 2017)

Neoliberalism, often called "modernization"[7] in mainland China, shows similar trends: As a result of the modernization, mental health disorders have surpassed cancer and the cardiovascular diseases and become the leading cause of burden. . . . Autism, schizophrenia, depression and dementia, four brain disorders occurring at different stages across the lifespan, are considered as prioritized disease areas. These diseases are emerging mental health issues, and efforts to scientific research may provide important implications for neuropsychiatric medicine, in particular for developing novel strategies for effective therapeutic and preventive intervention, to fight against mental health disorders in China.

(Zhao, 2015)

Wenzhou Kangning Hospital Company, a chain of psychiatric hospitals, shows how rapid change has

improved living standards while fraying social ties and creating new social pressures. A once rural society held together by extended families is now an urban one in which single children compete fiercely from preschool onward. Depression, anxiety, and insomnia are increasingly common among the young, while dementia increases among China's growing ranks of elderly.

(Minter, 2018)[8]

One meta-study argues the suicide rate

in the general population of China has decreased in recent decades over previous urban and rural areas, . . . Differences in suicide rates amongst the elderly exist between rural and urban areas. Addressing the high suicide rate amongst the elderly in rural China requires a policy response.

(Katikireddi, 2019)

But the competitive nature of the new economy increasingly affects the young and may be underreported (Yan, 2018).

The World Federation of Mental Health has declared "suicide prevention" its theme for 2019:

Suicidal behavior has existed throughout human history, but due to several complex factors it has increased gradually in *all parts of the world* and, in the past few decades, has reached *alarming statistical levels. . . .* According to the WHO, more than 800,000 people die by suicide a year, making it the principal cause of death among people fifteen to twenty-nine years old. It is often believed that it is only adults who exhibit suicidal behaviors, but it should be known that children and young people engage in this kind of behavior as a result of violence, sexual abuse, bullying and cyberbullying.

(Trimboli, 2019, emphasis added)

In 2001, the WHO predicted that mental and neurological diseases could afflict 25 percent of world population by 2020, with the poor often bearing the

greater burden of mental disorders, both in terms of the risk in having a mental disorder and the lack of access to treatment. Constant exposure to severely stressful events, dangerous living conditions, exploitation, and poor health in general, all contribute to the greater vulnerability of the poor. The lack of access to affordable treatment makes the course of the illness more severe and debilitating, leading to a vicious circle of poverty and mental health disorders that is rarely broken.

(2001)

## A note on the political economy of the *emotariat*

The scope and ambition of the neoliberal programme to *restore what could never be expunged* can be summarised by Margaret Thatcher's infamous remark that method was economics, the goal was to change the soul – the slogan of market Stalinism. The libidinal metaphysics that underlies neoliberalism might be called *cosmic libertarianism . . .* a constructive project: the competitive economic subject was the product of a vast ideological and libidinal engineering project.

(Davies and Fisher, 2018)

"To be able to work 996 is a huge bliss. . . . If you want to join Alibaba, you need to be prepared to work 12 hours a day, otherwise why even bother joining.

(Jack Ma, quoted in Denning, 2019)

This overview demonstrates a consistent correlation between the public and private health aspect of a global psyche and a host of socio-environmental factors stemming from the transition to global capitalism. This correlation can no longer be ignored. At the dataist,[9] political and conceptual levels, the Foucauldian "disciplinary" industrial societies have given way to the neoliberal digital, hyper-dynamic Deleuzian *Societies of Control,* where desire-mongering reigns supreme. If the exploited of the disciplinary society were exemplified by the proletariat, the exploited of the control society may be exemplified by the cognitariat[10] and *emotariat.*

I focus here on the *emotariat,* a burnout condition stemming from the relentless exploitation of affect and desire emerging from the unceasing production of subjectivity of global capitalism, together with its deleterious impact on the psychosomatic body of contemporary individuals. In choosing this name, I want to emphasize the distinctive affective register of today's corporate capitalism[11] and to follow in the footsteps of a critical tradition that has called the exploited industrial worker *proletariat* and, more recently, the exploited knowledge worker *cognitariat.* I conflate the three within the *precariat* worker (Lazar, 2019), toiling under a generalized neoliberal post-Fordist control regime of semio-capitalist precarity (Berardi, 2009b).[12] The "informal economies" of the Global South have, of course, known precarity since colonialism and its present-day extractocene,[13] a precarity that has been greatly intensified and accelerated in the current dataist economy. But even the more permanent formal work in the North seems to have been a mere temporary phenomenon, as demonstrated in the widely read Thomas Piketty *Capital in the 21st Century,* with its warnings on "patrimonial capitalism".[14]

Again, it could be argued that there is no need to coin a new word for what could be loosely accommodated within a proletariat categorization, as simply the accelerated exploitation of human affects by capital, but it is impossible to ignore some of the qualitative differences between the Fordist industrial capitalist economies of mass production and mass consumption, dominant up until the late 1970s, and the new techno-economic formations that have rapidly emerged since then. In this regard, French, German, and Italian theorists, in particular, have addressed the phenomenon of a global political economy dominated by cybernetics, artificial intelligence, and informatics, mobilizing what Marx's *Grundrisse* theorized as the "general intellect", which has given rise to the "control societies" already mentioned (Deleuze, 1990/1995, pp. 177–182). Just as *cognitariat* has been proposed for the knowledge workers of the "gig economy" and their "immaterial production", so, too, we could refer to the dynamic of a "soul at work", borrowing Berardi's evocative term, for the always on, 24/7, unpaid, and restless psychic contributors to the algorithmic platforms of "emotional capitalism" and its passion economy, as an *emotariat* condition. I believe it is important to emphasize this distinction, even though, de facto, all these categories are mixed within the current global regime.

## An economy of *Eros* and the *emotariat*

> Over and over again we find, when we are able to trace instinctual impulses
> back, that they reveal themselves as derivatives of Eros. . . . [W]e are driven

to conclude that the death instincts are by their nature mute and that the clamour of life proceeds from the most part from Eros. The Moerae were created as a result of a discovery that warned man that he too is a part of nature and therefore subject to the immutable law of death. Something in man was bound to struggle against this subjection.

(Freud, 1923/1992, pp. 118–119)

To say that desire is part of the infrastructure comes down to saying that subjectivity produces reality. Subjectivity is not an ideological superstructure.

(Guattari, April 3, 1984)

We are no longer dealing with a duality of mass and individual. Individuals become "*dividuals*," and masses become samples, data, markets, or *banks*.

(Deleuze, 1990/1995, p. 180, emphasis in original)

Eros,[15] following a known hermeneutical tradition, as foundational libidinal energy and divinity, becomes reified, quantified, commodified, accelerated, automated, monetized, and weaponized in contemporary capitalism. Thus, we begin this short exploration, where under emotional capitalism (Illouz, 2007), this Eros energy is constantly teased and withdrawn through imposed scarcity and lack, to efficiently fuel a kind of frenzy, a *dyseros*, a dystopian delirium, betrayal, and consumption of the "common man". Its dividual-ized[16] algorithms act as a recurrent "dream catcher", a libidinal enclosure platform (Srnicek, 2017) of subjectivity and a master of the "soul at work" (Berardi, 2009a), for maximum profit, power, and exploitation. Its erotic, libidinal repression lights up a torch, which, like climate-induced wildfires, threatens to engulf the entire body organic and body politic of the planet.

If, as a thought experiment of associations and analogies, we reflect on the *macchina mitologica* (Jesi, 2013) or "mythological engine"[17] at work in liberal, capitalist modernity and, more recently, on the play of the intensities of emotional capitalism and the passion economy[18] and return to the ancient mythical origins of this powerful Greek divinity in search of his genealogical ancestry, we will see a series of relevant insights and metaphors come to mind.[19] He was variously associated with Aphrodite (Venus) and Ares (Mars), as brother to Pothos (longing) and Anteros (mutual love). In yet other nomenclatures, he was the sibling of Harmonia, Phobos (fear), Deimos (dread, terror), and Adestria or Nemesis (the inescapable goddess of retribution against arrogance before the gods). In Plato's *Symposium*, through the voice of mantic Diotima, he was the grandchild of the Oceanic Titaness Tetis (wisdom, skill, craft, magical cunning), whose son Poros (expediency, resourcefulness, plenty) was father to Eros. Penia (poverty, lack, need) was his mother, who, uninvited to the birth of Aphrodite, found a way to sleep with Poros. Hesiod, much earlier, placed him as one of the five original gods and goddesses emanating from the initial Void of Chaos, along with Gaia (the Earth), Erebus (darkness), Nyx (night) and Tartarus (the abyss). In the

Orphic tradition, close in time to Hesiod's story, Eros emerges from the Cosmic Egg (Harrison, 1922, 3rd Ed, 1991; Burkert, 1985; Woodard, 2007).

This compact story of Eros's parentage brings to our attention a topology of vectors and meanings at play in the opaque field of desire and its siblings and how these representations are still deeply meaningful to us. A recurrent theme is at once evident: at the *ursprung* moment, when ancestral infinitesimal fluctuations "break the symmetry" and "swerve" into existence the five original gods, Eros is among them. This account is not unique to ancient Greece, as each culture in its own way imagines, venerates, loves, and fears, then and now, this basic biological, social, and psychological drive, becoming a complex evolutionary mechanism deeply connected to our survival.[20] This is why a sophisticated ability to tap into this vast reservoir may give the upper hand to those able to appropriate this energy for their own purposes, individually, culturally, economically, and politically.

In fact, even a superficial analysis of this primal ancestry and erotic propellant reads like a recurrent litany of many present-day red-hot libidinal vectors at the communal and psychological levels. It also shows how, in the hands of clever and knowledgeable manipulators, these libidinal signifiers can be activated and become a powerful and combustible mix, which can only be partially harnessed, as the historical record abundantly demonstrates. In this contradictory delirium, the multiple energies of Eros are absorbed and crunched within the machinery of corporate ideology and capital accumulation, "social subjection". and "machinic enslavement", in the words of Félix Guattari and Gilles Deleuze (Lazzarato, 2014, p. 23), leading to an *emotariat* symptomatology of anxiety, depression, addiction, grief, and other maladies of the soul, discussed earlier.

"For Freud, the human psyche is a kind of thermodynamic mechanism in which libido, [is] a generalized, mobile, pleasure-seeking energy" (Scarborough, 1994, p. 24), susceptible to blockage and repression that can burst out if undue internal or external pressure builds up without any cathartic outlet. Dreams are symbolic stratagems from the id, which try to elude the censorship of the superego; more expansively, "myths are public collective dreams", that can carry the neurotic contents of the unconscious. In this vein, for Carl Jung,[21] the "collective unconscious" becomes the repository of humankind's fears and hopes and is directly related to a mythic dimension expressed in the "archetypes", resembling Plato's ideal forms, but also providing an entry point to the enduring power/discourse of the religious question. Regrettably, for lack of space, the topic cannot be discussed here, though in the context of the rising power of religious fanaticism and its unsavory connections with populism, it deserves an extended treatment.

Circa 494–434 BCE, Empedocles's *Love and Strife* provides a helpful bridge between the Eros story and the fascination Freud had with this pre-Socratic philosopher. Sarah Kofman, noted Freudian scholar, gives us a clue about Freud's interest in Empedocles, rendering a key connection between myth and psyche for purposes of my own argument:

As the unconscious projections of the instincts, distorted by displacement, into the external world, the Empedoclean *myth* would simultaneously *reveal* and *conceal psychic truth*. . . . Henceforth, it is easy to understand why Freud favors Empedocles. *What is determinant here is the mythical element.* In as far as every myth contains a psychic truth, a mythical philosophy is more symptomatic, more revealing of the unconscious, and closer to primary processes than a purely speculative philosophy would be. . . . By concealing, myth reveals more than the supposed conceptual clarity of the philosophers. And if Freud selects Empedocles . . . it is primarily because [he] is the only one to apply *"double causality"* to all things, and also because we only know him in fragments. "This fragmentary character is itself, in effect already an image of the lacunar character of the psychic self." Also, because Empedocles was a polymath, learned, yet "fond of popular superstitions . . . believing in an animate universe.

(Kofman, 1974/1991, pp. 27–28, emphasis added)

Angie Voela, in her recent *Psychoanalysis, Philosophy and Myth in Contemporary Culture*, has added a Lacanian and Stieglerian dimension to popular culture, science fiction, and the "abyss of the Other's desire, or Greek Myth for (neoliberal) children" (2017, p. 137), proving how insightful this line of analysis continues to be – playing into the persuading libidinal hands of AI, behavioral economics, neuro-marketing, and politics.

This Eros genealogy, as primary processes and transforming elements, can be seen as a-historical projections, but as part of the double Eros/Thanatos, love/strife dynamic, they can also be regarded as expressing the radical precarity of the living human condition (Butler, 2004) within the context of culturally and socially constructed forces co-evolving within the framework of specific modes of production, technical relations of production, and ecological relations of production, comprising a *"capitalocene*, a 'world-ecology' of wealth, power, and nature" (Moore, 2015). This world-ecology of primary processes mined as raw material for alluring consumption, profit maximization, and recursive psychic angst become an increasing source of *emotariat* burnout, though, these primary elements can also be a hopeful source of Spinozist potentiality (Negri, 1981; Lordon, 2010).

## The republic of data and the *legitimation crisis*

It is not clear if and how representative democracy will survive in the 21st century. New "smart" technologies such as AI, robotics, social media and automation are threatening to fundamentally disrupt our politics, economy and society. Pessimistically, these advances will only exacerbate existing inequalities and injustices linked to corporate globalization. However, they also hold the positive potential to radically transform our democracies and civic societies, creating ones that are more responsive, egalitarian and accountable. In these turbulent times for governing . . . we are confronted with dramatically

opposed futures for conceiving how technology will reshape civic participation as well as economic and political governance . . . perhaps the most
profound techno-political struggle of the 21st century [will be] between a
progressive "techno-democracy" and a regressive "techno-populism".

(Bloom, 2019, p. 5)

Once adopted into the production process of capital, the means of labor
passes through different metamorphoses, whose culmination is the machine,
or rather an *automatic system of machinery* (system of machinery: the automatic one is merely its most complete, most adequate form, and alone trans-
forms machinery into a system), set in motion by an *automaton*, a moving
power that moves itself; this automaton consisting of numerous mechanical
and intellectual organs, so that the workers themselves are cast merely as its
conscious linkages. . . . [I]t is the machine which possesses skill and strength
in place of the worker, is itself the virtuoso, with *a soul of its own*, in the
mechanical laws acting through it; and it consumes coal or oil as the worker
consumes food to keep up its *perpetual motion*.

(Marx, *The Grundrisse*, 1858, pp. 692–693, emphasis added)

Marx's economic theory was based on the labor theory of value: that the
value of a good is, at its simplest form, the necessary labor time to make it. In
"The Fragment on Machines", Marx tackles a question that is more relevant
today than ever: how do we define value when the human labor required to
create goods rapidly approaches zero? Or, put more apocalyptically: when
AI have taken all the jobs, who is left to buy goods?"

(McBride, 2017)

"Are we all going to be working for a smart machine, or will we have smart
people around the machine?" The question was posed to me in 1981 by a
young paper mill manager. . . . I recognized the oldest political questions:
Home or exile? Lord or subject? Master or slave? These are eternal themes of
knowledge, authority, and power that can never be settled for all time. There
is no end of history; each generation must assert its will and imagination as
new threats require us to retry the case in every age.

(Zuboff, 2019, p. 3)

Over the last century technological acceleration has transformed our planet,
our societies, and ourselves, but has failed to transform our understanding of
these things. . . . Our technologies are complicit in the greatest challenges that
we face today: an out-of-control economic system that immiserates many
and continues to widen the gap between rich and poor; the collapse of political and societal consensus across the globe resulting in increasing nationalisms, social divisions, ethnic conflicts and shadow wars; and a warming
climate, which existentially threatens us all.

(Bridle, 2018)

Enterprises embarking on the AI and ML journey should not rely solely on
data scientists to see the bigger picture. . . . Successful cognitive application

in production is not just a data science problem, but also a software engineering problem that involves several key roles. What is needed is a phased approach that uses different disciplines and collaborative processes within the organization, ensuring everything from the creation of the models, to the real-world testing and integration into the business processes, is handled successfully. The essential players are referred to as the 4Ds: data scientists to leverage data and create models designers to work on UI and UX, developers to develop the right software or application that applies the models to business processes, DevOps to manage and update the infrastructure, integrations, deployments and model management.

(Phukan, 2019)

Horkheimer and Adorno view Odysseus's legendary cunning, which is a "kind of thinking that is sufficiently hard to shatter myths", as the precursor of instrumental reason and the technical domination of nature. . . . In the face of the hard totalitarianism of fascism and the soft totalitarianism of an administered world, [they] held that the "moment of critical thinking", of the capacity for independent political judgment, however limited, had to be preserved. . . . Through an immanent critique of Freud, [Marcuse] sought to break the identification of civilization with repression and to prove that a "non-repressive" society was, at least in principle, possible. . . . Against Freud's claim, [he] set out to demonstrate that the reality principle, which he took as the principle governing social life, is historically contingent and can assume different forms under different social conditions.

(Whitebook, 2004)

The term democracy sounds a false note wherever it crops up in debates these days because of a preliminary ambiguity that condemns anyone who uses it to miscommunication. . . . [I]t might mean one of two different things: a way of constituting the *body politic* . . . (public law) or a *technique of governing* . . . (administrative practice) . . . the form through which power is legitimated and the manner in which it is exercised. Since it is perfectly plain to everyone that the latter meaning prevails in contemporary political discourse, that the word democracy is used in most cases to refer to a technique of governing (something in itself not particularly reassuring).

(Agamben, 2001)

[T]he logic of *computation* and its ingression into culture . . . describes a world in which algorithms are no longer or are not simply instructions to be performed, but have become performing entities: actualities that select, evaluate, transform, and produce data. . . . This is not to contend that algorithms are the building blocks of a physical universe in which any kind of thought can be fully computed. Instead, a closer look at algorithmic procedures shows that incompleteness in *axiomatics* is at the core of computation. . . . Algorithms expose the internal inconsistencies of the rational system of governance, inconsistencies that correspond to the proliferation of increasingly random *data* within it. Instead of granting the infallible execution of automated order and control, the entropic tendency of data

> to increase in size, and thus to become random, drives infinite amounts of
> *information* to interfere with and reprogram algorithmic procedures. . . .
> The system of governance defined by the digital world of data can therefore
> no longer rely upon the smooth programming tasks, the exact reproduction
> of rules, and the optimization of conducts, habits and behaviors.
>
> (Parisi, 2013, p. viii, emphasis in original)

Giorgio Agamben reminds us of a dualist "ambiguity" at the origin of democracy: 1) *formal*, or "juridico-political" constitution, and 2) *instrumental*, or "economic-managerial" governance. Much later, in liberal democracy, this ambivalence allowed to either separate political democracy from economic democracy or, worse, to obfuscate their intimate connection, leaving in many instances a "democratic" political shell of empty rhetorical tropes like "freedom" and "liberty" and weakened institutions, increasingly devoid of legitimacy or perversely conflating monopoly capitalism with individualism, into the managerialist, instrumentalist oxymoron known as "free market democracy".[22] With Adam Smith, David Ricardo, and Karl Marx, even within all their differences of outlook, we had an explicit integration in the field of political economy, the later iterations of positivist law, political science, and neoclassical economics during the 19th and 20th centuries, divided and separated this historical dynamic, and lulled us into the ideologically comfortable cocoon of "objective" sciences and amoral econometrics.

Such rhetorical sophisms of truth-telling and truth-tellers, as Foucault's governmentality expounded and Plato's *Republic* long-ago discussed, have exploded in the face of our latter-day neoliberalism since its 2008 Great Recession legitimation crisis. Brexit, Trump, Modi, and Bolsonaro, to mention just some of the most prominent examples, show how running on a populist legitimation platform won over opponents merely running on an instrumentalist governance platform. Jürgen Habermas foretold this at the start of the Fordist/post-Fordist transition, which uncannily speaks of the

> controversy over the *truth-dependency* of legitimation . . . ignited at the
> sociological level by Max Weber's ambiguous conception of "rational
> authority", that is, the legally formed and procedurally regulated type
> of authority characteristic of modern societies. . . . [I]f belief in legitimacy is conceived as an empirical phenomenon without an immanent
> relation to truth, the grounds upon which it is explicitly based have only
> *psychological* significance. Whether such grounds can sufficiently stabilize a given belief in legitimacy depends on the *institutionalized prejudices* and *observable behavioral dispositions* of the group in question.
>
> (Habermas, 1973, 1975, p. 97, emphasis added)

Needless to say, that the contemporary controversies over "fake news", the climate change "hoax", racism and xenophobia, Zuboff's "behavioral futures" in "surveillance capitalism", and my own reflections on *emotariat* burnout, through which platform capitalism seduces and persuades us to go into a predictable direction, have resulted in the troubling rise of a generalized fear, depression, anxiety, grief, and alienation, a severe acceleration of ecological disruptions, and new kinds of neo-fascist populism and nationalism throughout the world. But, hey, why worry? The casino stock market for the 1 percent, in spite of bumps, is at unheard-of heights.

Thus, we come to the idea and practice of democracy under the shadow of high-tech and a legitimation crisis, facing a double-bind with the data set appropriated by platform capitalism and AI – another expression of the bifurcation I suggested at the beginning of this chapter: 1) a mere instrumentalist data republic: data governance, an unprotected, uncritical clearing house of data, massively used for obscure power grabs, control, and manipulation or 2) a hopeful means of greatly expanding the reach of the *demos*, what I call the *Republic of Data*. So far, the first option seems to have the upper hand, in ways that even Zamyatin, Orwell, or Huxley could not have imagined.

Function, Control, Option, Command, Shift, Caps Lock, Tab, Delete, Return. . . . A fast world at our fingertips full of options, letters, numbers, emojis, brushes, sounds, possibilities, and the always present Escape key . . . "dataset augmentation", (Bastone, 2019, June 12) and 3D illusions, faux depths and Deep Fakes. A world at our immediate command, but the real in the shadows, flattened by the algorithms and the hurricane-force gales of data and a-signifying semiotics.

> Digitality radically restructures the Lacanian triad of real, imaginary, and symbolic. It dismantles the real and totalizes the imaginary. As a digital reflector, the smartphone serves to renew the mirror stage after infancy. It opens up a narcissistic space – a sphere of the imaginary – in which one encloses oneself. The other does not speak via the smartphone.
> (Han, 2017b, p. 22)

So the stage is set for a treadmill of the soul, where the whole being is disembodied, trapped, and then thrown off to the four winds, like a medieval quartering machine, but now fueled with unconscionable speed – a segment of the millennial generation is already ensnared in too many options (Brigham, 2019). Yet, as Han's *Psychopolitcs* reveals, TINA (There Is No Alternative) neoliberalism has, de facto, vastly narrowed our legitimate democratic options.

Because the purpose was always a singlehanded option – what Mark Fisher brilliantly called "market Stalinism", a free market neoliberalism 'constructed' as a "psycho-political" engineering project conflating a libidinal economy with libidinal politics, encapsulating Margaret Thatcher's dictum – the *method* is *economics*, but the goal is to *change the soul* – an *emotariat* program indeed. This is a crystal-clear "rational" management strategy of "governmentality" and a particular management of the soul: the "entrepreneur of the self" or "achievement-subject", as Foucault and Han put it. And, being an "engineered" politics of the soul, it must rely on an internalized calculable soul that is externally actioned: thus, the contemporary emphasis on Big Data platforms, artificial intelligence, and automaticity. It is a massive Pavlovian experiment, where the libidinal red meat algorithm acts as a trigger for the dividualized self, now converted into a mere conveyor belt of desires, anxieties, ICTs and IoTs shopping sprees, deep fakes, Twitter tirades, and Cambridge Analyticas – a generalized hyper-reality that leads to "social subjection" and "machinic enslavement" and a wide *crise de production de subjectivité*, in Félix Guattari's insightful analysis (Lazzarato, 2014).

We can further envision this subjection and enslavement of subjectivity, through the unconscious liminality of the opaque and powerful libidinal energies released by hyper-modernity's "lost spirit of capitalism", and its sublime Other's aesthetic alienation and repression, as a vast planetary Greek Tragedy of the Common(s), now in full view as the digital *Eumenides*, unleashed by the hubris of patriarchal cybernetic algorithms, wreak havoc on democracy, governance, and the *demos* at a global scale.[23]

The repressed collective unconscious of the patriarchal symbolic order, Cixous *écriture féminine* (Cixous, 1976), can be seen as "feminized madness and terror". The archaic allusion to the *Eumenides* (Cixous, 1992) is a libidinal reference to the foundational challenge that the "Furies" pose to the dominant calculative order of Enlightenment rationality, even more so now than when she first posited her *écriture*. In our hyper-rational, seemingly controlled, contemporary algorithmic dataism, an unmanageable non-linear furious virality has the world on edge – ergo, too many "choices" repressed into one single cybernetic path: TINA neoliberalism. The built-in biases of the algorithmic systems needed to appropriate private citizens' information in order to maximally monetize their clicks has brought about a deep dark side that is threatening the very foundations of the world polity, a veritable anxious moment of *emotariat* exploitation and precariousness, as Shoshana Zuboff's *The Age of Surveillance Capitalism* (2018) has eloquently exposed.

The golden age of technology, the computational paradise, and communicative spell of choice is no more; we have bitten the poisoned apple (or is it *Apple*?), lost once more our techno-innocence, (Facebook, anyone?), and have been expelled to a dystopian hinterland very far from the promised "singularity". The Amazon River, now tamed by global warming and by giant Amazon warehouses, with their myriad servers, standing in some frosty, out-of-the-way cold desert (better for the heat-devouring cloud servants), has dried out the old urban Main Street and laid waste to an entire way of life, much like a new "Ali Baba and the Forty Thieves". The Arabian myth is a cautionary tale of serendipity, greed, and systematic elimination of contenders privy to the dual secret password codes: "open sesame" and "close sesame", leaving one single winner in possession of all the loot.

Amazon? (Ye, 2019). Ali Baba the woodcutter? Or is it the other Alibaba of 996 frenzy? (Chiu, 2019). Are these the new "satanic mills?"[24]

Nobody asks in the old tale how those "forty thieves" got hold of their original loot: it simply appeared inside the cave, magically, not unlike what they have us believe about the capitalist process of primary accumulation. It just happens because of a clever combination of 996 work, entrepreneurial ingenuity applied to technology, and *voilà*, goodness and the billionaires appear by spontaneous generation, out of the ether (the cloud?) like pre-Pasteurian microbes. This loot is the result of a massive social appropriation, cloaked beneath a naturalized Newtonian world, ignoring the source of capital accumulation. Michael Taussig's classic, *The Devil and Commodity Fetishism* – where indigenous victims of Colombian sugar plantations and Bolivian tin mines, undergoing a transition from pre-capitalist to capitalist forms of production and exchange, bring up magic, the devil, as an explanation for the destruction of their world and the coming into being of a harsh new one, where all personal agency is lost – is still relevant. Taussig adds:

> For William Blake, Newton was the symbol of market society and its oppressive use of technology and empire, and he assailed those very "principles of union" that Adam Smith found so congenial. . . . It was this reciprocating replication of market society in nature and of nature in market society that allowed Newtonianism to triumph and consummate the mechanical "principles of union" into a wholly and scientifically impervious truth of all being.
>
> (Taussig, 1980, p. 34)

Newton, Blake, and a peasantry forcibly integrated into market capitalism from a corner of South America can help us visualize the ravages of major capitalist transitions, which Marx already foresaw in his famous expression: "All that is solid melts into air". Today, a new global process of transformation occurring from one economy, industrial Fordism, to another, post-Fordist neoliberalism – impacting social class, ecology, technology, geopolitics, public life, democracy, and human subjectivity – has given rise to new misery amidst opulence, contradictory popular expressions, and perilous world tensions, which seem to be signaling the arrival of yet another phase centered on fanatical tribalism, increased regional strife, big power blocs, and accelerated climate change. The kind of Western liberal order in place since World War Two, which decayed into neoliberal globalization's legitimation crisis, is now stricken by its own Faustian bargain of internal contradictions, in spite of all the "rule of law", "free trade", and techno-fixes promised. The Old *Res-Publica* as a contract for governance centering on the public-thing, has given way to the insidious rejection of the commons and all things public in favor of neoliberal privatization and its magic "free" market Stalinism.

These magical explanations further depicted in fanatical racialized populism and nativism, hoping to be saved from the unsettling effects of a fast-changing world, occlude a devious "stealth neoliberalism" unbeknownst to many as a causative factor (Wendy Brown, 2015). The great popularity of superhero, zombie, bot, and vampire movies worldwide betrays a magical libidinal desire of "becoming great again": that is, returning to a mythical paradise, away from thieves and dangerous others, returning to a certainty in the future that has been robbed by a menacing dark Other. Unconsciously acknowledging, on the one hand, a vampiric process of exploitation[25] that it is leaving us undead, zombielike, contingently floating, and unmoored on a sea of *emotariat* precariousness and, on the other, compulsively searching for a superego, superhero savior or the cavalry, the navy, a demagogue, to save the day and restore us to our safe Eden.

Today's roster of "savior" authoritarian strongmen (and they are all men) depicts a world in open conflict, incapable – worse, unwilling – of reflecting on the true causes of popular despair. Africa, Asia, and Latin America are more than ever coveted for their mineral and ecological riches, permanently in danger of ruling class self-serving deals. Or even shorter: the Global South is more than ever coveted for their mineral riches and in permanent danger of ruling class self-serving deals.

In turn, Davos World Economic Forum founder Klaus Schwab in his *The Fourth Industrial Revolution*, reads Western history as a "man over nature" techno-centric narrative: Industrial Revolution 1.0 replaced animal power, IR 2.0 brought about mass production, IR 3.0, the digital revolution, and now IR 4.0, the fusing of physical, digital, and biological, impacting economies, industries, even what it is to be human (Schwab, 2016). Bloom and Sancino offer four loosely corresponding stages leading to Democracy 4.0, where a clash between "Techno-Populism" and "Techno-Democracy", potentially resolves into a "disruptive democracy" that could correspond to IR 4.0, following the "revolutionary stage" of IR 1.0, the "social democratic stage" of IR 2.0, and the "liberal stage" (really the neoliberal stage) of IR 3.0, where "human and social rights were expanded alongside the spread of the free market". They emphasize "how democracy is always a historically specific phenomenon that is usually at once both socially innovative and politically disruptive". Their D 4.0 "will be premised upon the core disruptive values of radical openness, personalization, and emancipation" (Sancino, 2019, p. 62).

William Davies's *Economic Science Fictions* is a search for alternative worlds, insisting on

> the possibility that imagination can intrude in economic life in an uninvited way that is not computable or accountable. *To imagine wholly different systems and premises of calculation*, for example, is in itself to resist the dystopian ideal promised by Wall Street and Silicon Valley, that there is nothing that can evade the logic of software algorithms, risk, and finance. *At a time when capitalism and socialism have*

*collapsed into each other*, obliterating spaces of alterity or uncalculated discourses in the process.

(Davies, 2018, pp. 22–23)

Bloom and Sancino further suggest that

> crucial for all these future-oriented politics is the radical democratisation of the present. ICTs have produced novel modes of . . . "virtual power" . . . *current technologies contain the seeds of new radical presents and futures to bloom and flourish*. . . . Fortunately, there are vibrant democratic movements and technologies. . . . Civic technologies (or) *Civtech* . . . reconceiving *public participation* . . . and the reach of *democratic* power.

Moreover, the use of social technologies encourages "participatory futures", helping

> to inform existing experimentation with radical democratic community building around the world.

(Sancino, 2019, pp. 67–69, emphasis added)

*Citizen Cyborg* (Hughes, 2004) illustrates an "updated version of citizenship . . . around the use of technology for expanding human potentiality", leading to "alternative realities [that] expand local knowledge as well as foster solidarity within and among marginalised groups across the globe. . . . [W]here a global civic society is networked to foster a collective and place-based leadership" (Sancino, 2019, p. 69).

Complementary alternatives, relevant to the earlier discussions, from Colombia, Peru, Argentina, Canada, Portugal, China, Cameroon, South Africa, Spain, and the United States are encountered, for example, in the recent work of Arturo Escobar's *Designs for the Pluriverse* and *Territories of Difference*, Boaventura de Sousa Santos's *The End of the Cognitive Empire*, Marisol de la Cadena and Mario Blaser's *A World of Many Worlds*, Yuk Hui's *The Question Concerning Technology in China*, Achille Mbembe's *Critique of Black Reason* and "Politics of Viscerality", Luis I. Prádanos's *Postgrowth Imaginaries*, Jason M. Hanania's *Architecture of a Technodemocracy*, and Donna J. Haraway's *Staying with the Trouble*. Space constraints prevent me from expounding on their insights, but each one depicts potential critical avenues for emancipatory futures that center on a democratic transversality of environmental, philosophical, political, indigenous, creative, economic, and technological questions. In my opinion, authors like these can crucially enrich the "disruptive" relevance of Democracy 4.0, with which an empowering Republic of Data – in the form of an EcoDomic aesthetic(s) of the common(s) – would align (Valero, 2015).

## Epilogue

This chapter has been ultimately a meditation on the soul of a living democracy in the midst of a massive global legitimation crisis caused by the accelerated neoliberal capitalocene experiment. How the falling dominoes of a multiplicity of world authoritarianisms is leaving behind a charred democratic shell devoid of ethical and emotional meaning, endangering the future project of a democratic pluriverse and its attendant rhizomatic transversalities. More specifically, to suggest that without economic democracy, there can be neither political democracy nor ethical democracy, but also that without a psychological democracy, ecological democracy, cultural democracy, and data democracy, a pluriversal[26] democracy cannot survive and flourish. I have chosen to emphasize democracy, along with these fundamental building blocks, only as an analytical strategy, for in a real democratic practice, the ethical, political, economic, psychological, ecological, cultural, and data rhizomes are transversally interrelated.

At the same time, the idea of an *emotariat* burnout, ever accelerating because of the runaway expansion of social subjection and machinic enslavement (Guattari, 1984), enabled by the "ingression of computational logic into culture" (Parisi, 2013, p. xiii), has led to a suffocating neofeudal, neoliberal a-signifying dataism and precarity. This seems to me to be one of the key elements at the core of the present democratic crisis of legitimacy. The authoritarian despots, whether state or corporate, intuitively, but also intentionally and cynically, understand that a major underbelly of power legitimacy rests in weaponizing the "soft" areas of discourse and practice pertaining to Eros, affect, emotion, repression, the Freudian pleasure and reality principles, and the Lacanian real, symbolic, and imaginary, deviously prolonging a mirror stage, lack, and consumerist stupor. However, the insertion of such algorithmic randomness into the socio-cultural, psychological, economic, ecological, and political process is leading to an abyssal incompleteness of deleterious unknowns like global warming, terrorism, white supremacy, populism, and a global angst that no amount of "software engineering" or geo-engineering will ever be able to "innovate" or "correct".

Marcuse, Habermas, Foucault, Derrida, Negri, Deleuze, Guattari, Berardi, De Sousa Santos, Escobar, Mbembe, Han, Hui, and Zuboff, among others, in their own approaches, helpfully reflect on the European enlightenment project of rationality, its various truth regimes, and confrontational politics. But one thing seems clear to me: that the psychic economy or psycho-political has attained an outsize importance in the management of contemporary populations, helped and abetted by the instantaneous speed of big data regimes, mostly at the service of power and profit. As the so-called Industrialization Revolution 4.0 has been shifting more and more toward the visual, multi-sensorial, and visceral components, the erotic-affective and emotional has been rapidly displacing the "cooler" waters of cognition and "dispassionate" empiricism, directly impacting as well the socio-environmental, psycho-cultural, and political-economic. So it should not come as a surprise that all forms of power monopolies should be availing themselves of these powerful emotional tools with the toxic results we are witnessing today. It is critical for them that an *emotariat* regime of burnout should prevail, by becoming an ongoing condition of exploitation, agitation, fear, anxiety, grief, drug addictions, and manufactured madness, perversely watering and softening the grounds of high-tech/low-tech authoritarian governmentality.

What to do, then, in the midst of these unsustainable circumstances? A doubling down on democracy, confronting head on the poisonous fumes of *emotariat* exploitation and precarity, first, by actually giving it a name and then, searching for alternative healing processes and worlds-other. Easier said than done, of course, but if we carefully look around, we may see myriad democratic seeds sprouting and coming forth in various guises, reminding us of Guattari's call for molecular revolutions, social movements that I can imagine as multiple "aesthetic(s) of the common(s)" (Valero, 2014) and post-growth "*affective ecologies* . . . emanating a deep corporeal communication among bodies of different kinds that crystallize the qualitative multifolded dynamic of place" (Cajigas, 2019). They are beginning to give us new visions and hopes throughout the planet, a sort of dialectical *aufheben*, resisting and equally empowering the possibility of a new democratic dawn, a *Tao* of democracy, what was referred to earlier both as Democracy 4.0 and as Techno-Democracy, or perhaps even an EcoDomic democracy. (Valero, 2015) They should not be seen merely as virtual interventions in cyberworlds, but as vital placed-based complements to the painstaking labor of relentless building, canvassing, and integrating diverse eco-political constituencies at the local and global level. This is what I have briefly tried to imply with the *Republic of Data*, a discourse and practice where, paradoxically, the precarious suffering of the proletariat, cognitariat, and *emotariat* may serve as trigger and transforming fuel, a non-repressive *enantiodromia*, to the democratic engines of this new "Data Publics" *Res-Publica*.

As a final hopeful note, I close this chapter with the voices of several astronauts and cosmonauts, because it shows how one of the most iconic data-heavy technological pursuits of the last 62 years, space exploration, can help us visualize a kinder future past many present techno-dystopias. Franklin Chang Diaz: "I think of myself as a citizen of the world, of the planet, and many astronauts will tell you that. They come back realizing that they really are citizens of the planet and not citizens of a country" (Hatzipanagos, 2019. His experience is echoed in a group recently interviewed by the *Washington Post*, summarized by Chris Hadfield:

> At one point I just sent out a [tweet] at the suggestion of my son and just said to everybody, "What do you want me to take a picture of?" And the overwhelming result from everywhere around the world was "my hometown". That means people are proud of where they live. . . . But the flip side of that is they also want to see how they fit, and how their

hometown fits, into the big kaleidoscope of all the hometowns in the world. I found that really unifying.

It is an emancipating bookend to the words of Yuri Gagarin, the first man in space: "Orbiting Earth in the spaceship, I saw how beautiful our planet is. People, let us preserve and increase this beauty, not destroy it" (Vitkovskaya, 2019).

## Notes

1 A word of special gratitude to the editors of the book, professors Peter Mörten-böck and Helge Mooshammer, for their very gracious invitation to London and Vienna and for their continued support of my work.

2 For a period of time I was working in my country of origin, Colombia, with the government body in charge of science and technology and with the Organization of American States, both trying during interminable negotiations to extract more favorable "technology transfer" terms from US corporations and the US government that often led to a dead end. My subsequent engagement in development and environment policies at the national and international levels further gave me a close understanding of nascent neoliberal policies, promising an early escape from "underdevelopment", packaged as *"modernización"* and *"sociedad del logro"*, or achievement society, which Foucault theorized as the "entrepreneur of the self".

3 See also Leswing (2019).

4 Stiegler recalls in "Plato's Pharmacy" (Derrida, 1981, pp. 61–171) Derrida's reading of Plato's *Phaedrus* concept of the *pharmakon* within the context of a critique of Western metaphysics, in his introduction to a "Pharmacology of the Proletariat".

5 "Ecological grief" or "environmental grief" is a deeply meaningful emotion within the context of a widening climate crisis and sixth mass extinction, inequality, and other "hyper-object" calamities (Morton, 2013; Stevens, 2019).

6 The global "war on drugs" and the scandal of multinational pharmaceutical companies' complicity in the American opioid crisis, which have claimed thousands of lives so far, gravely disrupting entire societies and vulnerable groups, are major instances of such tragic pharmacopeia.

7 Modernization is a highly contested concept in the social sciences. It basically refers to the transition to a capitalist market economy. It is different from modernity and modernism, theorized in the humanities, though all three are conceptually related to the European Enlightenment.

8 "The number of Chinese registered as suffering from depression, anxiety, alcohol abuse, dementia, and other mental illnesses increased by 25 percent between 2014 and 2016, according to Chinese authorities. By one recent accounting, they number 173 million. Only 20 million receive professional treatment" (Minter, 2018).

9 My own adjectival form of "Data", taken from Dataism, a term that has been used to describe the mindset or philosophy created by the emerging significance of Big Data. It was first used by David Brooks in the *New York Times* in 2013 [1]. More recently, the term has been expanded to describe what social scientist Yuval Noah Harari has called an emerging ideology or even a new form of religion, in which "information flow" is the "supreme value" [2].

10 The *cognitariat* is a concept primarily theorized by Italian *postoperaismo*, which attempts to understand the "immaterial production" and value of the "general intellect" under the precarious labor conditions created by digital network capitalism, questioned by exponents of the Marxian value-form theory, particularly

on immeasurability. Given that background, it is perhaps daring on my part to attempt to develop yet a new concept related to this new data capitalism. By calling *emotariat* a general condition of emotional exploitation that has greatly intensified in this new economy, I am just initiating a conversation around emotional suffering and its amelioration and not entering at this point into a complex discussion on the labor theory of value, which is nevertheless of crucial importance.

11 Contemporary TINA (There Is No Alternative) capitalism has many guises: neoliberalism, globalization, platform capitalism, algorithmic capitalism, emotional economy, passion economy, attention economy, cloud economy, gig economy, shared economy, knowledge economy, immaterial economy, semio-capitalism, capitalocene.

12 These nomenclatures are more readily found within the intellectual discourse, popular imaginary, and political movements of continental Europe than in the Anglo-Saxon sphere "where the English-speaking world has had thirty years to get more used to a more 'flexible' labor market" (Grizziotti, 2019, p. 1).

13 The *extractocene* is a concept being developed by artist/scholar Praba Pilar. See also Gómez-Barris (2017) and Singham, June 09, 2019).

14 Thomas Piketty's work generated much controversy among the wealthy leading to, for example, *Anti-Piketty*, a "rebuttal" by a group of conservative writers supported by the Koch brothers–financed Cato Institute.

15 For my purposes here, I have chosen to explore the Eros saga, primarily because of his importance within the Western hermeneutical tradition. "God of love, late 14 c., from Greek *eros* (plural *erates*), literally 'love,' related to *eran* 'to love,' *eresthai*, 'to love, desire,' of uncertain origin. Freudian sense of 'urge to self-preservation and sexual pleasure' is from 1922". (Google, *eros*, etymology).

16 "Dividualism is a way of seeing personhood usually attributed to Melanesian cultures but seen in many others, which includes partibility and relational personhood in its model. A person is not seen as a separate entity from the rest of the world, but as a complex of relationships interlinked with the world" (Salisbury, n.d.). Marilyn Strathern's *Partial Connections* and *The Gender of Gift* are key interventions in this context. However, Deleuze gives *Dividualism* a different connotation: "We are no longer dealing with a duality of mass and individual. Individuals become '*dividuals*', and masses become samples, data, markets, or '*banks*'" (Deleuze, 1990/1995, p. 180, emphasis in original). I believe the complementarity of those two views may be helpful to understand the increasing power and reach of platform capitalism.

17 "In one of his most notable books Furio Jesi speaks of the language of 'publicity,' as the new way of communication used by right-wing culture: the culture of ideas without words". / "*In uno dei suoi libri più noti Furio Jesi parla del linguaggio della pubblicità come del nuovo modo di presentarsi della cultura di destra, la cultura delle "idee senza parole*" (Jesi, 1979, https://it.wikipedia.org/wiki/Furio_Jesi.

18 Here I am referring to the turn of the 20th century work of Gabriel Tarde, long forgotten in social thought but influential on Sigmund Freud, Gilles Deleuze, Félix Guattari, and more recently Bruno Latour (Latour & Lépinay, 2009).

19 It should be noted, again, that this type of archaic mythical excavation has a long tradition in the hermeneutical tradition of the West, but also in other non-Western traditions as well, though they are not explored here.

20 Cf. The upper paleolithic "Venus Figurines" (Vandewettering, 2015). Mozi, the fourth century BCE Chinese philosopher talks about *Ai*, love, and "universal love" or *jiān'ài* in contrast to the more restricted "benevolent love" of Confucianism. "Later in Chinese Buddhism, *Ai* was adopted to refer to passionate, caring love and was considered a fundamental desire . . . seeing as capable of being either selfish or selfless, the latter being a key element toward enlightenment"

(Wikipedia, 2019). There is the "Lady Rainbow", the Maya Ixchel, later adopted by the Aztecs as "Precious Feather Flower"; and Xochiquetzal, goddess of love, fertility, flowers, vegetation, prostitution, and pleasure, who never aged or lost her beauty, patron of weaving and the arts. Oshun, a Black Madonna from the Yoruba Lands and Afro-America, the great Isis from ancient Egypt, or Guan Yin, the Bodhisattva of Compassion. In fact, anthropologists have never found a society that did not have romantic love (Fisher, 2014, 2008).

21 In many scholarly quarters, in spite of his contributions, Jung is ignored, still bearing the "brutal and sanctimonious Jung" Freudian remark, uttered upon their break, his problematic relations to women and the Nazis keep alive the controversy, not unlike Heidegger's case.

22 "Democracies cannot survive on norms alone. When markets are left under-regulated – and workers, unorganized – the corporate sector becomes a cancerous growth, expanding until it dominates politics and civil society. An ever-greater share of economic gains concentrates in ever-fewer hands, while the barriers to converting private wealth into public power grow fewer and farther between. Politicians become unresponsive to popular preferences and needs. Voters lose faith in elections – and then, a strongman steps forward to say that he, alone, can fix it" (Levitz, 2018).

23 "The Eumenides function for Cixous as the repressed other of contemporary patriarchal culture. They represent a world of feminized madness and terror, from the perspective of our dominant symbolic order . . . one in which the opposition of subject and object, masculine and feminine, no longer mark stable points of reference, but dissolve into an open field of relations that is at once exhilarating and terrifying. . . . [T]he possibility of a fundamental different relation to being, to the repressed that is constitutive of our present psychic order . . . a moment of orphic ambiguity, one that is *lived* rather than thought *about*" (Miller, 2016, p. 26).

24 The November 2019 *Scientific American* article, "The Inescapable Casino", by Professor Bruce M. Boghosian, describes a "novel approach developed by physicists and mathematicians, [depicting] wealth distribution in modern economies with unprecedented accuracy". It demonstrates that "the unfairness inherent in market economies" inexorably leads to an oligarchy and concludes reiterating "the fact that a sketch of the free market as simple and plausible as the affine wealth model gives rise to economies that are anything but free and fair should be both a cause for alarm and a call for action" (Boghosian, 2019). An *Ali Baba* update for the 21st century?

25 Here it may be relevant to recall Marx's vivid metaphor describing capital as "dead labour which, vampire-like, lives only by sucking living labor, and lives the more, the more labour it sucks" (Marx, 1867/1976, I, p. 342).

26 I am here inspired by Arturo Escobar's *Designs for the Pluriverse*, with his plural ontological and epistemological call for a "real world autonomous design", within a "politics of relationality and the communal".

# References

Agamben, G. (2001), 'Introductory note to the concept of democracy', in *Democracy in What State?* New York: Columbia University Press, pp. 1–2.

Aristophanes. (414 BCE), *Birds*. Athens Dionisya: s.n.

Bastone, N. (2019), 'A former Google product exec just raised millions from Eric Schmidt and Khosla Ventures to liberate AI from Big Tech's grip', *Business Insider*. Available at: www.businessinsider.com/former-google-product-exec-raises-seed-from-khosla-and-schmidt-2019-6?r=DE&IR=T.

Berardi, F.B. (2009a), *The Soul at Work: From Alienation to Autonomy*. Los Angeles: Semiotext(e), distributed by MIT Press.

Berardi, F.B. (2009b), *Precarious Rhapsody: Semiocapitalism and the Pathologies of the Post-alpha Generation*. London: Minor Compositions.

Blaser, M. and de la Cadena, M. (2018), *A World of Many Worlds*. Durham, NC and London: Duke University Press.

Bloom, P. (2019), *Disruptive Democracy*. s.l.: SAGE Swifts. Kindle Edition, p. 5.

Boghosian, B. (2019), 'The Inescapable Casino' in Scientific American. Volume 321, Issue 5.

Bridle, J. (2018), *New Dark Age: Technology and the End of the Future*. London and Brooklyn, NY: Verso.

Brigham, T. (2019), 'I've been a "millennial therapist" for more than 5 years – and this is their No. 1 complaint', *CNBC*. Available at: www.cnbc.com/2019/07/02/a-millennial-therapist-brings-up-the-biggest-complaint-they-bring-up-in-therapy.html?__source=iosappshare%7Ccom.apple.UIKit.activity.Mail.

Brown, W. (2015), *Undoing the Demos: Neoliberalism's Stealth Revolution*. New York: Zone Books.

Burkert, W. (1985), *Greek Religion*. Cambridge, MA: Harvard University Press.

Butler, J. (2004), *Precarious Life: The Powers of Mourning and Violence*. London and Brooklyn, NY: Verso.

Cajigas, J.C. (2019), *Vitality: Emanation-of-place*. Davis, CA: UC Davis.

Chiu, K. (2019), *Tech Titans Defend 996. Jack Ma and Richard Liu Defend China's Overtime Work Culture, But Ordinary Workers Can't Relate*. s.l.: Abacus.

Cixous, H. (1976), *The Laugh of Medusa*. Chicago: University of Chicago.

Cixous, H. (1992), *Les Euménides d'Eschyle*. Paris: Théâthre du Soleil.

Daily, M., Rao, A. and Kantrowitz, L. (2018), 'We are all burnout and trying to escape it', *VICE Magazine, Burnout and Escapism Issue*. Available at: www.vice.com/en_us/article/j5zjay/were-all-burned-out-and-trying-to-escape-it-v25n4.

Davies, W. (2018), 'Mark fisher, foreword', in *Economic Sciece Fictions*. London: Goldsmiths Press.

Deaton, A. and Case, A. (2017), 'Mortality and morbidity in the 21st century', *Brookings*. Available at: www.brookings.edu/bpea-articles/mortality-and-morbidity-in-the-21st-century/ [Accessed 5 July 2019].

Deleuze, G. (1990/1995), 'Postscript on control societies', in *Negotiations*. New York: Columbia University Press, pp. 177–182.

Denning, S. (2019), 'The rumored roots of Alibaba's results: The "996" work culture', *Forbes*. Available at: www.forbes.com/sites/stephaniedenning/2019/04/16/the-rumored-roots-of-alibabas-results-the-996-work-culture/#7aa07b684eec [Accessed 7 July 2019].

Derrida, J. (1981), *Dissemination*, trans. Barbara Johnson. Chicago: Chicago University Press, pp. 61–171.

Entralgo, P.L. (1958, 1970), 'Inside cover', in *The Therapy of the Word in Classical Antiquity*. New Haven and London: Yale University Press.

Escobar, A. (2008), *Territories of Difference: Place, Movements, Life, Redes*. Durham, NC and London: Duke Unversity Press.

Escobar, A. (2018), *Designs for the Pluriverse: Radical Interdependence, Autonomy and the Making of Worlds*. Durham, NC and London: Duke University Press.

Fisher, M. (2018), in Economic Science Fictions ed. by William Davies. London: Goldsmiths Press.

Fisher, H. (2014, 2008), *The Brain in Love* [Online]. Available at: www.ted.com/talks/ helen_fisher_studies_the_brain_in_love?language=en [Accessed 2 August 2019].

Freud, S. (1923/1992), *The Ego and the Id, Cited in V P Gay Freud on Sublimation Reconsiderations*. Albany: SUNY Press, pp. 118–119.

Gómez-Barris, M. (2017), *The Extractive Zone: Social Ecologies and Decolonial Perspective*. Durham, NC and London: Duke University Press.

Griffith, R. (trans.). (1896/ 2019), *The Hymns of the Rig Veda, Book 10*. Kotagiri, Nilgiri: Wikepedia/Public Domain.

Grizziotti, G. (2019), *Neurocapitalim: Technological Mediation and Vanishing Lines*. Colchester, NY and Port Watson: Minor Compositions/Autonomedia, p. 1.

Guattari, F. (1984), 'La Crise de production de subjectivité', in *Seminar*. s.l.: Revue Chimeres.

Habermas, J. (1973, 1975), *Legitimation Crisis*. Boston: Beacon Press.

Han, B.C. (2017a), *In the Swarm: Digital Prospcts*. Cambridge, MA: MIT University Press.

Han, B.C. (2017b), *Psychopolitics: Neoliberalism and New Technologies of Power*. London and Brooklyn, NY: Verso.

Hanania, J.M. (2018), *Architecture of a Technodemocracy*. San Francisco: www.tech nodemocracy.us.

Haraway, D.J. (2016), *Staying With the Trouble: Making Kin in the Chthulucene (Experimental Futures)*. Durham and London: Duke University Press.

Harrison, J.E. (1922 3rd ed./1991), *Prolegomena to the Study of Greek Religion*. Princeton: Princeton University Press / Mythos – Cambridge University Press.

Hatzipanagos, R. (2019), '"A citizen of the world": NASA's first Latino astronaut reflects on how space changed his immigrant identity'. Available at: www.washingtonpost. com/nation/2019/07/12/citizen-world-nasas-first-latino-astronaut-reflects-how-space-changed-his-immigrant-identity/?utm_term=.096fea613ad3-

Hughes, J. (2004), *Citizen Cyborg*. Cambridge, MA: Westview Press.

Hui, Y. (2016), *The Question Concerning Technology in China: An Essay in Cos-motechnics*. Windsor Quarry, UK: Urbanomic Media, Ltd.

Illouz, E. (2007), *Cold Intimacies: The Making of Emotional Capitalism*. Cambridge, UK and Malden, MA: Polity Press.

Jesi, F. (1979), *Cultura di Destra*. Milano: Garzanti.

Jesi, F. (2013), *Il tempo della festa*. Roma: Nottetempo.

Jones, E. (2018), *The Burnout and Escapism Issue* [Online]. Available at: www.vice. com/en_us/article/3k9vj3/take-a-trip-through-vice-magazines-latest-issue-v25n4. [Accessed 19 June 2019].

Karni, A. (2019), *Trumps Scraps Trip to Denmark, as Greenland Is Not for Sale* [Online]. Available at: www.nytimes.com/2019/08/20/us/politics/trump-cancels-greenland-trip.html?action=click&module=Top%20Stories&pgtype=Homepage [Accessed 20 August 2019].

Katikireddi, S.V. and Meizhi, L. (2019), 'Urban-rural inequalities in suicide among elderly people in China: A systematic review and meta-analysis', *International Journal for Equity in Health*, 18. [Online] Available at: https://equityhealthj. biomedcentral.com/articles/10.1186/s12939-018-0881-2 [Accessed 5 July 2019].

Kofman, S. (1974/1991), *Freud and Fiction*. Boston: Northeastern University Press, pp. 27–28.

Latour, B. and Lépinay, Vincent Antonin. (2009), The Science of Passionate Interests: An Introduction to Gabriel Tarde's Economic Anthropology. Chicago: Prickly Paradigm Press.

Lazzarato, M. (2014), *Signs and Machines: Capitalism and the Production of Subjectivity*. Los Angeles: Semiotext(e), distributed by MIT Press, p. 23.

Leswing, K. (2019), 'Here's how big tech companies like Google and Facebook set salaries for software engineers', *CNBC*. Available at: www.cnbc.com/2019/06/14/how-much-google-facebook-other-tech-giants-pay-software-engineers.html.

Levitz, E. (2018), 'America's version of capitalism is incompatible with democracy', *New York Magazine* [Online]. Available at: http://nymag.com/intelligencer/2018/05/americas-brand-of-capitalism-is-incompatible-with-democracy.html [Accessed 30 October 2019].

Lordon, F. (2010), *Capitalisme, désir et servitude. Marx et Spinoza*. Paris: La Fabrique éditions.

Mackay, R. and Avenessian, A. (eds.). (2014), *#ACCELERATE# the Accelerationist Reader*. Windsor Quarry, UK and Berlin: Urbanomic Media and Merve.

Marx, K. (1848), *Communist Manifesto*. Available at: marxist.org.

Marx, K. (1858), *The Grundrisse* [Online]. Available at: http://thenewobjectivity.com/pdf/marx.pdf [Accessed 6 July 2019].

Marx, K. (1867/1976), *Capital, Vol.1*. New York: Penguin, p. 342.

McBride, M. (2017), 'Did Karl Marx predict artificial intelligence 170 year ago', *medium.com* [Online]. Available at: https://medium.com/@MichaelMcBride/did-karl-marx-predict-artificial-intelligence-170-years-ago-4fd7c23505ef [Accessed 6 July 2019].

McDougall, D. (2019), 'Life on thin ice', *theguardian.com* [Online]. Available at: www.theguardian.com/society/ng-interactive/2019/aug/12/life-on-thin-ice-mental-health-at-the-heart-of-the-climate-crisis [Accessed 20 August 2019].

Miller, P.A. (2016), *Diotima at the Barricades: French Feminists Read Plato*. Oxford: Oxford University Press.

Minter, A. (2018), *Mental-Health IPO Is a Leap Forward for China* [Online]. Available at: www.bloomberg.com/opinion/articles/2018-01-01/mental-health-ipo-is-a-leap-forward-for-china [Accessed 5 July 2019].

Moore, J.W. (2015), *Capitalism in the Web of Life: Ecology and the Accumulation of Capital*. London: Verso.

Moore, J.W. and Patel, R. (2018), *A Histroy of the World in Seven Cheap Things*. London and New York: Verso.

Morton, T. (2013), *Hyperobjects: Philosphy and Ecology after the End of the World*. Minneapolis: University of Minnesota Press.

Negri, A. (1981), *L'anomalia selvaggia. Saggio su potere e potenza in Baruch Spinoza*. Milan: Giangiacomo Feltrinelli Editore.

Nova, A. (2019), 'Many Americans say their financial situation is worse since the Great Recession', *CNBC*. Available at: www.cnbc.com/2019/06/14/many-americans-say-their-finances-are-worse-since-the-great-recession.html.

Overing, J. (ed.). (2000), *The Anthropology of Love and Anger: The Aesthetics of Conviviality in Native Amazonia*. London and New York: Routledge.

Parisi, L. (2013), *Contagious Architecture: Computation, Aesthetics, and Space*. Cambridge, MA: MIT Press.

Phukan, R. (2019), *Thinking about AI and ML? You'll Need More than Data!*. [Online]. Available at: www.devopsonline.co.uk/thinking-about-ai-and-ml-youll-need-more-than-data/ [Accessed 9 July 2019].

Prádanos, L.I. (2018), *Postgrowth Imaginaries: New Ecologies and Counterhegemonic Culture in Post-2008 Spain*. Liverpool: Liverpool University Press.

Salisbury, R. (n.d.), 'On dividualism', *Post-Scarcity Anarchism*, Vol. 1.

Sancino, A. and Bloom, P. (2019), *Disruptive Democracy: The Clash Between Techno-Populism and Techno=Democracy*. Los Angeles: Sage Swifts, pp. 62–69.

Santos, B. (2018), *The End of the Cognitive Empire: The Coming of Age of Epistemologies of the South*. Durham and London: Duke University Press.

Scarborough, M. (1994), *Muth and Modernity: Postcritical Reflections*. Albany, NY: SUNY Press, p. 24.

Schwab, K. (2016), *The Fourth Industrial Revolution*. Geneva: World Economic Forum.

Sian Lazar, A.S. (2019), 'Understanding labour politics in an age of precarity', *Dialectical Anhtropology*, 43(1).

Singham, N. (2019), 'How powerful mining corporations flagrantly plunder the global south without consequence', *truthout.org*. Available at: https://truthout.org/articles/how-powerful-mining-corporations-plunder-the-global-south-without-consequence/.

Sloterdijk, P. (1989/2000), 'My translation', in *La mobilisation infinie. Vers une critique de la cinétique politique*. Paris: Seuil/Christian Bourgeois.

Srnicek, N. (2017), *Platform Capitalism*. Cambridge: Polity Press.

Stevens, K. (2019), *Longreads* [Online]. Available at: https://longreads.com/2019/08/19/greenlands-deepening-ecological-grief/ [Accessed 20 August 2019].

Stiegler, B. (2010), *For a New Critique of Political Economy*. Cambridge: Polity Press.

Taussig, M. (1980), *The Devil and Commodity Fetishism in South America*. Chapel Hill: University of North Carolina Press.

Trimboli, A. (2019), *World Mental Health Day: Focus on Suicide Prevention* [Online]. Available at: https://wfmh.global/world-mental-health-day-2019/ [Accessed 5 July 2019].

Valero, I. (2014), 'How free is free? Property, markets and the aesthetic(s) of the common(s)', in *What We Want is Free: Critical Exchanges in Recent Art*. Albany: SUNY Press.

Valero, I. (2015), 'EcoDomics: Life beyond the Neolibbera Apocalypse', in P. Mörtenböck, H. Mooshammer, T. Cruz and F. Forman (eds.), *Informal Markets Reader: The Architecture of Economic Pressure*. Rotterdam: nai010.

Vandewettering, K.R. (2015), 'Upper paleolithic venus figurines and interpretations of prehistoric gender representations', *PURE Insights*, 4, Article 7.

Vitkovskaya, J. and Davenport, C. (2019), 'What's it really like to live in space?', *The Washington Post* [Online]. Available at: www.washingtonpost.com/graphics/2019/national/50-astronauts-life-in-space/?utm_term=.1d34c228e9ba [Accessed 14 July 2019].

Voela, A. (2017), *Psychoanalysis, Philosophy, and Myth in Contemporary Culture*. London: Palgrave Macmillan, p. 137.

Watters, E. (2010), *Crazy Like Us: The Globalization of the American Psyche*. New York: Free Press, p. 1.

Whitebook, J. (2004), 'The marriage of Marx and Freud: Critical theory and psychoanalysis', in *The Cambridge Companion to Critical Theory*. Cambridge: Cambridge University Press, pp. 74–102.

WHO. (2001), *Mental Disorders Affect One in Four People* [Online]. Available at: www.who.int/whr/2001/media_centre/press_release/en/ [Accessed 5 July 2019].

Woodard, R.D. (2007), *The Cambridge Companion to Greek Mythology*. New York: Cambridge University Press.

Yan, A. (2018), 'Child suicide covered up in China, says think tank as it calls on authorities to publish figures', *South China Morning Post* [Online]. Available at: www.scmp.com/news/china/society/article/2145372/child-suicide-covered-china-says-think-tank-it-calls-authorities [Accessed 5 July 2019].

Ye, J. (2019), 'Amazon China ends its market place. Consumers say Amazon failed in China because it didn't adapt'. s.l.: Abacus.

Zhao, J. and Zhang, F. (2015), 'China is prepared to fight against emerging mental health disorders?', *International Journal of Emergency Mental Health and Human Resilience*, 17(3), p. 628.

Zuboff, S. (2019), *The Age of Surveillance Capitalism*. New York: Public Affairs, Kindle Edition, p. 3.

# Part II

# Environments

# 4 Unearthly domain

## The enigmatic data publics of satellites

*Stephen Graham*

There comes a point, as one ascends into the sky from the Earth's surface – and the largely upright human experience of living on it – when the conventions that surround the human experience of the vertical dimension must inevitably break down. At the margins of the Earth's atmosphere and the threshold of the vast realms of space, we enter a world of orbits. At this point we start to encounter the crucial but neglected manufactured environment of satellites and space junk.

"Verticality pushed to its extreme becomes orbital", multimedia artist Dario Solman reflects. At such a point, "the difference between vertical and horizontal ceases to exist". Such a development brings with it profound and unsettling philosophical challenges for a species that evolved to live upright on *terra firma*. "Every time verticality and horizontality blend together and discourses lose internal gravity", Solman argues, "there is a need for the arts" (2001).

The Earth's fast-expanding array of around 1,900 active satellites – over 800 of which are owned by the United States – are central to the organization, experience, and destruction of contemporary life on the Earth's surface. And yet it remains difficult to visualize and understand their enigmatic presence. Mysterious and cordoned-off ground stations dot the Earth's terrain, their futuristic radomes and relay facilities directed upward to unknowable satellites above. Small antennae lift upward from a myriad of apartment blocks to silently receive invisible broadcasts from transnational television stations. Crowds might even occasionally witness the spectacle of a satellite launch atop a rocket.

Once aloft, however, satellites become distant, enigmatic, and, quite literally, "unearthly" (Oberg, 2012, p. 2). At best, careful observers of the night's sky might catch the steady march of mysterious dots across the heavens as they momentarily reflect the sun's light. Such a small range of direct experience fails to equip us easily with the skills to disentangle the politics of this huge aerial assemblage of circling and (geo)stationary satellites. It doesn't help that the literature on satellites in the social sciences is startlingly small. Communications scholars Lisa Parks and James Schwoch suggest that this is because social researchers, too, struggle to engage with satellites because they lie so firmly beyond the visceral worlds of everyday experience and visibility. "Since they are seemingly so out of reach (both physically and financially)", they point out, "we scarcely imagine them as part of everyday life" at all (2007, pp. 207–208).

The continued tendency of many scholars of the politics of geography to maintain a resolutely horizontal view compounds our difficulties in taking seriously the crucial roles of orbital geographies in shaping life (and death) on the ground. Only very recently have critical geographers started to look upward to the devices circling our Earth in their first tentative steps toward a political geography of inner and outer space.

Such a project emphasizes how the regimes of power organized through satellites and other space systems are interwoven with the production of violence, inequality, and injustice on the terrestrial surface (Sage, 2014). But it also attends to the importance of how space is imagined and represented as a national frontier, a birthright of states, a sphere of heroic exploration, a fictional realm, or a vulnerable domain above through which malign others might stealthily threaten societies below at any moment.

The invisibility of the Earth's satellites and their apparent removal from the worlds of earthly politics have made it very easy to remove their organization and governance far from democratic or public scrutiny. Such a situation creates a paradox. On the one hand, widening domains of terrestrial life are now mediated by far-above arrays of satellites in ways so fundamental and basic that they have quickly become banal and taken for granted – when they are even noticed or considered at all.

The data publics surrounding global communication, navigation, science, trade, and cartography have, in particular, been totally revolutionized by satellites in the last few decades. Military GPS systems, used to drop lethal ordnance on any point on Earth, have been opened up to civilian uses. These GPS systems now organize the global measurement of time as well as navigation of children to school, yachts to harbors, cars into supermarkets, farmers around fields, runners and cyclists along paths and roads, and hikers up to mountaintops.

Widened access to powerful imaging satellites, similarly, has allowed high-resolution images to transform urban planning, agriculture, forestry, environmental management, and efforts of NGOs to track human rights abuses.[1] Digital photography from many of the prosthetic eyes above the Earth, meanwhile, offer resolutions that Cold War military strategists could only dream of – delivered via the satellite and optic fiber channels of the internet to anyone with a laptop or smartphone. A cornucopia of distant TV stations are also now accessible through the most basic aerial or broadband TV or internet connection. Virtually all efforts at social and political mobilization rely on GPS and satellite mapping and imaging to organize and disseminate messages.

Satellites, in other words, now constitute a key part of the public realms of our planet. The way they girdle our globe matters fundamentally and profoundly. And yet, satellites are regulated and managed by a scattered array of esoteric governance agencies. They are developed and engineered by an equally hidden range of state and corporate research and development centers. When the obsessive secrecy of national security states is added to this mix, it becomes extremely hard to pin down even basic information about the ownership, nature, roles, and capabilities of the crucial machines that orbit the Earth.

Such a situation has even led media theorist Geert Lovinck to suggest that it is necessary to think of the figure of the satellite in contemporary culture in psychoanalytical terms – as an unconscious apparatus that lurks away from and behind the more obvious or "conscious" circuits of culture (2005). "Publics around the world have both been excluded from and/or remained silent within important discussions about [the] ongoing development and use [of satellites]", Parks and Schwoch stress. "Since the uses of satellites have historically been so heavily militarized and corporatized, we need critical and artistic strategies that imagine and suggest ways of struggling over their meanings and uses" (2007, pp. 207–208).

Given such a context, this chapter explores the complex data publics of reconnaissance, communication, military, and navigation satellite systems. It does so in five parts. These address, in turn, the geopolitical dimensions of nation-state reconnaissance satellites; the secretive "black" reconnaissance satellites run by the United States National Reconnaissance Office (NRO), the politics of US satellite ground stations, the prospects for armed military satellites, and, finally, the complex cultural, visual, and vertical politics surrounding the extraordinary mainstreaming of Google Earth.

## "Ultimate high ground": space geopolitics[2]

> Space superiority is not our birthright, but it is our destiny. . . . Space superiority is our day-to-day mission. Space supremacy is our vision for the future.
> (Lord, cited in Weiner, 2005)

Even a preliminary study of the world of satellites must conclude that they have contributed powerfully to the extreme globalization of the contemporary age. Nowhere is this more apparent than in the murky and clandestine worlds of military and security surveillance satellites. Not surprisingly, the idea of colonizing inner space with the best possible satellite sensors has long made military theorists drool. Their pronouncements revivify long-standing military assumptions that to be above is to be dominant and in control of the subjugation of enemies.

The extraordinary powers of globe-spanning military and security satellites are only occasionally hinted at by whistleblowers or leaks. By communicating details about the Earth's surface to secretive ground stations – its geography, communications, and attributes – and by allowing weapons like drones to be controlled anywhere on Earth from a single spot, military and security satellites produce what geographer Denis Cosgrove calls "an altered spatiality of globalization"(2001, p. 236).

German thinker Peter Sloterdijk stresses the way the increasing dominance of the view of the Earth from satellites since the 1960s has revolutionized human imagination about the Earth through a form of what he calls "inverted astronomy". The view from a satellite makes possible a Copernican revolution in outlook, Sloterdijk writes.

> For all earlier human beings, gazing up to the heavens was akin to a naive preliminary stage of a philosophical thinking beyond this world and a spontaneous elevation towards contemplation of infinity. Ever since the early sixties, an inverted astronomy has . . . come into being, looking down from space onto the earth rather than from the ground up into the skies.
>
> (1990, p. 111)

This sense of global, total, and seemingly omniscient vision from above allows military satellite operators in particular to render everything on the Earth's surface as an object and as a target, organized through near-instantaneous data transmission linking sensors to weapons systems (Harris, 2002). Crucially, such "virtual" visions of the world, wrapped up in their military techno-speak, acronyms and, euphemisms, are stripped of their biases, selectivity, subjectivity, and limits. The ways in which they are used to actively and subjectively manufacture – rather than impassively "sense" – the targets to be surveilled – and, if necessary, destroyed – are, consequently, denied. A further problem, of course, is that satellite imaging efforts also completely ignore the rights, views, and needs of those on the receiving end of the technology on the Earth's surface, far below satellite orbits – the people who are most affected by the domineering technology above.

This imperial trick manufactures the world below as nothing but an infinite field of targets to be sensed and destroyed, remotely, on a whim, as deemed appropriate by operators in distant bunkers. "All the various aspects of satellite imagery systems . . . work together", writes communications scholar Chad Harris. They do this, he says, to create and maintain "an imperial subjectivity or 'gaze' that connects the visual with practices of global control" (2002).

Militaries and security agencies portray satellite visioning as an objective and omniscient means for a distant observer to represent the observed, rather than a constructed and subjective system. The God-like view of satellite imagery is often invoked by states as evidence of unparalleled veracity and authenticity when they are alleged to depict weapons of mass destruction facilities, human rights abuses, or nefarious military activities.

It does not help that many critical theorists mistakenly suggest that contemporary spy satellites effectively have no technological limitations or that a hundred Hollywood action movies – erroneously depicting spy satellites as being capable of witnessing anything – do the same. All too often, critics depict satellite surveillance as being totally omnipotent and omniscient – a world of complete dystopian control with no limits to the transparency of the view and no possibilities for resistance or contestation (Kingsbury and Jones, 2009). In suggesting, for example, that "the orbital weapons [and satellites] currently in play possess the traditional attributes of the divine Omnivoyance and omnipresence", French theorist Paul Virilio radically underplays the limits, biases, and subjectivities that shape the targeting of the terrestrial surface by satellites (2002, p. 53).

Instead of invoking satellites as an absolute form of imperial vision, it is necessary, rather, to see satellite imaging as a highly biased form of visualizing or even simulating the Earth's surface rather than some objective or apolitical transmission of its "truth" (Pickles, 1995). It is also, as we shall see shortly, necessary to stress the potential that satellites offer for those challenging military-industrial complexes, environmental and human rights abuses, and all manners of political and state repression.

While maps are now widely understood to be subject to bias and error, satellite images are still widely assumed to present a simple, direct, and truthful correlation of the Earth. This occurs even when there is a long history of such images being so imperfect and uncertain – and as so manipulated, mislabeled, and just plain wrong – that it's necessary to be skeptical of such claims.[3]

US military theorists offer an excellent case study of how attempted domination of satellite sensing is being combined with long-standing metaphors about the strategic power of being above one's enemies. In 2003 the US military's RAND think tank declared that space power and its attendant satellites offered the "ultimate high ground" in struggles for military superiority (Lambeth, 1999).[4]

The US military's vision for dominating space is characterized by dreams of being able to see anything on the Earth's surface at any time, irrespective of enemies' efforts to occlude their targets.[5] This is linked with an obsession with the ability to use GPS satellites to organize the dropping of lethal ordnance on those self-same spots. Satellite dominance is seen as a critical pre-requisite to the dominance of airspace, land space, and maritime space below.

Finally, satellites are deemed by US military theorists to be a crucial means of reducing the vulnerability of the home nation. This is done by using satellites to target incoming missiles – and, possibly in the future, by launching specialized weapons from one's own satellites, against the satellite fleets of enemies.

## "Black" satellites: the other night sky

How might critical scholars and activists penetrate the "Black" world of secret military satellites? Two linked strategies emerge here. On the one hand, a secretive group of satellite activists have done much recent work to expose the daily trajectories or geostationary orbits of the fleets of military spy satellites as they operate high above.

Working with this community, artist and geographer Trevor Paglen – who helped to expose the CIA's system of extraordinary rendition in 2006 – has spent many cold nights peering through sophisticated tracked telescopes in California's Sierra Nevada mountains and other sites around the world. With his colleagues (Paglen, 2012a), he has been able to track, photograph, catalogue, and calculate the orbits of 140 or so of the classified "Black" US satellites known to orbit the Earth at any one time.

Paglen and his colleagues have been able to do this because of a paradox: whilst "Black" satellites are so secret they aren't even supposed to exist, their large size means that, if you are able to calculate the certain places and times where they become clearly visible because they reflect sunlight, tracking orbital spy satellites is relatively simple. (Geostationary orbits, or GSOs, at exactly 35,787 km up, plus or minus a kilometer or two, are much harder to spot.)

Pulling scraps of data from satellite enthusiasts, publicly available military budgets, and federal regulators' flight plan information, Paglen and his colleagues have done much to piece together what he calls the "other night sky" – the clandestine world of US radar, radio, infrared, and visual light-based military satellites. They even glean useful clues as to the location and latitude of the US National Reconnaissance Office's (NRO's) launched satellites by decoding the military cloth badges that are made public about each launch.

Paglen's sketchy time-delay images offer a fleeting glimpse of a world that supposedly does not even exist – a world that, paradoxically, can be witnessed by anyone on the earth's surface simply by looking up on a clear night and catching the sun's reflections on the satellite body. "The other night sky", Paglen writes:

> is a landscape of fleeting reflections: of giants, glimpses, traces and flares. Of unacknowledged moons and "black" space craft moving through the pre-dawn and early evening darkness, where the rising and setting sun lights up the stainless steel bodies, and they blink in and out of sight as they glide through the backdrop of a darkened sky hundreds of miles below. In most cases, the reflection is all we get.
>
> (2012a, p. 244)

Like the whistleblowing leaks of Chelsea Manning and Edward Snowden, Paglen's work is an example of what has been sous-surveillance – literally, "under surveillance" or "surveillance from below". In challenging the cloak of invisibility and secrecy that obscures top-down surveillance by the latest secret satellites, the work of Paglen and the satellite tracking community fleetingly exposes one crucial material embodiment of the increasingly secretive and authoritarian nature of security politics (Lynch, n.d.).[6]

Predictably, further exposures come from the United States' strategic competitors. Between 2005 and 2010, for example, Russia managed to obtain detailed images of the NRO's enormous 'Lacrosse' radar reconnaissance satellites by using high advanced ground-based telescopes in Siberia. These rare images, which can be contrasted with pictures of the satellites on the ground, were released for propaganda purposes.

Such tactics inevitably emerge, of course, as a reciprocal world of "watching the watchers". After completing his photographs, Paglen reflected that his project was "not a passive exercise: as I photograph the night sky, the other night sky photographs back" (Lynch, n.d.). There is also evidence that the US has responded to the satellite tracking community by reorienting some of their most secretive satellites – those of the multibillion dollar "Misty" program – so that they don't reflect sun down to the areas of the world where the main trackers live. "We would prefer that these things not end up on the internet", an NRO spokesperson said dryly in 2006 (Keefe, 2006).

## Ground stations: "fragments of America"

A complementary approach is to explore and map the ground-level infrastructure necessary to allow military spy satellites to function. Steve Rowell, an artist affiliated with the Center for Land Use Interpretation (CLUI) in Los Angeles, has completed one of the most thorough studies here. His analysis of the distribution of US satellite stations – both unmanned and manned – across the world is especially significant because such installations are not normally counted within conventional analysis of US military bases.

As Rowell puts it, "Every satellite in orbit requires a tremendous amount of infrastructure on the ground" (2008). He estimates that the US alone has around 6,000 ground-based installations around the world. "These sites", he writes, "whether radar-detection posts, satellite-tracking bases, telecommunications-intercept centers, space ports, unmanned transmitter arrays, or overcrowded field offices, are fragments of America".

Whilst they are fixed at the ground level, Rowell emphasizes the changing roles of ground and earth stations in the shifting geopolitical strategies of the United States and other powers. Fenced off, patrolled, and enigmatic, their radomes and aerials can but hint at the roles of such facilities within a vast, largely unknowable, and infinitely larger data-scape of instant, encrypted, imaging, sensing, targeting and communication.

The satellite stations of the US combine stations inherited from the British after World War Two, a wide range of bases set up during the Cold War, and a newer set of installations that evidence that dramatic growth of the military-intelligence industry in the wake of the "war on terror". Steve

*Figure 4.1* Image of Menwith Hill ground station
*Source*: Public domain – attributed license

Rowell's mapping of these facilities gives an indication of their reach and density across the Earth.

Usefully, Rowell's work connects the abstract cartographies of the satellite-based surveillance with face-to-face confrontations with the eerie installations on the ground that sustain it. As part of his research, Rowell paid particular attention to the largest and most important of the National Security Agency's global satellite surveillance stations: the notionally "Royal Air Force" base at Menwith Hill in North Yorkshire, England.

Menwith Hill is one of three key US satellite bases at the heart of the globe-spanning communications surveillance system known as PRISM, a system powerfully exposed by the NSA whistleblower, Edward Snowden, in 2011.[7] Like a dystopian film set, the base's architecture of over 30 Kevlar radomes sits rather incongruously within the pastoral landscapes of North Yorkshire's valleys. It's razor-wired peripheries are circled by US military guards; its 2,300 employees are drawn from all three key players in the US satellite-surveillance complex.[8]

Menwith Hill's recently expanded and modernized fields of radomes house extraordinarily powerful systems for scooping up all electromagnetic wireless and satellite phone calls and data and video transmissions over large geographical areas. Linked as well with the NSA's systems for tapping terrestrial communications over optic fiber systems, bases like Menwith Hill allow for the covert collection of large swathes of the traffic from vast swathes of the internet. This is done with agreement from large Internet providers such as Microsoft, Google, Yahoo!, Facebook, PalTalk, YouTube, Skype, AOL, and Apple. Combined with supercomputers and classified decryption software, Menwith Hill and its allied bases thus provide automatic analysis and classification of a huge range of intercepted data in order to track identified "targets". These range from alleged insurgent leaders to terrorist "cells" in the Middle East to European politicians and businesses to entirely legal and legitimate civilian protest groups and social movements within the UK, Europe, and North America.

Menwith Hill's systems are also pivotal in globe-spanning systems organized to support the detection of ballistic missiles and the prosecution of lethal drone strikes. Indeed, Menwith Hill is a crucial hub in a massive US effort to be able to launch lethal power at any spot on the Earth's surface at very short delay. Such so-called "time-critical targeting" is deemed a crucial response to a world where non-state terrorist and insurgent threats are very hard to distinguish from the background of "civilian" societies within which they hide. The aim of such global targeting is to build a fully integrated network, combining satellite imagery with interception of all types of electronic communications, in a way that provides the real-time intelligence necessary to identify targets and to carry out attacks anywhere in the world without the need for conventional armies (Yorkshire CND, 2013). Menwith Hill has thus played a pivotal role in the continuous prosecution of routine violence across vast geographic areas that have characterized the United States' global covert wars over the past sixteen years.

## Weaponizing space

> Let's hope the words "commence the orbital bombardment" don't enter our vernacular in the near future.
>
> (Sager, 2014)

Since Sputnik was first launched in 1957, the orbits of satellites have given geopolitics a radically vertical fourth dimension (Caracciolo, 2004). Indeed, the last half century has made the orbital domains of inner space a profoundly contested zone dominated – despite notional international agreements, such as the 1967 Outer Space Treaty, prohibiting the process – by increasing processes of militarization and weaponization. As well as secretive launches of more sophisticated and powerful spy satellites and an extending range of ground stations, evidence of the deployment of armed satellites is emerging. Way back in 2003, for example, the US military undertook research on the lethal effects of an orbiting satellite simply letting go of long, inert tungsten rods, targeted using simple gravitational force, to any spot on Earth with unprecedented speed.

Targeted especially at destroying the deeply buried bunkers of adversary states, they calculated that a six-meter-long rod, nicknamed the "Rod from God", would impact the Earth at ten times the speed of sound, unleashing energy on impact equivalent to a small nuclear explosion (U.S. Air Force Transformation Flight Plan, 2003).To bolster the militarization of space, a new field of "astro-geopolitics" has emerged, largely in the United States. This is fueled heavily by the use by metaphors linking the domination of inner orbits with both the reach of empires across the horizontal planes of oceans in pre-industrial eras and the competitive scramble between European empires in the 18th and 19th centuries. To the Heritage Foundation, a think tank on the Republican right in the US and a key player in deploying such metaphors, "space is the high seas of tomorrow" (Johnson, 1999).

A range of hawkish astro-geopolitical theorists, meanwhile, now herald the domination of space as the key to controlling the Earth below. Their thesis is a classic tautology, as a wider range of nations emerge to launch their own military space programs, space will be weaponized; therefore, space must be weaponized most powerfully and quickly by the United States in a pre-emptive effort to maintain power. "He who controls the lower orbits controls the near Space around Earth", writes Everett Dolman of the School of Advanced Air Power Studies at Maxwell Air Base in Alabama – one influential theorist. "He who dominates the Earth determines the future of mankind" (2002, p. 8).

Given the reliance of contemporary societies and economies on satellite-based communication, navigation, and information, they constitute a clear Achilles heel, as their destruction would bring extraordinary disruption and economic destabilization. Italian journalist Lucio Caracciolo sees the orbital skein of communications and navigation satellites as an "indispensable strategic nerve system of the more developed economies" (2004) – one that is highly vulnerable to anti-satellite weapons fired from the ground, aircraft, or, conceivably, other satellites. "Satellite constellations set up in peace are the fixed coastal defenses of the modern age", the US Naval Institute argues. They are "easy to target and plan against – and most likely first on an enemy's targeting priority list" (Salamander, 2015).

Worryingly, the centrality of satellites to contemporary imperial power is being used by military leaders to urge the exploration of a wide range of lasers and "kinetic" (i.e., physical) weapons that can actually hit the Earth's surface from satellite orbits. "We will fight from Space and in Space", then–Commander in Chief of the United States Space Command, General Joseph Ashby, said, contemplating the future of his organization, way back in 1996. "One day we will hit earthbound targets – ships, aircraft, objects on the ground – from Space. We will hit targets in Space from Space" (Heronema, 1996, p. 4).

Anti-satellite weapons launched from below, in fact, have a long history. In the early days of the Cold War, their lack of accuracy was compensated for by huge nuclear warheads attached to modified ballistic missiles (Mackey, 2009). In 1962, to test such ideas, the United States exploded a 1.4 megaton nuclear weapon known as Starfish at an altitude of 400 km above Johnston Island in the Pacific Ocean (Bhalla, 2014). Over the last 40 years, the US, Russia, and China have all deployed a suite of anti-satellite missiles launched from ships, aircraft, or ground stations.

These systems are now so accurate that they use conventional explosive warheads. Whilst testing of such systems is not as common as it was between 1970 and 1990, anti-satellite missiles have been used on several occasions to destroy satellites deemed either to be a risk to inhabitants of Earth or an intelligence risk, when the satellites fall back through the Earth's atmosphere after their operational lives are over or following a malfunction.

Such attacks create huge debris fields, which, in turn, become a major hazard to other satellite and space operations. In 2007, the first Chinese anti-satellite launch, which destroyed a meteorological satellite, created a debris field of between 20,000 to 40,000 fragments of one centimeter or greater in size. In one fell swoop, the Chinese caused a 20 percent increase in the number of small objects in lower Earth orbit – each one travelling at around eight miles a second – which need to be tracked in order to minimize the damage to, or destruction of, other satellites or space vehicles. Twenty-two years earlier, a similar US anti-satellite launch created 250 pieces of trackable debris, one of which almost collided with the International Space Station in 1999.

In total, there are already 500,000 fragments of potentially damaging space debris in orbit around the world. Such debris is a grave concern because its impacts on states' satellites and other orbiting vehicles could easily be mis-interpreted as deliberate anti-satellite warfare by adversary states. In 2016 the Russian Academy of Sciences warned that debris impacting on orbiting vehicles might even provoke quick escalation toward global conflict because "the owner of the impacted and destroyed satellite can hardly quickly determine the real cause of the accident" (Spacedaily, 2016).

Other development efforts in anti-satellite warfare center on the use of high-powered lasers located on the ground, on ships, or in aircraft. Micro-waves, particle beams, or electromagnetic pulse devices have also been explored as ways to damage or disable both incoming ballistic missiles and orbiting satellites.

Another strategy is to launch anti-satellite satellites. Satellite researchers think that the highly secretive fleet of tiny 250-kilogram US experimental geostationary satellites under the program name "MiTex" are already capable of stealthily tracking, inspecting, intercepting, and even knocking out or disrupting the geostationary craft of adversary nations. One such interception has already been observed by the South African satellite observer Greg Roberts (Paglen, 2012b).

Whilst weapons, as far as publicly known, have yet to be deployed into space itself, President Reagan's ambitious "Star Wars" Strategic Defense Initiative in the 1980s and 1990s involved wide-scale research and development of armed satellites as well as ground-based anti-missile and anti-satellite systems. Indeed, the proliferation of ground-based anti-satellite weapons has rekindled the fear that weapons systems will soon be deployed into orbit around the world.

Many US military theorists consider such deployments inevitable and suggest that the United States needs to lead such a move pre-emptively in order to maintain the nation's long domination of the "ultimate high ground" (Bhalla, 2014). It is clear, at least, that the US is now developing a secret, reusable "space-bomber" (the Boeing X37) and a range of satellites designed to destroy other satellites whilst in orbit have also been mooted.

Looking beyond the reliance of the military and security services on satellites, the prospect of the use of anti-satellite weapons in conflicts is a daunting one. Such weapons contravene all of the key principles of international humanitarian law. In increasingly high-tech and automated societies, where more and more infrastructure and services rely continuously on GPS and satellite mapping and imaging in order to function, their use would cause widespread, immediate, and potentially even fatal disruptions.

Destruction of a nation's satellites, Theresa Hitchens, director of the UN Institute for Disarmament Research (UNIDIR) warns, would leave "an entire country without effective communication systems, with very little access to the internet and phones, for a certain period of time". It would also disrupt financial systems, telemedicine, ATMs, and so-called "just in time" logistics and delivery systems, as well as the water supply, power grids, and search and rescue operations (World Economic Forum, 2012).[9] As societies automate rapidly, further impacts can be envisaged. How murderous might a future highway system used by fleets of driverless satellite-guided cars become were those satellites to be suddenly disabled or hacked?

Anti-satellite attacks would also likely trigger waves of unstoppable tit-for-tat escalation between the main satellite powers. Many US war games simulating such attacks quickly escalate to nuclear exchanges. Arms control lawyers are therefore now arguing that the proliferation and possible use of anti-satellite weapons are so significant that they need to be subject to a range of treaties, proscriptions, regulations, and inspections similar to those that have long attempted to regulate nuclear, biological, and chemical weapons.

"Given the nearly unstoppable advance of modern military technology", international lawyer Robert David Onley writes, "if space weapons are not banned, countries will be forced to build satellites equipped with counter-measures that destroy incoming anti-satellite missiles – and as a consequence, effectively guarantee the permanent weaponization of space". At such a point, he suggests, "there exists only a small leap in logic between the prospects of satellites armed with missiles for self-defense, to satellites (or space-bombers/orbiters) armed with missiles and bombs for offensive purposes" (2013, p. 739).

## World-zoom: Google Earth

> Today the aerial view – the image of everywhere – seems to be everywhere.
>
> (Dorrian and Pousin, 2013, p. 295)

Perhaps the most profound effect of the contemporary proliferation of satellites centers on the way their extraordinary powers of seeing from above are now harnessed to computers and smartphones.

Google Earth is obviously especially pivotal here. As a system of systems linked to a computer or mobile smartphone, it offers almost infinite possibilities of zooming in to and out of views of the Earth's surface at local, regional, and global scales (Heise, 2008, p. 11). It does this by "mashing up" global satellite imagery, geopositioning coordinates, digital cartography, geolocated data, three-dimensional computerized maps, architectural drawings, street-level digital imagery, and other social media, data, and software. These are configured together as an "always-on", interactive, and boundless data-scape – a flexible and multi-scaled portal of largely vertical images which now mediate life in profoundly new and important ways.

The apparently infinite "scale-jumping" possibilities of Google Earth force us to revisit, and update, a very long-standing debate about the politics of the aerial, "God's eye", or top-down view (Tong, 2014, pp. 200–201). Many cultural theorists argue that the new ubiquity of the digital view from above is an important part of contemporary shifts away from a world dominated by a stable and single sense of ground and horizon organized through linear perspective. Instead, contemporary societies are saturated by a multitude of "always on" digital and screen-based perspectives; extending armies of prosthetic eyes laid across entire volumes of geographic space; intense and real-time globalization; and, for many, unprecedented human mobility. Satellites and satellite vision are absolutely pivotal to this new sense of vertical "free-fall" that attends this new age (Steyerl, 2011).

Google Earth is pivotal to these transformations. It is the prime means through which vertical and oblique views of our worldview have rapidly become radically accessible, zoomable, and pannable in a myriad of ways. Many researchers suggest that mass public access to Google Earth fundamentally challenges long-standing assumptions that the view from above necessarily involves dispassionate, technocratic, or privileged visual power (Dorrian, 2011, pp. 164–170).

In presenting a "virtual globe" that can be navigated on screen and repeatedly zoomed, Google Earth presents a powerful imagination of the planet – one that is simultaneously global, corporate, and saturated with commercial data and corporate location-based advertising. It is thus "closely related to the production and movements of contemporary urbanization" (Laforest, 2014). The active shaping of this "virtual globe" by the viewer is crucial, however. In contrast to media like aerial or satellite photographs, users of Google Earth are no longer simply passive viewers witnessing the world as a zoom.

Instead, participants actively customize their own experience of Google Earth by building their own interfaces and adding their own data and imagery. Indeed, the frame-by-frame animation of the Google Earth interface works to provide viewers and users with a virtual globe, which they can manipulate to provide their own personal cinematic rendition of the planet that they can then view and manipulate in a decidedly God-like way. Media scholar Leon Gurevitch calls this the "divine manufacturer of the very [Google Earth] environments [viewers] wish to travel through" (Gurevitch, 2014, p. 97).

The addition of street-level visuals through Google Street View however, grounds this virtual world with imagery of current and historical street scenes. Now "cloud" level and "street" level worlds work seamlessly together, shimmering visual surfaces that occlude as much as they reveal to the inspecting subject. The system's interface "provides the ability to come and go freely within a completely controlled universe", media scholar Daniel Laforest emphasizes, "while maintaining the sense of distance as a constant promise, a source of leisure, or even as an unexpected pleasure" (2015, p. 6).

Despite its flexibility, the cultural and political biases of Google Earth are not hard to spot. Until recently, the system defaulted to a view that placed the US at the center of the screen. The interface offers little evidence of the source or accuracy of the global surveillance that sustains Google Earth. The way that Google Earth itself handles the reams of data that is passed on to commercial information markets or security and surveillance services like the NSA is also carefully obscured.

Many areas are also censored or offered at deliberately low resolution. Under US law, for example, Google must represent certain parts of Israel/ Palestine at low resolution. States have also been found to doctor Google Earth images. Hawkish security commentators, who stress the usefulness of Google Earth to those planning terrorist attacks, are now urging that such censorship be extended. "Terrorists don't need to reconnoiter their target", Russian security official Lieutenant General Leonid Sazhin said in 2005. "Now an American company is working for them" (Stahl, 2010, p. 66).

The social and cultural biases of Google Earth can also be stark. In post-Katrina New Orleans, for example, efforts to use Google Earth to allow communities affected by the crisis to share information and support across the various neighborhoods of the city inevitably ended up being geared overwhelmingly toward more affluent and whiter neighborhoods because of wider geographies of the so-called "digital divide" in the city (Crutcher and Zook, 2009, pp. 523–534).

Certain information, moreover, is dramatically prioritized within the system – information for users of corporate services, automobile drivers, and so on. Google Earth's dominant, de facto data sets are heavily dominated by a cluster of key transnational corporations. To sustain their competitive advantages in tourism, travel, leisure services, oil consumption, and food provision, these companies overlay the satellite surfaces with geolocation data geared toward exploiting this new screen interface.

Other information – say, of human rights abuses or the installations of national security states – is obviously obscured or inaccessible, sometimes through the crudest of censorship. Extreme biases in access and use, meanwhile, mean that user-generated content of Google Earth strongly reflects wider social and ethnic inequalities in society.

Beyond this lies a burgeoning politics of urban legibility and camouflage, as state, commercial, and non-state actors work to appropriate the new vertical views to conflicting ends. As financial collapse hit the Greek state in 2009, for example, the government tried to locate wealthy Athenians guilty of tax avoidance by using Google Earth to find their swimming pools. The immediate response was to drape tarpaulins over the telltale azure rectangles.

Meanwhile, many social and political movements have mobilized Google Earth and satellite imagery in their efforts to expose war crimes and state violence in places as diverse as Darfur, Zimbabwe, the Balkans, Syria, Burma, and Sri Lanka (Parks, 2009; Herscher, 2010). Satellite images have been very helpful in securing prosecutions against war criminals at the International Criminal Court in The Hague (Walker, 2014).[10]

Activists in Palestine, meanwhile, have actively used the system to generate maps that depict widening Israeli control as an effort to undermine the cartography produced by the Israeli state to legitimize or minimize its degree of colonial control (Quiquivix, 2014, pp. 444–459). The system has also been a boon to those aiming to expose, hack, and contest the scale and power of national security states, military forces, and corporate power (Perkins and Dodge, 2009, pp. 535–545). Perhaps the most famous example here was the discovery in China in 2006 of a military training area that mimicked precisely the exact terrain of part of the Indian-Chinese border that has been in dispute since 1962.

In Bahrain, in 2011, meanwhile, Google Earth's ability to trace aggressive efforts to vertically build up "reclaimed" land to fuel elite real estate speculation had a huge impact on the mass uprisings in the island-state.[11] The mobilization of the Shiite majority against the dictatorial Sunni elite – brutally suppressed by local security forces with the help of Saudi paramilitaries – was ignited partly by the circulation of Google Earth images depicting the scale of corrupt land "reclamation" by Sunni elites to radically remodel and further privatize the tiny nation's coastline.

More broadly, the vertical gaze of Google Earth helped the poor Shiite majority in Bahrain to fully realize that the nation's tiny Sunni elite owns and controls 95 percent of the country's land and has, along with wealthy tourists, exclusive private access to 97 percent of its beaches. The geographies of exploitation and repression became startlingly clear in full color, high-resolution imagery. "When Google Earth was introduced", Middle East specialist Eugene Rogan relates, "Bahrainis for the first time could see the walled palaces and rich homes that normally were hidden from view. Bahrainis got a bird's-eye view of how rich people there lived". Whilst the Bahrainian state blocked Google Earth in response, activists beyond the country merely circulated the same images in PDF form (quoted in Byrne, 2011).

Whilst Google Earth clearly has enormous potential as a support to activism and critique, it is easy to forget that such new, GPS-enabled activism relies fundamentally on "dual-use" devices that can only function as the result of military rocket launches. Such efforts are also based on the deployment of a series of 24 geosynchronous satellites used continually to drop murderous ordnance on a wide range of countries. And they are inevitably mediated through imperial networks of militarized ground stations and data centers. And they even rely fundamentally on a network of atomic clocks run by the US Air Force.

In such a context, media theorist Roger Stahl emphasizes the military origins of the whole aesthetic of Google Earth. This "began its life as the very picture of war", he stresses. During the 2003 Gulf War, he relates:

> a certain 3D aesthetic appeared in the form of virtual flybys, as part of more complex computer animations, in studio surveys of bomb damage, in speculations on the whereabouts of Saddam Hussein, and a range of other uses. It is not an exaggeration to say that this aesthetic took center stage in the high-tech spectacle of U.S. television coverage.
>
> (2010, p. 67)

Such a perspective forces a deep appreciation of the ways in which, despite its widening civilian use, Google Earth remains a highly militarized domain embedded fundamentally within a broader military-technology-geotechnology-security complex. This means that the system is a key means through which citizens now consume state military violence, a process that adds to the mythology of "clean" war and "precision weapons" that contemporary US militaries are eager to circulate. "Rather than say that the 3D satellite image has been 'demilitarized' as it has entered civilian life", Stahl emphasizes, "it may be more accurate to say that the transference has draped the planet with a militarized image of itself".

The militarized nature of GPS systems – a crucial basis for Google Earth – also needs emphasis. Media activist Brian Holmes, for one, questions the powers of GPS-based art and activism in a world where the broader technological structures of power are dominated powerfully by what he calls a "hyper-rationalist grid of Imperial infrastructure". When you use a GPS-locating device such as Google Earth, he argues, "you respond to the call. You are interpellated into Imperial ideology" (Holmes, n.d.).

Finally, the vertical gaze of satellite imagery, now suddenly so remarkably accessible, offers important new perspectives on how the horizontal geographies of our planet's surface are changing. For it is only from such distant heights that we can possibly begin to make sense of the extraordinary territorial formations currently being created by the rampant growth and sprawl of the world's urban areas.

"To truly exist", Rice University architecture professor Lars Lerup writes, "every city needs its perspective. Its point of view. Its eyes" (2006, p. 242). And yet the dominant experience at the edges of many sprawling urban areas – beyond the clusters of rapidly rising skyscrapers and elite housing towers – is one of apparently endless horizontality. In such landscapes, obtaining a sense of the wider, sprawling city becomes very difficult.

Google Earth allows such landscapes to be understood. Only the zoomable and extending top-down gaze of the satellite can really stretch to encompass what Lerup calls the "striated, spread-out geographies" of contemporary urbanized regions and "megalopolitan" corridors. Writing about Alan Berger's remarkable maps of the geographies of sprawl and wasted land in urban America, Lerup points out that "from a satellite, this neglected in-between [of drosscape or 'pure unadulterated waste'] is the real grammar of the horizontal city, requiring a new mathematics whose nature, strength and intelligence lies embedded in its apparent incoherence" (2006, p. 243).

With the satellite view of the city now a normal way of representing urban areas for mass consumption, navigation, planning, and, increasingly, marketing, it is perhaps now the way in which cityscapes are increasingly engineered to be brand-scapes visible from space that is the most immediate example of Google Earth's impacts on the ground.

Mark Dorrian points out that "the terrestrial surface itself becomes manipulated as a media surface, not just virtually on the Google Earth interface, but literally" (2011). This democratization of verticality has important effects: in this new, mass-market medium, corporations are now concerned with how their spaces and buildings look from satellites and aircraft.

On the one hand here, there is growing evidence that city booster-ists increasingly work to ensure that their branded, spectacularized urban "products" work well when viewed through Google Earth. (The construction of corporate advertising for aerial and satellite consumption is also increasingly common.) A consultant involved in the staging of the 2012 London Olympics, for example, remarked that "it's a media event, so it will look great from the air" (Dorrian, 2013, p. 169). Sometimes city authorities, keen to vertically show off their new developments, are unhappy at the slow updating of the vertical imagery of their cities.[12]

And already, commentary is emerging of the relative aesthetic merits of the "fly-through" experience above and through the increasingly 3D virtual renditions of major global cities. "As a city to fly through or play with", geographer David Gilbert remarks, "London works better than the homogeneity of Haussmann's Paris or the regular order and rectilinear street plans" of Manhattan. Gilbert argues that both Paris's long boulevards and Manhattan's endless avenues through canyons of high towers "become less interesting than a cityscape of roads that change direction or end unexpectedly, of labyrinthine lanes and alleys that repay close investigation, and of rapid variety in the characteristics of districts and built forms" (2010, pp. 289–299).

On other occasions, artists and activists are undertaking ambitious projects to use the very surface of the Earth as a canvas for their efforts to be consumed, via the Google Earth system, using the laptops and smartphones of a global audience. Most notable is a project by the Chilean activist and poet Raul Zurita – who suffered incarceration and torture at the hands of the Pinochet regime – to use earth-moving machinery to inscribe a four-word poem in a three-kilometer-long stretch of the bone-dry Atacama Desert. The line – *ni pena ni miedo* ("no pain no fear") – is a deep reflection of Zurita's response to his experience of political tyranny.

More familiar is the widespread engineering of manufactured Earth to create distinctive mega-structural urban brand-scapes which are carefully designed with their representation through Google Earth in mind. Most notable here, as we have seen already, are the "Palm" and "World" developments in Dubai – gargantuan projects marketed as "today's great development epic". Here, civil engineering, land art, and landscape architecture blur together. They do so to create vast manufactured islands designed as gigantic vehicles for real estate speculation whose prime marketing advantage is their unique appearance, via satellites, on the mobile Google Earth interfaces carried on a billion smartphones in a billion pockets and a billion laptops in a billion bags.

NOTE: This chapter is based on a chapter in Graham, S. (2016), *Vertical: The City from Satellites to Bunkers*, Verso: London.

## Notes

1 On the latter, see Science and Human Rights Program, American Association for the Advancement of Science, "Geospatial technologies and human rights", 2015.
2 Adding to this subject's relevance is the recent creation (on paper, at least) of the US "space force" by the current US administration. See Erwin, 2020, "US Space Force has lifted off, now the journey begins" in *Space News*.
3 The satellite images of the imagined "WMD" facilities presented by the US government to justify the 2003 invasion of Iraq are a sobering example here. See David Shim, "Seeing from above: The geopolitics of satellite vision and North Korea", *GIGA Institute of Asian Studies*, August 2012.
4 Benjamin S. Lambeth, *Mastering the Ultimate High Ground: Next Steps in the Military Uses of Space*: This "high ground" of terrestrial space is split into three zones. "Low" Earth Orbits (LEOs) – between 150 and 2,000 kilometers up – are dominated by fast-moving reconnaissance and communications satellites and inhabited craft for living astronauts. Here, the latest reconnaissance satellites – such as the US GeoEye-1, which can spot objects on Earth that are only 30 to 40 centimeters in size – operate. Higher up – between 800 and 36,000 kilometers away from the Earth's surface – are a range of communications, GPS, and navigation craft orbiting at medium Earth orbit (MEOs). (GPS satellites orbit at

around 20,200 kilometers.) Finally, geostationary satellites – used for weather forecasting, satellite TV, satellite radio, most other types of global communications, and military and security eavesdropping – orbit the equator at exactly 35,786 kilometers, a distance that allows them to remain permanently over the same part of the Earth – or "footprint".

5 Subterranean burrowing has long been the best strategy to challenge satellite surveillance.
6 The disclosing by Trump of a satellite image of an Iranian launch site earlier this year seems to have offered a glimpse of this secretive technical infrastructure.
7 The others are in Australasia and Hawaii.
8 These are the National Security Agency (NSA, which runs the site), the National Reconnaissance Office (NRO, which runs surveillance and military satellites), and the National Geospatial Intelligence Agency (NGIA, which runs geographic intelligence of many kinds). Staff from US military corporations and the UK's GCHQ are also present at the base.
9 See Stephen Graham (ed.), *Disrupted Cities: When Infrastructure Fails.*
10 See also the Terrapattern project (2016), www.flong.com/projects/terrapattern/, which aims at making some of the technologies for recognition more widely available.
11 This case is described in more detail in Stephen Graham, *Vertical: The City from Satellites to Bunkers,* Chapter 11.
12 An example is Liverpool in 2006. See *BBC News*, "Online map 'misses' regeneration".

## References

Anon. (2006), 'Online map misses regeneration', *BBC News*, 26 November.

Bhalla, P. (2014), *Weaponisation of Space*. New Delhi: Centre for Land Warfare Studies.

Byrne, M. (2011), 'Google Earth and the Bahraini uprising', *Motherboard*. Available at www.vice.com/en_us/article/pggzgg/why-google-earth-now-has-the-whole-industrialized-world-terrified.

Caracciolo, L. (2004), 'Assault on the sky', *Heartland*. Available at: http://temi.republica.it.

Cosgrove, D. (2001), *Apollo's Eye: A Cartographic Genealogy of the Earth in the Western Imagination*. Baltimore: JHU Press.

Crutcher, M. and Zook, M. (2009), 'Placemarks and waterlines: Racialized cyberscapes in post-Katrina Google Earth', *Geoforum*, 40(4), pp. 523–534.

Dolman, E. (2002), *Astropolitik: Classical Geopolitics in the Space Age*. New York: Frank Cass Publishers.

Dorrian, M. (2011), 'On Google Earth', *New Geographies*, 4, pp. 164–170.

Dorrian, M. and Pousin, F. (2013, ed. 2015), *Seeing from Above: The Aerial View in Visual Culture*. London: IB Tauris.

Erwin, S. (2020), 'U.S. Space Force has lifted off, now the journey begins', *Space News*. Available at: https://spacenews.com/u-s-space-force-has-lifted-off-now-the-journey-begins/.

Gilbert, D. (2010), 'The three ages of aerial vision: London's aerial iconography from Wenceslaus Hollar to Google Earth', *The London Journal*, 35(3).

Graham, S. (2009), *Disrupted Cities: When Infrastructure Fails*. New York: Routledge.

Graham, S. (2016), *Vertical: The City from Satellites to Bunkers*. London and New York: Verso.

Gurevitch, L. (2014), 'Google warming: Google Earth as eco-machinima', *Convergence*, 20(1), pp. 85–107.

Harris, C. (2002), 'The omniscient eye: Satellite imagery: Battlespace awareness, and the structures of the imperial gaze', *Surveillance & Society*, 4(1/2). Available at: https://ojs.library.queensu.ca/index.php/surveillance-and-society/article/view/3457/3420.

Heise, U. (2008), *Sense of Place and Sense of Planet: The Environmental Imagination of the Global*. Oxford: Oxford University Press.

Heronema, J. (1996), 'A.F. space chief calls war in space inevitable', *Space News*, p. 4.

Herscher, A. (2010), 'From target to witness: Architecture, satellite surveillance, human rights', in B. Kenzari (ed.), *Architecture and Violence*. Barcelona: Actar.

Holmes, B. (n.d.), *Drifting Through the Grid: Psychogeography and Imperial Infrastructure*. Available at: www.springerin.at/dyn/heft_text.php?textid=1523&lang=en.

Johnson, B. (1999), 'The new space race: Challenges for US national security and free enterprise', *The Heritage Foundation, Backgrounder*, 25 August, vol. 1316.

Keefe, P.R. (2006), 'I spy', *Wired*, 2 January.

Kingsbury, P. and Jones, J.P. (2009), 'Walter Benjamin's Dionysian adventures on Google Earth', *Geoforum*, 40(4).

Laforest, D. (2014), 'The satellite, the screen, and the city: On Google Earth and the life narrative' *International Journal of Cultural Studies*, 19(6), pp. 659–672.

Lambeth, B.S. (1999), *Mastering the Ultimate High Ground: Next Steps in the Military Uses of Space*. s.l.: RAND Corporation.

Lerup, L. (2006), 'Vastlands visited', in A. Berger (ed.), *Drosscape: Wasting Land in Urban America*. New York: Princeton Architectural Press.

Lovink, G. (2005), *Out There: Exploring Satellite Awareness* [Interview], 1 November 2005.

Lynch, L. (n.d.), '"As I photograph the night sky, the other night sky photographs back": Surveillance, transparency, and the frenzy of disclosure,' Available at: https://www.academia.edu/1718979/_As_I_photograph_the_night_sky_the_other_night_sky_photographs_back_Surveillance_transparency_and_the_frenzy_of_disclosure.

Mackey, J. (2009), 'Recent US and Chinese antisatellite activities', *Air & Space Power Journal*, Fall 2009.

Oberg, J. (2012), citied in Trevor Paglen, *The Last Pictures*, New York: Creative Time Books, p. 2.

Onley, R.D. (2013), 'Death from above: The weaponization of space and the threat to international humanitarian law', *Journal of Air Law and Commerce*, 78(4), p. 739.

Pagen, T. (2012), 'AFP 731 or the other night sky: An allegory', in L. Parks and J. Schwoch (eds.), *Dow to Earth: Satellite Technologies, Industries, and Cultures*. New York: Rutgers University Press.

Paglen, T. (2012a), 'Chapter one', in *The Last Pictures*. New York: Creative Time Books.

Paglen, T. (2012b), *The Last Pictures*. New York: Creative Time Books.

Parks, L. (2009), 'Digging into Google Earth: An analysis of "Crisis in Darfur"', *Geoforum*, 40(4), pp. 535–345.

Parks, L. and Schwoch, J. (2012, ed.), Down to Earth: Satellite Technologies, Industries, and Cultures, New York: Rutgers University Press

Perkins, C. and Dodge, M. (2009), 'Satellite imagery and the spectacle of secret spaces', *Geoforum*, 40(4), pp. 546–560.

Pickles, J. (1995), *Ground Truth: The Social Implications of Geographic Information Systems*. Guilford: Guilford Press.

Quiquivix, L. (2014), 'Art of war, art of resistance: Palestinian counter-cartography on Google Earth', *Annals of the Association of American Geographers*, 104(3), pp. 444–459.

Rowell, S. (2008), *Ultimate High Ground* [Online]. Available at: http://steverowell.com/index.php/archive/ultimate-high-ground/.

Sage, D. (2014), *How Outer Space Made America*. Farnham: Ashgate Publishing Limited.

Sager, C. (2014, April 14), *Death Metal from Space*. s.l.: Genius Stuff Blog.

Salamander, C. (July 2015), *But You Can Sling One Under a F-18 About to Shoot Off a CVN*. s.l.: U.S. Naval Institute Blog.

Shim, D. (2012), 'Seeing from above: The geopolitics of satellite vision and North Korea', *GIGA Institute of Asian Studies*.

Sloterdijk, P. and Sacks, W. (1990), *Planet Dialectics: Explorations in Environment and Development*. London: Zed Books.

Solman, D. (2001), *Airfiles Blog* [Online]. Available at: http://filmlog.org/airfiles/dat-nav/t-s-htm/attf/attf07.html.

Staff Writers (2016), 'Will space debris be responsible for World War III?', *Spacedaily*, 1 February.

Stahl, R. (2010), 'Becoming bombs: 3D animated satellite imagery and the weaponization of the civic eye', *Media Tropes*, 2(2).

Steyerl, H. (2011), 'In free fall: A thought experiment on vertical perspective', *E-Flux Journal*, 4.

Tong, C. (2014), 'Ecology without scale: Unthinking the world zoom', *Animation*, 9.

U.S. Air Force Transformation Flight Plan (2003). Available at: www.au.af.mil/au/awc/awcgate/af/af_trans_flightplan_nov03.pdf.

Virilio, P. (2002), *Desert Screen: War at the Speed of Light*. New York: A&C Black.

Walker, J. (2014), *Archimedean Witness: The Application of Remote Sensing as an Aid to Human Rights Prosecutions*, Ph.D. Thesis. Los Angeles: UCLA.

Weiner, T. (2005), 'Air Force seeks Bush's approval for space weapons programs', *New York Times*, 18 May.

World Economic Forum (2012), 'What if space was the next frontier for war?', *Time Magazine*, 3 October.

Yorkshire CND (June 2013), *www.yorkshirecnd.org.uk* [Online]. Available at: www.yorkshirecnd.org.uk/menwith-hill-and-the-national-security-state/.

# 5 Sensing air, creaturing data

*Jennifer Gabrys*

If you should find yourself standing outside the Hobgoblin Pub on New Cross Road in the Borough of Lewisham, London, you might notice a grayish-white box approximately two-and-a-half meters high scrawled with a faded and cascading line of graffiti. Wedged in the space between buildings and facing outward toward the road, the air vent and monitoring equipment at the top may be one of the few details that betray the purpose of this structure, which is to measure air quality at this fixed spot in London. One of the stations in the London Air Quality Network (LAQN), which covers 33 boroughs, this monitoring station contributes to the hourly indexes of air quality and news of pollution "episodes" in London. Detecting sulfur dioxide ($SO_2$), particulate matter 10 and 2.5 (PM 10, PM 2.5), as well as nitrogen oxide (NO) and nitrogen dioxide ($NO_2$), the station generates data that indicate whether the UK is meeting EU air quality objectives for both short- and long-term emissions of pollutants.[1] The data also contribute to environmental science research and are managed and made available by the Environmental Research Group (ERG) at King's College London, where this network is managed and run.

Passersby may experience, in a potentially fleeting way, the connection between this station, the local air quality, and the data it generates, which typically circulate in spaces of environmental science and policy. The air quality data that are generated at this fixed site are black-boxed and located in spaces somewhat remote from experiences of air quality on the street. Air quality data are not typically present at the point of encounter with this station, but instead are located in more distant spaces of laboratories and servers, where data are gathered and processed to influence the management of environments and air quality.

In order to make air pollution data gathered by this station and the approximately 100 other stations in the LAQN more accessible, King's ERG has designed a London Air app to allow people to observe emissions levels at key monitoring sites and to make inferences about their own personal exposure when passing through these sites. While this strategy moves toward making the data of fixed sites more accessible through an air quality app, the pollution that individuals experience in their everyday trajectories may be quite different than the types of pollution that are captured through fixed

*Figure 5.1* Citizen sense, 2013
*Source*: Citizen Sense Project

monitoring sites generating data that are averaged over set monitoring periods. The New Cross Road station, for instance, typically records an annual exceedance of $NO_2$ at this fixed point – a pollutant formed through combustion of fuel that is largely the result of high levels of automobile use in the city.[2] Yet all along New Cross Road, individual moments and locations of exposure may give rise to a far different set of pollution "episodes", with much different consequences for urban dwellers in these areas.

Inevitably, the question arises as to how individuals may generate data about their own mobile exposure to air pollution, which is likely to differ from the fixed sites of the official monitoring stations. As discussed throughout this study, environmental monitoring is proliferating from a project undertaken by environmental scientists and governmental agencies to a practice in which DIY groups and citizen sensors are now engaged. Many recent citizen-sensing projects that deploy lower-cost digital sensors and smartphones have focused on monitoring air quality levels in ways that attempt to make environmental data more immediate and connected to experienced conditions. One of the primary ways in which such citizen-sensing projects have sprung up is through direct engagement with monitoring environmental pollution. While some citizen-sensing projects use the itinerant aspects of individual exposure to environmental pollution as a way to experiment with mobile-monitoring practices with which fixed sites of detection cannot compare, other projects suggest that official or government data may not always be available or trusted, so alternative data sources may be necessary in order to gauge exposure to pollutants of immediate concern.

Whether displaying pollution levels or developing platforms to make pollution information more readily available, many citizen-sensing pollution projects attempt to make the details of environmental pollution more instantaneous and actionable. An even more extensive range of pollution-sensing projects has turned up in this area, from devices that use low-cost electronics, including Speck (for PM 2.5 sensing) and AirBeam (for NOx sensing), as well as Citizen Sense kits using Shinyei PM 2.5 sensors. Citizen sensing is a strategy that often attempts to translate practices of monitoring pollution from the spaces of "expert" scientific and government oversight into practices and technologies that are available to a wider array of participants. As the EPA has noted in its work on surveying and assessing the rise in citizen-sensing practices and low-cost monitoring equipment, air pollution monitoring is no longer confined just to official networks and the professional practices of scientists and technicians, but is proliferating into new types of uses that might, they anticipate, even begin to "supplement" regulatory approaches to air pollution. "New breakthroughs in sensor technology and inexpensive, portable methods", one U.S. EPA (2013, p. 2) report notes, "are now making it possible for anyone in the general public to measure air pollution and are expanding the reasons for measuring air pollution".[3] With these citizen-sensing practices, data shift from having to meet a regulatory standard to ensure policy compliance to proliferating and indicating change, hence perhaps instigating different citizen-led actions.

In citizen-sensing projects, more extensively and democratically gathered data are typically presented as "the reasons for measuring air pollution", since it is through collecting data that everything from enhanced participation in environmental issues to changes in policy are hoped to be achieved. The impetus to monitor and gather data is bound up with established (and emerging) processes of understanding environments as information-based problems. Within citizen-sensing projects, data are intended to be collected in ways that complement, reroute, or even circumvent and challenge the usual institutions and practices that monitor environments and manage environmental data. Data are seen to enable modes of action that are meant to offer effective ways to respond to those problems. With more data, and potentially more accurate and extensively distributed data, environmental problems such as air pollution are intended to be more readily and effectively addressed. Data are intertwined with practices, responses to perceived problems, modes of materializing and evidencing problems, and anticipations of political engagement. But how are air quality data constituted, through expert or citizen practices? How do differing practices of environmental monitoring inform the character and quality of data gathered, as well as the possible trajectories and effects of those data? What are the instruments, relations, and experiences of air quality data generated through these distinctive engagements with environments and technology? And in what ways do environments become computational through the use of low-cost air pollution monitoring technologies?

In the process of monitoring air pollution, citizen-sensing practices experiment with the tactics and arrangements of environmental data. These monitoring experiments, however, are not just a matter of enabling "citizens" to use technology to collect data that might allow them to augment scientific studies or to act on their environments. Rather, as I suggest throughout *Program Earth*, computational-sensing technologies are bound up with the generation of new milieus, relations, entities, occasions, and interpretive registers of sensing. The becoming environmental of computation describes this process. Sensor-based engagements with environments do not simply detect external phenomena to be reported; rather, they bring together and give rise to experiencing entities and thereby actualize new arrangements of environmental sensing and data. The production of air quality data through environmental monitoring generates distinct subject-superject entities and occasions for generating and making sense of that data – as scientific facts, matters of concern, or even as inchoate patterns produced through unstable technologies or sporadic monitoring practices.

As a central point of focus, this chapter then crucially asks in what ways environmental sense data emerge not through universal categories or forms, but as concrete entities – or *creatures* – that concresce through processes of subjects participating in environments and environmental events. "The actual world is a process", Whitehead writes, and this "process is the becoming of actual entities. Thus actual entities are creatures; they are also termed 'actual occasions'" (1929, p. 22). Actual entities are creatures or lively meetings of entities that form routes of experience. In this sense, the process of gathering air pollution data might be identified as more than documenting static facts of air quality at any given time or place and instead be approached as a practice that gives rise to entities and modes of participation that transmit data in particular ways and along distinct vectors of environmental participation.

Working with this Whitehead-inspired analysis of how concrete entities of environmental data materialize through pollution sensing, I then consider how environmental-sensing projects are processes of what I call *creaturing data*, where the actual environmental entities that come together are creations that materialize through distinct ways of perceiving and participating in environments. These creatures may have scientific legitimacy. Or they may form as alternative modes of evidence presented in contestation of scientific fact. But in either or both capacities, they are *creaturely* rather than universal arrangements of data.

The point of attending to the creaturing of data is to at once draw attention to the concrete actual entities of data – even the "accidents" of data, as Whitehead would have it – and to take into account the "conditions" that give rise to and sustain these creatures of environmental data. Creatured data are not an abstract store of information or something to be coherently visualized, but rather are actual entities involved in the making of actual occasions and material processes. Data may typically appear to be the primary objective of environmental sensing projects, which focus on obtaining data to influence environmental policy and practices, but along the way, the relations and material arrangements that data gathering sets in place begin to creature new entities that concresce through monitoring practices.

The general ethos of many DIY and citizen-sensing projects has been that by enabling and democratizing the monitoring of local environments, it may also be possible to achieve increased engagement with environmental concerns. These projects test, experiment with, and mobilize alternative modes of environmental citizenship. Yet in what ways do practices of environmental monitoring with sensing devices give rise not just to experimental modes of participation and civic engagement but also to different modalities for experiencing environmental pollution through monitoring practices that generate air quality data? Within these projects, how does the experience and experiment of air pollution and air quality data become a site of political, as well as potentially affective, engagement? How do the creatures of environmental data become points of attachment for influencing and informing environmental concern and politics?

## Citizen data and environments of relevance

While in *Program Earth* I discuss a range of citizen-sensing projects as a way to engage with these questions, I also take up these questions to discuss the specific creatures of data that could be seen to emerge within Citizen Sense research. Within this abbreviated discussion of the "pollution sensing" aspects of the Citizen Sense research project, I consider how the generation of citizen data became entangled with the creation of environments of relevance, which were required in order for citizen data to take hold and have effect. I take up a more extensive discussion of these aspects of the Citizen Sense research in collaboratively written project articles on citizen and collective forms of monitoring and in an investigation of the "just good enough data" that citizen monitoring mobilized in order to make claims to policymakers and regulators.[4] But to briefly mention this Citizen Sense research work here, I would note that the processes of citizens gathering data through kits that we collaboratively developed did not only involve working with sensors to tune in to air and emissions. These processes also involved arranging data as evidence, putting together data stories that were ways of "figuring" the problems of air pollution and the worlds that might come together in order for this air pollution to register, and forming extended social environments in and through which citizen data could gain a foothold and become relevant for addressing problems of air pollution.

As citizen sensing and citizen data collection practices demonstrate, defining what counts as air pollution is not always a straightforward matter. This is particularly the case when attempting to establish evidence of harm or possible harm.[5] Institutional and governmental monitoring networks typically identify pollutants of concern in response to health research that provides evidence for levels of harm caused by particular pollutants. As part of the Global Burden of Disease 2010 study, outdoor air pollution was identified as a leading cause of death, contributing to heart, lung, and cardiopulmonary disease, which are now particularly linked to PM 2.5 exposure, which are also less evident as pollutants.[6] In many ways, health research influences environmental policy, which sets targets in relation to which monitoring networks set criteria for monitoring, as well as providing air quality forecasts, management, and mitigation.

While the impacts of air pollution on human health are one of the key motivators for establishing air quality standards, often the means of monitoring and enforcing these standards can miss the localized pollution experienced by individuals. Environmental and individual health are bound up with articulations of what does and does not count as a pollution *episode* and what may constitute an excessive level of pollutant *exposure*. Emissions of a certain pollutant at a given site in a city may be within an acceptable range, but individual exposure may vary considerably. Air, noise, and water pollution are local if distributed environmental disturbances that many urban dwellers experience on a regular basis, although for some more than others since sites of pollution are often concentrated in lower-income urban areas. Emissions and exposure mitigation have then been identified as two different ways in which to monitor and manage air quality: one addresses fixed sites and reductions of air pollutants; the other attends to how individuals may manage their individual experience to lessen air pollution exposure, such as monitoring and taking alternative routes through cities, although not necessarily attending to overall reductions of air pollutants.

Articulations of personal, urban, and environmental health shift across these different strategies for addressing air pollution. Practices of monitoring pollution at the citizen or individual level are ways to counter or redress the possible gaps in data, but there is more to these projects than this, since in mobilizing sensors to bring environmental monitoring into a more democratic, if often individual, set of engagements, new material-political actors, engagements, and experiments concresce – along with new political (im) possibilities. The question arises as to how data become relevant. Air pollution data might become relevant through health research that establishes high levels of morbidity due to particular air pollutants, through scientific monitoring networks that identify pollutants exceeding accountable limits, or through concerns for certain environmental effects, from acid rain to eutrophication, which unfold with excessive levels of pollutants.

*Relevance* is a term that Whitehead uses to address the ways in which facts have purchase, and the "social environments" that are set in place in order for facts to mobilize distinct effects (1929, p. 203; cf. Stengers, 2011, p. 259). Relevance is a critical part of the process of creaturing, since creaturing involves the ways in which creativity is conditioned or brought into specific events and entities. The ways in which creatures gain a foothold, in other words, are expressions of relevance. Social environments are integral to the immanent processes that condition and give rise to creatures – they do not exist without the formation of creatures, and they continue to co-evolve as the situations in which creatures make "sense" and have effect.

Environments, as understood within Citizen Sense research and throughout *Program Earth*, are then at once an "object" of study as well as a mutually informed and coproduced relation through which monitoring practices and gathered data take hold and gain relevance. The relevance of air quality data is not determined through absolute criteria, since these criteria shift depending on modes of governance, location, and more. If data are understood instead as perceptive entities, it then becomes possible to attend to how data are differently mobilized and concresce within and through practices.

Data in one context might have the status of facts and in another context might galvanize a much different set of a/effects. As the US EPA has expressed in its analysis of new modes of environmental monitoring, "types of data" and "types of uses" are interlinked (2013, pp. 2–5). Data typically only become admissible for legal claims when gathered through specified scientific procedures and with quite precise (as well as expensive) instrumentation. There may also be situations in which data are "just good enough" for establishing that a pollution event is happening, for instance.[7] Yet it remains a relatively open question as to what the uses and effects of data gathered through citizen-sensing technologies might be, since these creatures have arguably not yet settled into entities for which relevance is expressible. In other words, how do citizen sensors undertake actions with and through air pollution sensing practices and data? Could it be that the environments of relevance for this data are still in formation? This is something that the Citizen Sense Data Stories attempt to work with and through, not just in order to understand environments of relevance on a descriptive level, but also to contribute to practice-based formations of such environments through citizen-sensing engagements.

## Conclusion

At this point, it might be easy enough to make a statement about the ways in which environmental monitoring technologies "construct" the air and the problem of air quality. While this inquiry works in a way parallel to constructivism, it also attempts, following Stengers, to think of constructivism as a process not of making *fictions*, but rather of making realities concresce and take hold – or gain a "foothold" (2011, pp. 163–164, 518). Sensors are part of generative processes for making interpretative acts of sensation possible and for attending to environmental matters of concern in particular ways. The environments, arrangements, and practices that are bound up with how facts take hold, and even potentially circulate with effect, are then a critical part of any study into how expanded and differently constituted air pollution data and data-gathering practices might have relevance and be able to make claims on that data to effect change.

This approach to constructivism is different from a poststructuralist rendering, since ideas and language do not *mediate* things, but rather things concresce as propositional effects (Stengers, 2011, p. 252). As Whitehead notes, every fact must "propose the general character of the universe required for that fact" (1929, p. 11). Here is another aspect of *tuning*, which is not just a process of making particular modalities of sensing possible across subjects, environments, and experiences (cf. Gabrys, 2012), but also involves the tuning of facts and the conditions in which those facts have relevance. If facts require particular social environments in order to have relevance, this does not make them illusory (Whitehead, 1929, p. 203; Stengers, 2011, p. 259). Rather, it draws attention to the conditions needed for facts to have effect. In this way, facts are creatures, since, as Whitehead elaborates:

> Each fact is more than its forms, and each form "participates" throughout the world of facts. The definiteness of fact is due to its forms; but the individual fact is a creature, and creativity is the ultimate behind all forms, inexplicable by forms, and conditioned by its creatures.
> (Whitehead, 1929, p. 20)

The creatures of facts – and data – constitute entities that bring worlds into being – and also require worlds for these processes to unfold. Sense data are productive of new environments, entities, and occasions that make particular modalities of sensibility possible. A social environment then plays a formative part in conditioning and supporting creatures of fact and creatures of data.[8] These are creatures of data because they are involved in creative processes in bringing sensing to possibility and of informing the environments where these modes of sensing have relevance.

A process of creaturing data then attends to the ways in which data are not fixed objects gathered through universal criteria but instead are entities through which forms and practices emerge as creatures, and through creaturely processes. As discussed throughout *Program Earth*, perceiving subject-superjects combine as *feeling* entities through actual occasions. These entities might otherwise be termed creatures, since they are formations of conditioned creativity. Furthermore, the "datum", as Whitehead discusses it, is not simply an external array of objects awaiting conceptual classification by a human subject. Instead, the datum is that which subject-superjects feel and, through this experiencing (and so processing and transforming) the datum, generate actual entities, or creatures.

Data are always felt and experienced by and as creatures, which through feeling further give rise to distinct forms of data. A process of transforming the datum into felt experience is a process of creaturing data. What materializes through this process are subjects-superjects involved in processes of being and becoming creatures, thereby expanding what might count as "data publics" to a wider array of entities and relations. Perhaps in the most concisely stated version of this insight, Whitehead writes, "An actual entity is an act of experience" (1929, p. 68). Feeling the datum is a process of transforming the datum into experience, which concresces as an actual entity or creature. Creaturing is then the description of this process of *feeling the datum*, where creatures are the actual entities formed through creaturing the datum.

If we consider the "data" that digital sensors generate, then these devices might be understood less as technologies for gathering (particularly quantitative) data and more as technologies for processing, transforming, and creaturing data – as a felt form of the datum. While it may be easy enough to query the assertion that more data and more democratically gathered data might lead to action and engagement, an approach to creaturing data suggests that it might be relevant to attend to the ways in which data are taken up, felt, experienced, taken into account, gain relevance, and attain "power" as the process whereby particular perceptions or modes of prehension involve or prevail over others (Whitehead, 1929, p. 219). These processes require the formation of social environments in order for data to have effect.

Why is this important? Because, on a concrete level, in order for citizen-generated data to be taken seriously and to inform environmental policy and politics, it is necessary to consider the infrastructures, environments, and practices that are bound up with the creaturing of data in order to understand how to make citizen-generated data (among other forms of data) relevant in ways that can effect change. In other words, this requires tuning our attention to which modes of experience count, and for which purposes. Citizen-sensing practices are information as experimental practices that test not just how environmental monitoring data might be differently gathered but also how such data might be mobilized within distinct environments of relevance and to what (political) a/effect. Within this space, the modes and practices of data – the creaturely entities in and through which data manifest and give rise to worlds – are arguably an area yet to be fully explored, since data are so frequently presented as the abstract and dematerialized evidence of environmental fact.

In this context, what does it mean to "sense" or experience air pollution with computational sensors? Monitoring air pollution with digital sensors is not just a way of obtaining a "result" or fact about a particular environment, but is also about the ways in which data are creatured and mobilized, the social environments that concretize and allow those facts to have relevance, and the additional attendant data practices that might come together to generate a/effects. Creaturing data is an approach that asks how we might consider much more than the "facts" gathered, since the extended social environments, practices, and speculative relations required to bring facts into a space of relevance are crucial to the creatures of data that materialize. Creaturing data is a way of attending to the processing and transforming of environmental data. This is not simply a matter of attending to the extended capacities of generating data but instead involves considering the creatures of data, the entities and situations that form and take hold, whether to solidify, experiment with, or change environmental practices and politics. As Whitehead writes: "We find ourselves in a buzzing world, amid a democracy of fellow creatures; whereas, under some disguise or other, orthodox philosophy can only introduce us to solitary substances, each enjoying an illusory experience" (1929, p. 50). These creatures, as Whitehead (following James) has reminded us, then settle into "a democracy of fellow creatures", where the shared experiences of air, pollution, and possibilities for engagement might even bring us into inventive modes of solidarity.

## Acknowledgments

The research leading to these results has received funding from the European Research Council under the European Union's Seventh Framework Programme (FP/2007–2013)/ERC Grant Agreement n. 313347, "Citizen Sensing and Environmental Practice: Assessing Participatory Engagements with Environments through Sensor Technologies". This chapter is an abbreviated and revised version of "Sensing Air and Creaturing Data", in *Program Earth: Environmental Sensing Technology and the Making of a Computational Planet* (Minneapolis: University of Minnesota Press, 2016). Thanks are due to the University of Minnesota Press for permission to reprint this material.

## Notes

1 While all these pollutants affect cardiovascular and pulmonary health, particulate matter (PM) is of particular concern. As the World Health Organization (WHO, 2014) notes in a fact sheet on air quality, "PM affects more people than any other pollutant. The major components of PM are sulfate, nitrates, ammonia, sodium chloride, carbon, mineral dust and water. It consists of a complex mixture of solid and liquid particles of organic and inorganic substances suspended in the air. The particles are identified according to their aerodynamic diameter, as either PM (particles with an aerodynamic diameter smaller than 10 µm) or PM (aerodynamic diameter smaller than 2.5 µm). The latter are more dangerous since, when inhaled, they may reach the peripheral regions of the bronchioles, and interfere with gas exchange inside the lungs". See WHO, "Air Quality and Health".
2 The EU air quality objective (2008) indicates that there should be no more than 40 µm/m$^3$ of $NO_2$ per year. The New Cross Road station (in the borough of Lewisham) recorded 51 µm/m$^3$ of $NO_2$ in 2013. Also see the London Air Quality Network (LAQN) and the European Commission, "Air Quality Standards".
3 See also Snyder et al. (2013).
4 For a more extensive discussion of these aspects of Citizen Sense research, see the articles Helen Pritchard and Jennifer Gabrys, "From Citizen Sensing to Collective Monitoring: Working through the Perceptive and Affective Problematics of Environmental Pollution", *Geohumanities* 2, no. 2 (2016), 354–371; and Jennifer Gabrys, Helen Pritchard, and Benjamin Barratt, "Just Good Enough Data: Figuring Data Citizenships through Air Pollution Sensing and Data Stories", in

the special issue "Practicing, Materializing and Contesting Environmental Data", *Big Data & Society* 3, no. 2 (2016), 1–14, as well as the project website, http:// citizensense.net.

5 For established limits for common pollutants, see the US EPA National Ambient Air Quality Standards (NAAQS) Table and the European Commission "Air Quality Standards". For a discussion of the ways in which legal disputes become entangled in establishing both the matters of fact and concern of air pollution, see Jasanoff (2010). For a discussion on how exposure and harm become increasingly difficult to link within newer regimes of chemical living, particularly in relation to indoor air quality, see Murphy (2006). For a discussion on evidencing harm through citizen-sensing practices, see Gabrys (2017).

6 Ambient PM pollution contributes to 3.2 million deaths annually, and there are increasing levels of heart disease, lung cancer, and cardiopulmonary disease in association with PM 2.5 exposure. See Lim et al. (2012). The WHO (2014) suggests that "exposure to air pollutants is largely beyond the control of individuals and requires action by public authorities at the national, regional, and even international levels".

7 For a more extensive discussion of the concept and practice of "just good enough data", see Gabrys et al. (2016).

8 As Whitehead notes, "The data upon which the subject passes judgment are themselves components conditioning the character of the judging subject. It follows that any presupposition as to the character of the experiencing subject also implies a general presupposition as to the social environment providing the display for that subject. In other words, a species of subject requires a species of data as its preliminary phase of concrescence. . . . The species of data requisite for the presumed judging subject presupposes an environment of a certain social character" (1929, p. 203).

# References

European Commission (2008), "Directive 2008/50/EC of the European Parliament and of the Council of 21 May 2008 on Ambient Air Quality and Cleaner Air for Europe." *Official Journal of the European Union*, 6 November. L 152/1.

Gabrys, J. (2012), 'Sensing an experimental forest: Processing environments and distributing relations', *Computational Culture*, 2. Available at: http://computationalculture.net/article/sensing-an-experimental-forest-processing-environments-and-distributing-relations.

Gabrys, J. (2016), *Program Earth: Environmental Sensing Technology and the Making of a Computational Planet*. Minneapolis: University of Minnesota Press.

Gabrys, J. (2017), 'Citizen sensing, air pollution and fracking: From "caring about your air" to speculative practices of evidencing harm', *Sociological Review Monograph Series*, 65(2_suppl), pp. 172–192.

Gabrys, J., Pritchard, H., and Barratt, B. (2016), 'Just good enough data: Figuring data citizenships through air pollution sensing and data stories', *Big Data & Society*, 3(2), pp. 1–14.

Jasanoff, S. (2010), 'Thin air', in Madeline Akrich, Yannick Barthe, Fabian Muniesa and Philippe Mustar (eds.), *Débordements: Mélanges Offerts à Michel Callon*. Paris: Presses des Mines, pp. 191–202.

Lim, S., et al. (2012), 'A comparative risk assessment of burden of disease and injury attributable to 67 risk factors and risk factor clusters in 21 regions, 1990–2010: A systematic analysis for the global burden of disease study 2010', *Lancet*, 380(9859), pp. 2224–2260.

London Air Quality Network (LAQN). Available at: www.londonair.org.uk.

Murphy, M. (2006), *Sick Building Syndrome and the Problem of Uncertainty*. Durham, NC: Duke University Press.

Pritchard, H. and Gabrys, J. (2016), 'From citizen sensing to collective monitoring: Working through the perceptive and affective problematics of environmental pollution', *Geohumanities*, 2(2), pp. 354–371.

Snyder, E.G., Watkins, T.H., Solomon, P.A., Thoma, E.D., Williams, R.W., Hagler, G.S.W., Shelow, D., Hindin, D.A., Kilaru, V.J., and Preuss, P.W. (2013), 'The changing paradigm of air pollution monitoring', *Environmental Science and Technology*, 47, pp. 11369–11377.

Stengers, I. (2011), *Thinking with Whitehead: A Free and Wild Creation of Concepts*. Translated by M. Chase. 2002. Reprint, Cambridge: Harvard University Press.

U.S. Environmental Protection Agency (EPA) (2013), 'Draft roadmap for next generation air monitoring', 8 March. Available at: www.eunetair.it/cost/newsroom/03-US-EPA_Roadmap_NGAM-March2013.pdf.

U.S. Environmental Protection Agency (EPA) (n.d.), 'National Ambient Air Quality Standards (NAAQS) Table'. Available at: www.epa.gov/criteria-air-pollutants/naaqs-table.

Whitehead, A.N. (1929/1985), *Process and Reality*. New York: The Free Press.

World Health Organization (WHO) (2014), 'Ambient (Outdoor) air quality and health', *Fact Sheet No. 313*, March 2014. Available at: www.who.int/mediacentre/factsheets/fs313/en.

# 6 Offsite

## Data, migration, landscape, materiality

*Benjamin Gerdes*

Go to bed with the midnight sky above your head and if you can't fall asleep, try counting the stars. It usually helps! In the fall there are wild mushrooms that you'll enjoy foraging – from August to November you'll find a lot of delicious chanterelles on the ground.

Visit Sweden AirBnB listing, 2017[1]

Recently, we've been having difficult discussions within the party about the perception of reality.

Åsa Romson, Green Party, Deputy Prime Minister
of Sweden, announcing reductions in Sweden's
migration policies, 2015[2]

Just as the great Swedish company Ikea revolutionized how furniture is designed and built, we hope that Luleå 2 will become a model for the next generation of data centers.

Press release announcing construction of Facebook's
second data center in Luleå, Sweden, 201[3]

## Clip 1

A flat drawer opens slowly in front of a security kiosk at the entryway to a colocation data center, hold for a medium close-up of returning passports and fresh visitors' badges on branded lanyards. Shot/reverse shot here carries the camera through a security lock, a pair of translucent green cylinders that envelope two well-dressed men and then open for them to emerge out the other side. Inside, a conference room discussion yields a PR rep explaining the advantages of the Nordics for the expansion of a data center industry: a stable power grid with available electricity (much of it geothermal), a stable political economy, and a stable regional geological formation. The abundant energy comes from long-term state promotion of heavy industry. "So the risks are very low for basically anything". The CEO of a small IT company appears in a room of the colocation faculty: "We provide infrastructure as a service, and what we see here is part of our cloud. So this is really the cloud that you see in the back". He discusses the benefits of this particular center,

*Figure 6.1* One company's cloud, as referenced in Clip 1, Digiplex, Stockholm
*Source*: Photo taken by Benjamin Gerdes

security and stability (no center, of course, says otherwise; they only compete about who can be *more* secure or *more* stable; none are avowedly unsustainable, just achieving different levels of ultra-sustainability).

*Off-screen voice:* "Could you walk us around your cloud a little bit? We just want to get a sense of how big it is".

*CEO:* Everything is stored in these [computer] racks; we currently have seven of them up and running, but we grow it fast, so hopefully it will be many more racks in the near future.

### Framing

In these paratactic research notes for a film essay, I identify three recent and/or developing phenomena in Sweden, particularly in the north: the state-aided development of a world-class cluster of data centers just below the Arctic Circle in Luleå (presented via PR language as the "Node Pole"), migration policy and procedure such as refugee resettlement and rehousing industries, and migrant labor in the berry-picking industry, particularly recruitment of informal workers from Thailand under often exploitative conditions. Beyond examining these conditions in juxtaposition to offer a more nuanced understanding of capital accumulation and flow today, the project draws on one state or territorial context (here: Sweden) to suggest a more focused set of sites, struggles, and topics for collective contestation.

I am not alone in questioning the emerging contours of a particular set of lived relationships to data, labor, borders, infrastructural privatization, and the built environment, but I suggest a mode of inquiry that exists somewhere in between the site-by-site hyper-focus of many academic studies and the brevity and broadness of journalistic accounts of similar phenomena. Borrowing the term "offsite" from records management and data storage industries, and in general the prevalence of methods such as outsourcing or inversion in contemporary business practices, we could attempt to evaluate possibilities for the making visual (or making public) of complex phenomena like data centers, which are often rendered less visible in cultural terms by physical location.[4] My work then attempts to enact not only a process of extra-disciplinary juxtaposition, but one of insertion into industries and commercial practices underpinning wide swaths of cultural activity and everyday life, particularly those misunderstood as peripheral rather than central with regard to those public spheres.

## Clip 2

Image: overhead close-up of the front half of a bicycle, landscape orientation. As the bike rolls forward over a pebbled street, the image congeals into slow motion. Soundtrack: a distant mechanical whir and a series of beeps; the sound of automatic doors welcomes a drastic increase in the volume of the machinations. As a continuous shot of the rolling bicycle holds for over two minutes, the sound's volume remains constant while engaging subtle shifts in balance of treble and bass, clicks, whirs, and hums approach and recede as a suggestion of motion conveys a microphone traveling across machines in perceivably close proximity. This continues as the image jerks toward full speed as it cuts to a grassy path below a road overpass, then clouds, water, and northern land masses out a plane window. Blurred aspen forests from a train follow, arriving via cut to a wide shot of a wood and glass multi-story interior, a public library and cultural center with harbour-side side view out the window. Cut to grass and trees, more aspen' the camera pans up to an arrow sign innocuously directed toward "Facebook entrance (all deliveries here)". Wide shot as camera pans across vast built structure. A fence, large tract of muddy land, and slow-moving security vehicle in the foreground. Skies are wide and gray as a single vantage point struggles to convey the enormity of the data center, the setting bluntly industrial rather than majestic or distinguished by other features. The facilities are in a large unmarked field on popular mapping apps, but the name of the road is Datavägen ("Data Street").

### Bits

In 2013, Facebook opened its first data storage center outside the United States in Luleå, Sweden. According to Facebook, this was, upon opening, the most energy-efficient computer center ever built. In a fall 2015 article in *The Guardian*, this facility is described as being "set amid a green pine forest, lakes and an archipelago. The Arctic Circle is just down the road".[5]

*Figure 6.2* Entrance to Facebook's Luleå 2 data center, Luleå, Sweden

*Source*: Photo taken by Benjamin Gerdes

Facebook has since rapidly constructed a second 25,000 square meter facility using emerging pre-fabrication techniques. A press release announcing the construction of this center references the "Swedish" furniture design and manufacturing innovations of Ikea as an inspiration for Facebook's hopes to influence the design of pre-fabricated rapid data center construction.

In the wake of Facebook's initial investment in Luleå, a city of 75,000 with an industrial background in mining and steel mills, a consortium of public and private actors have cultivated and promoted an entire industry in the region ("the Node Pole") around data storage. Boosted by reduced operating costs via the natural cooling properties of the subarctic climate and recent incentives such as a June 2016 state plan to reduce electricity taxes on data centers, these sites are advertised as being the greenest and most cost effective in the world, additionally boasting by 2017 the lowest electricity rates in Europe. Marketing and growth via related business interests, including the Swedish state-owned utility Vattenfall (co-owner of the Node Pole consortium as of February 2017), are ongoing. In May 2018 Facebook announced plans for a third center of 97,000 square meters to be completed by 2021.

## Clip 3

> We saw an article about Google building data centers in Oregon. Of course the thinking then was why do they build data centers in Oregon along the river? Yeah, because it's a mission critical facility. They need a lot of power,

they needed the climate, etcetera. Then everybody understood, "OK this is something we have".

Tor Björn Minde, Research Institutes Sweden (RiSE), Luleå

Cut to: handheld camera follows Tor Björn into what looks like a large refrigeration unit. Pink plastic hangs from the ceiling as he explains this unit experiments with air flow control. A small number of computer rack servers become visible. "This is the first module we built and the first Facebook center is a thousand times bigger than this, but this is good enough for research".

*Question from behind camera*: "You were telling me earlier very few operations in Sweden would need more than this amount of space?"

*Tor Björn*: "This is very high end, so we try to think about what kind of operations in Sweden have more data than this. Of course, if you take the whole of Sweden, that would not fit in here, but there's a couple; Facebook is too big for this, of course. But this is a good one for studying how a data center works. . . . So one project is automation, controlling this environment. The long-term vision of that project is that these are autonomous data centers". Cut to: windy pan across Datavägen 15, portable guard rails, orange traffic cones, a pile of brown felled trees, and pop-up construction signs pepper a more suggestive structure, the architecture of the entrance to Facebook's Luleå 2, its earthen tones and angular roof suggesting a sustainable and welcoming open pizza box. Behind this facade, nearly camouflaged into the grayness of the sky, rests the wide and low-slung industrial mass.

### Found clip A

In the 2015 video clip of a press conference circulated widely in international news media under headlines such as "Sweden's deputy prime minister cries while announcing refugee U-turn", then-deputy prime minister Åsa Romsen begins to cry as she introduces restrictive immigration policy changes (*The Guardian*, 2015). In the Swedish media, this moment causes "Twitter to explode". The minister, co-leader of the Green Party in a ruling coalition with the more powerful Social Democrats, suggests the policy shift, which she describes the same day as "a terrible decision", emerges from intra-party conflict and discussion over a primarily political conception of reality. I find this clip ominously arresting, a different sort of signpost along the path of recent failure of democratic institutions in Western democracies. Compared to anti-government sentiment as expressed by rightward populisms – for example, the professional wrestling heel played by Donald Trump or Boris Johnson's loveable frumpy cad – Romsen's moment of public affect also breaks the norms of politics as usually practiced, but in a different manner. It is a speech act of failing from within policy that does not mask the violence of restrictive state immigration policies, nor does it excuse the state and its elected actors. (Notably, it reasserts the bordered state as the central agent in such matters.) While public and media responses express both support and criticisms of her position and public moment, one notable strain of responses describes this as a moment of weakness, seemingly reinscribing a gendered notion of state power.

### Bodies

Until announcing dramatic shifts in its asylum laws in November of 2015 (subsequently voted into law by Parliament in late June 2016), Sweden had long been seen internationally as a standard bearer for the humane acceptance of refugees. As artists who have long addressed immigration dialogues in the United States and abroad, we have firsthand experience of this: in August 2007, we interviewed a group of Iraqi refugees taking Swedish language classes at a Komvux in Sodertalje for the short video *Because there are so many: Iraq*. At that point, Sweden had accepted 12,259 Iraqis seeking asylum in the first eight months of 2007, whereas the United States had accepted 685. Prior to the legislative change, the country had, in fact, accepted the most refugees per capita of any European nation. As two components of the new platform are temporary (over permanent) asylum and individual (instead of family) asylum, Sweden is witnessing alterations to the process for refugee housing and resettlement. A developing trend is the temporary housing of newly arrived refugees in the Arctic North in converted hotels, conference centers, and other formerly non-residential buildings. For example, a fall 2015 article in the Canadian newsmagazine *Maclean's* profiled Mohammad Mahsoun, a Syrian refugee living close to the Arctic Circle in Porjus (resident population of 350, refugee population of 150). Porjus is, like Luleå, in Norrboten, the northernmost county in Sweden. Experiencing a decline in birth rate and generational labor migration toward the larger towns and cities, small villages are actively lobbying to be sent refugees in order to maintain sufficient populations to keep schools and hospitals open. The welcoming of difference in this context, although instrumental, offers a contrast to the anti-immigrant policies of the far-right Sweden Democrats who have gained a parliamentary foothold in recent national election cycles as well as come to municipal power in regions of southern Sweden (Nilsson, 2018).

### Found clip B

A tourism campaign initiated in 2016 by Visit Sweden, the national tourism organization owned 50/50 by the Swedish state and tourism industry, highlights the principle of *allemansrätt*, "freedom to roam" or the right of public access, guaranteed by the Swedish constitution. Yet this, too, becomes inflected through the logic of the digital platform, as Visit Sweden in 2017 initiated a campaign to draw attention to *allemansrätt* by listing "all of"

Sweden on the lodging platform AirBnB. Contrary to populist rhetoric of Sweden as a territory and state, under-resourced in the face of recent upswings in immigration, "Get Curious", a two-minute video produced by Visit Sweden in conjunction with this campaign, speaks of natural idylls through the eyes and mouth of children. The film opens with a shot of flight above the clouds and a small child's voiceover, "Of plants and animals please take care". Later, "I'm friends with a reindeer", says a slightly older child's voiceover. "The white one". As the story continues, images of child-led play in nature introduce us to a group: camping, hiking, meeting animals, and picnicking. It is a cosmopolitan collection of cross-racial friends or family; blonde children, parents, and grandparents mix with several non-white or mixed-race children. Tellingly, this perhaps family includes no adult men of color, and the one non-white adult in the piece, a woman with dreadlocks, is only seen seated with her back to the camera in a brief and wide-angle group shot. In contrast, the silver-haired grandmother figure appears in close-up and via voiceover. "We all get something from nature. . . . We can discover so many new things. . . . It enriches us all", says another child as the piece nears an end. This voiceover is delivered over a close-up of a blonde toddler plucking and then eating a single blueberry, then a shot of the white mother squatting on the forest floor to pick berries, holding the hand of the blonde toddler, who gazes up at the sky with a look of awe and childlike wonder. Acoustic guitar and angelic choral tones are present. Symptomatically, the absence of technology, infrastructure, less-assimilated figures of migration, or forms of labor (such as berry picking) that go beyond wide-eyed discovery render this fantasy-scape a different articulation of "Sweden" than that of the trade magazines or the xenophobic party. Migratory labor and over-all human migration correspond to industries such as data centers in their occlusion from the popular visual landscape. The alignment of an entrepreneurial urban business model with affirmations of sustainability and social tolerance render nature a non-populated space for temporary enjoyment and contemplation by cosmopolitan urban populations, the rougher yet quieter other to the slick and speedy smoothness of the city. It is rendered in terms of internal harmony and restorative power, to be taken care of, but to be taken from by the human (Lina Söderström (director), B-Reel films, 2017).

## Berries

Eighty percent of the more than 25,000 Thai people living in Sweden are women. Eighty-five percent of those women are married to Swedish men, and most of them live in rural areas of the country. Around the year 2000, Sweden experienced a reduction in the berry-picking labor force among white Swedes. Thai women married to Swedes began telling relatives and friends about a profitable, small-scale migratory labor practice picking blueberries, bilberries, cloudberries, and lingonberries. The berries are picked wild, primarily for cosmetics and health foods. They grow best in the north. The industry, whether the picking occurs in Norway, Sweden, or Finland, relies on the principle of *allemansrätten*, where any person has a right to pick berries on public lands. Beyond questions about the labor conditions, many in Sweden consider the berry industry – in the volume and scale of foreign labor recruitment – to be operating in bad faith regarding this right. After several summers of Thai workers visiting Sweden informally on tourist visas, labor recruiters became involved in both Sweden and Thailand. This saw an increase in Thai people going into debt – mortgaging farms and borrowing travel funds – to pick for the summer. Three-month work permits issued through the Swedish state via these recruiters excluded the workers from involvement in Swedish labor unions. This practice first received substantial press attention in the summer of 2009, when a bad crop year led to 80 percent of the 6,000 Thai workers failing to cover their costs. Recruiters had advertised higher pay and, once in Sweden, paid the Thai minimum wage. Four hundred people protested at the Swedish Embassy in Bangkok after returning, suing for wages and damages. While quotas had held at about 6,000 workers per summer, regulations tightened after public scrutiny in the years 2009 through 2012. Recent summers have seen a reduction in the number of workers in Swedish forests, with record numbers instead reported in the similar latitudes of Finnish Lapland, which presently enforces significantly fewer labor regulations.

The industry, whether the picking occurs in Norway, Sweden, or Finland, relies on the Swedish principle of *allemansrätten*, where any person has a right to pick berries on public lands. At the same time, the commercial demand for many of these berries increases, primarily for Asian "nutraceutical" consumer markets. How are those traversed paths materially manifested – both the transnational dimension of seasonal migratory labor and the repurposing and transformation of northern villages for life and work, including the occupation of closed schools and abandoned housing by berry pickers? How is rural Sweden influenced visually and socially through these interactions? (Hedberg et al., 2019).

### Borders

A May 2016 report on the "digitization of the European economy" commissioned by Google from the Stockholm office of the Boston Consultancy Group, in a perhaps unintentional nod to Vladimir Lenin, includes a section called "What Needs to Be Done" that encourages nations self-identifying as "European frontrunners" to "oppose data localization requirements" and "support cross-border initiatives" (Alm et al., 2019). The simultaneity of these recommendations, the prioritization of data migration, and the opening of borders at the same moment state policies on human migration enter a newly restrictive phase reveal a principle condition of the present.

## Logistical landscapes

In the same way that borders cannot be singular, but instead register as symbolic accretions of the political, material (human and inhuman), geographic, and technological, the landscape and territory "within" such a border also remains unstable and disputed. In Sweden, we locate two norths. Exploring the conditions of possibility for the data center industry and an accompanying re-scaling of territories, Asta Vonderau writes of the promotion of the north, a zone of high-tech innovation and future possibility, (2018) while Madeleine Eriksson and Aine Tollefsen write of the same north as a deteriorated resource periphery in relation to the low-tech low-wage berry-picking labor and supply chain (2018). Yet both studies share an interest in the production of the visible via landscape and infrastructure, with Vonderau drawing on a notion of "clouding" to discuss the visible and invisible aspects of data center infrastructural formations and Eriksson and Tollefsen referencing Don Mitchell understanding of landscapes when they describe them as "sites of struggle and places of resistance, [where] the reason for making a space into a landscape by those in power is to obstruct that struggle and to make power relations appear 'fully natural and timeless'"(2018, p. 71). In both instances, then, we could recognize the authors working along the lines of what a different set of scholars have recently called for as a "logistical gaze", an understanding of logistics and their emergent support infrastructures as not just material or circulatory networks, but in total, a bio-political apparatus that produces new forms of subjectivity (Benvegnù et al., 2019).

## "Folk" as visually and territorially boundaried

From a spatial and visual cultural studies perspective, housing refugee populations in villages in the far north arguably renders a less visible condition of access to rights and legality, a state of being "included" to only be rendered visible in the remote or peripheral regions. I would call this repopulation or resettlement by offsitedness. This situation proves particularly compelling given the prominent role of housing in prior moments of modern Swedish social and political history. Famously, the *Miljonprogrammet* (million program) built a million new units of housing in the years from 1965 to 1974. These were designed with the ideal of "mixed housing" to provide a spatial mixing of ages, household sizes, and tenures and included parks, public meeting spaces, schools, libraries, and churches. As a designed social program, these structures portray much about the aspirations and priorities of that era, which include access to affordable housing, while also showing the historical trajectory of such programs, which show today they constitute the base for Sweden's highly segregated non-white populations, with both Stockholm and Gothenburg now among the most segregated cities in Europe by some indexes. What are the similar social processes and norms we can glean today from examining the design, mobility, and spatial arrangement of

*Figure 6.3* In a deployment of benign "Swedishness" that occludes a more violent reality, Ikea references the principle of *allemansrätten* on packets of meatball sauce mix (notably to be eaten with lingonberries)

*Source*: Photo taken by Benjamin Gerdes

refugee housing facilities and locations? How do the trends of privatization and the selling off of state-owned apartments and housing affect the refugee and immigrant communities, respectively? What tensions and challenges can be traced to dominant narratives of the present and the past – particularly vis-à-vis long-held Swedish concepts and values such as *folkhemmet* ("the people's home") and *allemansrätten* ("freedom to roam" or "right of public passage")? (Thörn and Thörn, 2017).

## Clip 4

The camera pans down from within a rocky structure. No visual information indicates this installation squats within a former nuclear bunker or that one could walk up the ramp and exit to one of the hippest small squares in Stockholm. Instead, a careful hodgepodge of tinted fluorescent lighting, potted plants, massive color-coded metal overhead pipes, metal vault doors, and glass greet us. The camera pans left to a sign that, in balloon letters, reads "Reduce global warming – and get paid for it". A sticker on the glass outside the double sets of security doors informs us this is a "Triple Green Data Center". A series of static wide shots carries us into the ground floor of the small data center, with rows of racked servers fanning out, and the cave ceiling suspended at a great height above. The promotional materials and the "Data Centers by Sweden" marketing contact (who suggests I film here) both reference a villain's lair in a James Bond film. Cut to medium shot, angled down from a level above; we are in the conference room suspended above the server hall. Blue and magenta tones refract off glass and plexi, the repeated transparency of the catwalk, the enclosed pod, and the table. A small red-and-white-checkered rocket ship from *Tintin*, styled like a mid-century toy, sits atop the glass hexagon of the table, swivel chairs abandoned at skewed angles, while a cleaner in nothing-out-of-the-ordinary work clothes scrubs the table. The lanyard droops from his neck as he bends to wipe the glass back to an unsmudged state.

### "Swedish" sustainability

That "the great Swedish company Ikea" was until recently registered as a private Dutch family foundation, and that its founder was a tax exile from Sweden for many years, may reveal more about Facebook's motivations than the PR team intended in gesturing toward the innovations of flatpack shipping and transnational marketing of quasi-nonsensical Swedish product names and iconography. Similarly, the usage of Swedish locales as somewhat exotic in branding and the recruitment of data center business may have less to do with the actual geographic properties of the subarctic and more with the political economy of the Swedish data center industry: political stability, municipally backed land deals, the aforementioned low electricity rates, low latency via fiber connectivity, a robust power grid, and an existing English-language-proficient workforce. And yet, the deliberate linkage to Ikea's business model traces a line from consumer commodity sales to the production of virtual experience and user-generated data as value in themselves: two industry leaders enjoying the rhetoric of increasing consumption without consequence, where sustainability and profit are not at odds but promoted as co-mutual aspects of a core business model. The cultural signification of Ikea's "Swedishness" in language, visual design, and identification of Swedish product designers increasingly draws on Sweden's international reputation to promote a "green" business model. Similarly, the green forests of the "Node Pole" promote a place where data lives among the clean air, clean water, and clean power of the naturally cool north. For example, the cover of the 2017 promotional magazine *Data Centers in North Sweden*, a collaboration between Umeå University, Luleå University of Technology, and the Swedish Institute of Computer Science – three publicly funded institutions – shows a frozen landscape pocketed by a central body of water reflecting the aurora borealis occupying slightly more than half the image. This image, of course, conceals the comparatively less seductive material realities of industrial architecture, computing, and labor underpinning data center operations but pushes this promotion of more fluidity over solidity even further as the monochromatic frozen landscape surrenders to majesty of the water and sky (n.d.).

*Figure 6.4* Cover of the publication *Data Centers in North Sweden*
*Source*: Public domain

Even less visible is the manner in which the Swedish data center industry emerges not from nature, but from sites historically linked to heavy industry and national defense.[6,7] The state's preconditions reveal the paradox of logistics and nature in the data centre's imagelessness – a territory that delivers political stability, a power grid – not wild but highly regulated, a state that remains invisible but maintains order. The major occlusion then concerns the nature of data as a state-supported heavy industry, albeit in transition from industrial to "knowledge economy circles" as these public entities promote investment via an image similar to what their regional tourism councils would choose.

## *Migration*

It may initially appear too convenient to point to homologies in journalistic or everyday language used to describe persons and data storage, but given such overlaps, one could also suggest it remains surprising that certain overlaps are not explored more frequently. For example, data can be "housed" and "migrate", and the geographic location of data is every bit as subject to governance of political border crossings through treaties, privatized infrastructure, and so on. Therefore, on a primary level, questions of place, housing, and the built environment have historically not been addressed simultaneously when considering human migration and data, but one could read this as a symptomatic elision of these similarities in how seemingly discrete phenomena are popularly described, including how frequently landscape, location, geography, and state are invoked in corporate presentations of data centers.

If these overlaps in data-speak strike one as too coincidental a linguistic match with lived spatial trajectories of humans, we need only to point out the false dichotomy: to separate the human and the data at this point in industrialized nations contradicts a liberal notion of rights where privacy, production, and the right to mobility and work are inextricably linked to data relationships. Two examples carry us in different directions. First, the Estonian e-Residency program, a state priority, grants legal EU status to the Estonia-registered business dealings of "digital nomads" who may have no other legal or physical presence in the EU and are encouraged to conduct their work remotely (e-Residency, 2019). Meaning: some subset of rights and privileges once reserved for human-based activities derived from citizenship or physical residence within a particular territory have been decoupled from the physical, bodily requirement linked to place – for example, the use of biometric data to determine and affirm citizenship status – and instead transferred to the act of digital transmission by a body or its authorized agent. Second, beyond the state usage of biometric data, the recent attention paid to the role private tech firms like Palantir, Salesforce, and Amazon Web Services play in immigration detention operations in the United States points to the opposite effect: namely, that while mobility can be largely data driven, immobility and the carceral operations of the present are even more reliant on algorithmic background operations (Who's Beyond ICE? The Tech Companies Fueling Deportations, 2019).

*Field notes*

A primary topic of investigation in the video is the peculiar paradox of place in relationship to data centers: a placelessness or broad interchangeability of their interior functionality operates in contrast to their surrounding structures of secrecy, security, and public relations. Although most data centers remain difficult for researchers or the general public to access, an internal passage through banks of computing equipment still fails to convey the cultural and economic significance of these facilities.

In the summer of 2017, I was granted entry and permission to record in two data centers in the Stockholm region run by the Bahnhof and Digiplex firms, where after repeated attempts, I gained access through a marketing office. (There was little interest in public, artistic, or journalistic access.) I plan to explore these mid-size data centers in the larger project for which this piece constitutes a preliminary effort. To observe briefly: the contours of place and visibility register differently in mid-size data centers. First, these are not enterprise centers (purpose-built by a major industry player like Amazon Web Services, Google, Microsoft, etc). Particularly when these facilities offer colocation, the structure of address engages business clients on security, reliability, ecology, and fiscal viability while stopping short of the flagship-burnishing touches branded facilities deploy: name architects, wider-reaching "on brand" publicity, etc. Beyond these touches, the relationship to site and place often intensifies for the latter category as a result of their scale: the necessary acquisition of large plots of land favors regional contexts where these industries operate more prominently.

The two Facebook data centers proved more difficult to access, despite contact with some well-placed employees in the corporation outside Luleå. In that particular case, I am interested in a second paradox, one where Facebook relies on widespread participation and public accessibility, down to the level of Facebook's free, ad-supported model as an acknowledged component of their global expansion strategy, while maintaining a corporate rhetoric of impenetrability (terms like "mission critical" are common for data centers) around the facilities themselves. This becomes even stranger when one considers that the Luleå data centers have not one, but two public profile pages on Facebook, where one can, for example, message the data center or its staff. (I considered doing just this on my phone from a public road outside the fence on a cold and rainy August day in Luleå while being trailed by private security in a car at an appropriately hands-off Swedish distance.)

*Offsite*

In the same way that relocating persons from Syria to the subarctic north of Sweden could be said to traffic in climatological extremes, while one data center axis ("CENTRAL") follows a range of similar zones in suburban office parks and "innovation hubs" of major metropolitan areas (considerations of latency in financial industries, in particular, reportedly render this proximity necessary), the other axis ("REMOTE") yields extremes: cold and north, south and hot, and so on. In the United States, for example, one finds prominent data centers both in the cooler Pacific Northwest and in the deserts of the Southwest. In the former, energy and cooling costs remain comparatively low; the latter assumes higher energy costs offset by solar power. The both/and nature of these installations suggests a flexible and varied set of relations around energy, security, and presentation. In both cases they are remote, but in cases where a company may own and operate both types of data centers – for example, Google – it is worth noting the public relations prominence of the more ecological centers relying on passive cooling, etc. The degree to which a major corporation exhibits a capacity to embed a facility in a forest zone, to implicitly argue for the soft and non-destructive insertion of a massive complex into a natural landscape, plays better in the rugged geography of cooler climes than the optics of the desert, which immediately yield (entirely appropriate) comparisons to military bases and other highly securitized installations. Insofar as the nakedness of the desert then seems to make the centers too visible, the architectural dimension of these centers suggests that while their capabilities – in terms of energy, speed, and availability – can be widely touted, the structures themselves disinvite public attention to their visual design and scale.

It is also worth observing the proximity of data centers not only to necessary infrastructural supports, such as electricity, but also the connotation via proximity of movement of goods and high-performing workforces in and out of urban areas. For example, the 2018 Volume 1 of the publication *Advantage Sweden* by Business Sweden ("A magazine about expanding into Sweden") discusses data centers, Swedish start-up unicorns, digitization of construction, and green batteries on its cover with the tagline "Join Sweden in Designing a Digital Future", yet its first article concerns infrastructure projects in Sweden's two largest cities (Business-sweden.se, 2018).

### Footnote to clip 2

The video draws on multiple methodologies of representing data center operations on a firsthand, sensory level, such as audio field recordings of walk-throughs demonstrating the loudness of the environment and an interview with a related researcher within a research facility, also with significant background noise. Video images juxtaposed with these materials enact more typical manners of portraying "place" as a location and a public – the library, a cultural center, paths and roadways, the aspen from a moving train window – edited in an attempt to subtly engage the comingled mechanisms of security, publicity, and remoteness that often characterize the same centers on a broader cultural level. Before arriving at the recognizability and coherence of such scenes, however, the server hall walkthrough field recording overlays an extended slow motion shot of a bike moving above the pavement, documentation of travel from city center to data center. Interior bleeds into exterior; operation interrupts place. Aesthetically, this formal collision intends to convey the difficulty of making such connections, the complexity of understanding the multivalent operations of the data center as placed within a specific locality. On an epistemological level, I don't purport to gain much traction with larger structures via an exercise like this, but it does access the sensory to speak to a specificity that relocates these industries within the contours of specific times, places, and labor practices.

Place occupies a strange role in this equation. The subarctic climate, preferential land deals, political stability, and low tax and electricity rates (following Sweden's designation of data centers as a priority under state mechanisms previously designed to support heavy industry) render a specific location like Luleå strategically valuable for Facebook. Like many prior manufacturing industries, the lived social contexts in which these facilities operate remain impacted by their presence, now not so much in terms of mass employment but perhaps in offering politically or popularly a general affect regarding a viable local future. At the same time, storage industries currently rely on the offsite or the peripheral location as a principle – the physical and material location and footprint of data storage is occluded by design, unconsidered by a transnational general usership as a condition of its adoption as a fluid and always-available commodity. Strangely, we could almost consider this a lesson (as reversal) from the anti-nuclear movement, where the location of power generation facilities became a political issue and tactical ground for contestation. Here, consumer confidence appears boosted by a lack of knowledge regarding location, so peripheral invisibility broadly continues to support a highly visible industry locally.

My initial fieldwork in Luleå recognizes the conditions of this visibility as manifest most prominently on a municipal political level, rather than more pedestrian forms of social identification with the data centers. I failed to encounter substantial evidence of popular identification or alignment with the ideals or corporate identity circulated by Facebook beyond those directly working in economic development or related industries. The implicit character of this relationship between global corporation and locality, rather than one more publicly lived, encouraged me to tease out a more direct linkage in the video by beginning with an admittedly forceful sound/image juxtaposition, a dislocation of ambient sound that nonetheless invokes a fuller understanding of location.

### Compression, or to favor one landscape over another

To return to housing in multiple valences as I began, and in lieu of directly addressing the questions of human migration or broader forms of labor outside data centers, we can ask not just about the regional or state initiatives around data industries, but what we might term the transnational regulatory imaginary (or lack thereof). For example, Swedish authorities have expressed little interest in enforcing or revising agricultural policy in relationship to the berry-picking industry as this remains a low priority in relationship to rhetoric around creative economies and digital industries (Hedberg et al., 2019).[8]

## Clip 5

Medium shot of a man in front of a digital projection for the "Stockholm Data Parks" project: "Green Computing Redefined" explains how "our" next step is to capture the tremendous amount of heat produced by data centers. He explains that while it is concerning that energy demands are growing much faster than predicted, cryptocurrencies project to potentially reach 20 percent of global power consumption, and the energy that goes into data centers transfers predominantly to heat, given their very modest mechanical needs. Development of heat recovery systems allows a second use of this electricity as a thermal utility, washing the initial pass of Bitcoin's arguably excessive energy consumption of its "waste" tag. The project conveys recaptured heating to apartment blocks as a replacement for prior generative methods for district heating. It claims to be the first of its kind brought to market.

### *What is a data park?*

The integration of data with public infrastructure and traditional utilities takes on increasing ubiquity and integration not only in a business sense, but infiltrating spheres such as housing. In contrast to the north, which may privilege massive spatial scales, the Stockholm Data Parks effort involves heat recapture from submerged urban data centers to warm apartment buildings. This process draws on existing and newly constructed district heating networks, with excess energy from computing operations warming hot water for domestic heating purposes. While the footprint of data on the northern landscape remains most visible, the transfer of former state operations such as nuclear bunkers and the replacement of traditional heavy industries and heating operations with data facilities lead us to reconsider the connotations of the structures that underpin "the virtual", "the digital", or "the cloud". On an ontological level, the fact that living spaces can be indirectly heated through data usage signals a change to the moment we are not just logistically surrounded by our data, or algorithmically governed by it, but literally living it in a more animal sense, drawing bodily warmth from a collective offsite aggregation of data itself.

### *Acknowledgments*

The author wishes to thank the anonymous source who shared direct experiences of the international promotion of the Swedish data center industry, as well as Tess Takahashi for valuable editorial feedback.

# Notes

1 As quoted in www.businessinsider.com/sweden-lists-entire-country-on-airbnb-2017-5.
2 www.theguardian.com/world/video/2015/nov/24/asa-romson-sweden-deputy-prime-minister-cries-announcing-refugee-u-turn-video.
3 "Facebook Adopts IKEA-Style Pre-Fab Design for Expansion in Sweden", www.datacenterknowledge.com/archives/2014/03/07/facebook-adopts-ikea-style-pre-fab-design-expansion-sweden.
4 The artist and researcher Gerald Nestler recently suggested that Occupy Wall Street should have skipped Wall Street and occupied a site near the New York Stock Exchange's data centers as the primary site of value production for contemporary finance. The question then concerns the possibility of projects capable of connecting symbolic or abstract sites (Wall Street) to the obscured infrastructural base of operations (Mahwah, New Jersey). In this case, see the related performance and installation project by Johan Forsman and Anders Paulin, THREE WHITE SOLDIERS, particularly the section where the artists attempt to walk (including major bridges and freeways) from Wall Street to the suburban site of the Mahwah data center, underscoring the almost absurd impossibility of connecting certain transitions from urban to suburban in pedestrian time and space. In *Twin figure of mimesis I & II*.
5 www.theguardian.com/technology/2015/sep/25/facebook-datacentre-lulea-sweden-node-pole.
6 These preconditions are explored broadly in Tung-hui Hu's *A Prehistory of the Cloud*, MIT Press, 2015.
7 Consider the direct approach of the city of Boden, 36 kilometers from Luleå, where a former industrial and military stronghold has sought to replace ore mining with cryptocurrency mining, sometimes even inhabiting the same places as closed mines. www.economist.com/business/2015/01/08/the-magic-of-mining.
8 To implicate my own field, we could ask why the category of artistic research, for example is one of the four major fields funded by the Swedish Research Council.

# References

Alm, E., Deforche, F., Colliander, N., Lind, F., Stohne, V., and Sundström, O. (2019), 'Digitizing Europe: Why Northern European frontrunners must drive digitization of the EU economy', *www.bcg.com* [Online]. Available at: www.bcg.com/en-nor/perspectives/36553.
Benvegnù, C., Cuppini, N., Frapporti, M., Milesi, F., and Pirone, M. (2019), 'Logistical gazes: Introduction to a special issue of Work Organisation, Labour and Globalisation', *Work Organisation, Labour & Globalisation*, 13(1), p. 9.
Business-sweden.se. (2018), *Advantage Sweden a Magazine about Expanding into Sweden*. [Online]. Available at: www.business-sweden.se/en/Invest/news-and-down loads/publications/advantage-sweden-2018-1/ [Accessed 26 November 2019].
e-Residency. (2019), *What is e-Residency | How to Start an EU Company Online* [Online]. Available at: https://e-resident.gov.ee [Accessed 26 November 2019].
Eriksson, M. and Tollefsen, A. (2018), 'The production of the rural landscape and its labour: The development of supply chain capitalism in the Swedish berry industry', *Bulletin of Geography, Socio-economic Series*, 40(40), pp. 69–82.
The Government Offices of Sweden (2015), 'Sweden's deputy prime minister cries while announcing refugee U-turn – video', *The Guardian* [Image]. Available at:

www.theguardian.com/world/video/2015/nov/24/asa-romson-sweden-deputy-prime-minister-cries-announcing-refugee-u-turn-video.

Harding, L. (2015), 'The node pole: Inside Facebook's Swedish hub near the Arctic Circle', *The Guardian*, 25 September [Online]. Available at: www.theguardian.com/technology/2015/sep/25/facebook-datacentre-lulea-sweden-node-pole.

Hedberg, C., Axelsson, L., and Arabella, M. (2019), 'Thai berry pickers in Sweden: A migration corridor to a low-wage sector', *Stockholm: Delegationen för migrationsstudier*.

Hu, T.H. (2015), *A Prehistory of the Cloud* [Online]. Cambridge, MA: MIT Press. Available at: https://muse.jhu.edu/chapter/1622218.

Miller, R. (2014), 'Facebook adopts IKEA-Style pre-fab design for expansion in Sweden', *Data Center Knowledge*. Available at: www.datacenterknowledge.com/archives/2014/03/07/facebook-adopts-ikea-style-pre-fab-design-expansion-sweden.

Nilsson, P. (2018), 'Opening the door to the far right', *Jacobinmag.com* [Online]. Available at: https://jacobinmag.com/2018/09/sweden-election-sap-sweden-democrats-immigration-far-right/.

Paulin, A., Gross, A., Pristaš, S., Cvejić, B., Noys, B. and Phelan, P. (2018), *Twin Figure of Mimesis I & II*. Skogen.

Söderström, L. (director), B-Reel films (2017), *Visit Sweden – Get Curious* [Video]. Available at: https://vimeo.com/208520845.

Thörn, C. and Thörn, H. (2017), 'Swedish cities now belong to the most segregated in Europe', *Sociologisk Forskning*, 54(4), pp. 293–296. Available at: http://urn.kb.se/resolve?urn=urn:nbn:se:du-26854.

Umeå University, Luleå University of Technology, and the Swedish Institute of Computer Science (2017), 'Data Centers in North Sweden: Making data centers sustainable and energy efficient', *Itu.se* [eBook]. Available at: www.ltu.se/cms_fs/1.158617!/file/Data%20Centers%20in%20North%20Sweden.pdf.

Vonderau, A. (2018), 'Scaling the cloud: Making state and infrastructure in Sweden', *Ethnos*, 84(4), pp. 698–718.

# 7 Fracking sociality

## Architecture, real estate, and the internet's new urbanism

*Louis Moreno*

Common to technology, art, social practice. . . . Developments in architecture always have a symptomatic significance initially, and a causal one subsequently.

Henri Lefebvre

Fortunately, nobody owns the Internet.

Brian Carpenter

In June 1996 Brian Carpenter, a systems engineer at CERN, uploaded a memo called "Architectural Principles of the Internet". No more than seven pages, the purpose of the document was simple: to record the principles critical to the astounding connectivity which marked the internet's development. A collaborator and colleague of the web's inventor Tim Berners-Lee, Carpenter said, the "connectivity" that the internet gave society was demonstrably shown to be "its own reward . . . more valuable than any individual application such as mail or the World-Wide Web". Though a model of concision, the document contained a speculative question – "Is there an internet architecture?" Carpenter's answer was equivocal, opaque even: "Many members of the Internet community would argue that there is no architecture but only a *tradition*". What was interesting about this statement was the sense that what lay behind the protocol that so successfully enabled connectivity was a practice of cultivation rather than a feat of design. Thus, instead of thinking about the realization of this protocol in terms of the construction of a new building, Carpenter said that a more precise metaphor was a regenerative process of "constantly renewing the individual streets and buildings of a city, rather than razing the city and rebuilding it", which suggested that connectivity was better thought of as a process that was grown not designed, planted not planned.

Prompted by Carpenter's formulation, this chapter considers the architectural principles that have shaped the internet's urban development in recent decades. Though Carpenter's memo presents a dilemma: if the internet is better thought of as an organic system, why bother with the language of architecture? Why not adopt a metaphor directly from ecology, biology, chemistry, etc.? At one level the answer, as Carpenter said, was a matter of tradition. The metaphor was a hangover from the golden age of communications science, when architecture provided physicists, mathematicians, and engineers with a keyword to translate informatics in terms lay people – like investors, businessmen, politicians, consumers – could understand (Martin, 2005). But in the 1990s the question of the internet's architecture was more than just a matter of semantics; the impact the movement of information would have on the structure of everyday life was a topic of intense speculation. Bestsellers like *Being Digital*, written by architect and director of MIT's Media Lab Nicholas Negroponte (1995), sketched out the new urban opportunities that computer networks would present. And Manuel Castells (1989) argued that in a network based society, architecture would play a crucial role in ensuring that cities maintained a sense of place amid a torrential flow of information. The fact that such debates took place well before the internet was woven into the social fabric means that today they offer – like a mid-90s data glove – an antique sense of the future. As it is only very recently, over the last decade in fact, that it has become possible to consider the internet as an urban system that has finally acquired an architectural form.

Reflecting on the emergence of a new urbanism shaped by the internet's development, this chapter maps a set of tendencies that suggest that the internet's future is linked to changes in the urban processes and architectural practices of real estate investment. Though instead of merely assuming that new urbanism manifests the domination of internet connectivity by the spatial apparatus of financial capital (i.e. real estate), I shall consider the role that architecture played, and continues to play, in renewing the influence of real estate over the development of social space. Tracking the mid-20th-century critique of New Brutalism through to the recent implosion of WeWork, via debates on sensory systems, technological "decisionism" and Google's ad-space algorithms, I argue that what architecture has provided is an environmental medium to cultivate social space in such a way that the capitalization of land and knowledge is taken to be the cultural sign of technological "progress".

## Urban tendencies

Given that at least two generations have been raised online, the idea that the tools vital to the internet's navigation have only recently become concrete may seem counterintuitive; though there are a number of tendencies which index a new urbanism emerging from the internet's socio-spatialization. The first and most general trend is that internet companies have made real estate development a focal point of their competitive strategies. As Google's own head of real estate David Radcliffe admits, until recently "tech hasn't adopted a particular language for buildings, we've just found old buildings and moved into them" (Google, 2015). In practice, this has meant that companies like Google and Facebook have in the past adopted and adapted American

*Figure 7.1* Google's North Bayshore Estate

*Source*: Screengrab from video: www.youtube.com/watch?v=z3v4rIG8kQA, published by Google, 27 February 2015

suburban campus or business park typologies. The famous Googleplex in Mountain View, California, as Google's real estate team admits, comprises a university campus squeezed into a highway system, whose space is largely organized by a sprawl of parking lots. This is now changing. As a video promoting the development of its North Bayshore estate makes clear, Google is looking to create a new image of the city, one where nature, knowledge, and society circulate in a state of dynamic equipoise.

Which takes us to a second trend: internet companies have begun to hire architects and urban designers to give their technologies an environmental form. Again, to take the North Bayshore example, Google have hired what they describe as the world's "best in class" architects – the practices of Thomas Heatherwick and Bjarke Ingels – to construct urban ecologies that complement the communication of knowledge, which their products are intended to improve. Or as Heatherwick says in a promotional video, their role is to build "the best possible environment we can make to invent, engineer and most importantly make ideas happen and go out into the world" (Google, 2015). Back in the heart of the city, the notion that knowledge can be socially and spatially engineered through a mix of architecture and urban design marks out a new kind of real estate company. Mixing communitarian philosophy with urban economics, design fashion, and machine learning, companies like WeWork charge expensive "subscriptions" for the use of buildings that promise to network individuals and companies into urban circuits of conviviality, collectivity, and connectivity.

If internet companies like Google have asserted their urban presence through land acquisition and urban design, the buzz (and, as we shall see later, "mania") that has surrounded WeWork marks a third trend in the provision of real estate. As the authors of the Said Business School report

*PropTech 3.0: the future of real estate* argue, internet technology is finally beginning to "change the way real estate is traded, used and operated" (Baum, 2017). Though the influence of financial technologies – the so-called "FinTech" sector of "online payment systems, crowdfunding equity and debt platforms, and online exchanges" – has been gradually growing in scale over the last decade, the report says the industry of real estate has been slow to adopt these innovations. This inertia is largely a function of the peculiar nature of real estate as an asset class. As the report says, although financial deregulation, technological innovation, and internet communication have enabled the trade of real estate on financial exchanges, the material, spatial, and "illiquid" qualities of real estate make it less fungible than other forms of property like equities and bonds. But these barriers, real estate commentators argue, are beginning to dissolve because of a number of technological developments.

Technology constitutes then a fourth trend: the emergence of what the Said report calls "intelligent real estate" – sensor-based technologies said to improve the economic efficiency and profitability of a building – the growth of which was marked by Google's 2014 acquisition of NEST Labs, a start-up "producer of thermostats, sensors, lighting and other intelligent energy-saving home applications" (Baum, 2017). Thus, aside from a stated social commitment to community, what distinguishes the cutting edge of urban design, financial commentators argue, is investment in "data and tech . . . to create" a competitive "blueprint for optimal office design and superior worker productivity . . . that has taken an existing business – commercial real estate – and updated and scaled it for the tech age" (CB Insights, 2019).

Undercutting, however, the new urbanist ideology of collaboration and education is a fifth trend: a growing sense that what is driving the urbanization of internet-based technologies is a fundamentally divisive process. In Google's case, this is most clearly seen in urban housing and transport conflicts, with protests in San Francisco and Berlin over private shuttle services for Google workers and rent increases that price out the poor from urban centers (Streitfeld, 2018; Turk, 2018). All of which is set against a background of general labor conflicts over the precarious conditions generated by personal service platforms like Uber and Deliveroo (Baynes, 2018). Moreover, the revelations about Facebook's algorithms being used to manipulate voter patterns consolidates a pessimism, articulated even by Facebook's own founders, about the way their algorithms hack human emotion for political as well as financial gain (Vincent, 2017). Perhaps most disturbing of all is a growing body of research showing how the algorithmic architecture that supports internet search and social networking reinforces systems of racial and sexual domination that make the division of labor possible (Umoja Noble, 2017).

In what follows I want to consider what all these trends tell us about the way architecture networks the social protocols of commodification as well as communication. As what seems difficult to account for – in critiques of both information technology and gentrification – is a set of specifically architectonic practices that bind the spatial accumulation of capital to the temporal communication of information (and vice versa). Though I want to be careful not to assume that architecture is the servant of "smart" technology or a representation of digital capitalism. Rather, I want to focus on architecture to explore the nature of a process which, following Brian Carpenter, might be called a tradition of "urban renewal": one that has enabled internet companies to reformat social space. Later, we shall explore how the company WeWork represents a financial blurring of the lines that separate the social space controlled by internet companies and that of urban real estate. But to set the scope of the analysis, our point of departure is not the metropolis, but the arrangement of elements that constitute the building itself.

## Structures with feeling

Here it is useful to recall a debate that took place at the 2014 Venice Architecture Biennale. The theme of the Biennale, curated by Rem Koolhaas's Office for Metropolitan Architecture, was "Elements of Architecture: 5,000 years of history and now what?" For this, Koolhaas and his team produced an exhibition that broke down the fundamental elements that make the production of space possible in order to explore the forces affecting the practice of architecture. "Looking at the elements", Koolhaas said, two things struck home: first "we realized that, much more than we had previously thought, architecture is not defined as a comprehensive thing, but through the ingenuity of a collectively acquired overall intelligence". Second, that "each element is undergoing a transformation by digital technology" (Oosterman and Cormier, 2014).

In itself, the idea that architecture had been altered by the digital revolution was hardly a new hypothesis. It was an idea that galvanized the 1980 Biennale's infamous conception of a postmodern architecture trapped in time, set adrift from the architectonic traditions of city building which spatialized a sense of history (Szacka, 2016). Koolhaas's point though was not that the humanist attitude of architecture had been technologically overpowered, but that the built environment was undergoing a phase transition. And this realization only dawned on Koolhaas when, having laid out the components of the building, he noticed an anomaly. Surveying twelve building blocks of architecture – floor, door, wall, ceiling, toilet, facade, balcony, window, corridor, hearth, roof, stairs – one element stuck out. *The sensor.* Not only did it not belong to the history of architecture, this element had become so deeply embedded in the modern business of designing, constructing, and managing urban space, that it was almost impossible to conceive of a new building without a sensor installed in some nook or cranny. Koolhaas was concerned not simply with the design problems that digital technology presents for the architect; he was disturbed by something more pathological – the way the sensor had become a fundamental element of the building. Thus, what concerned Koolhaas was the care with which the practice of architecture had raised a parasite: the equivalent of a cuckoo's egg.

It may have been this avian analogy Koolhaas had in mind when he invited Tony Fadell, one of the developers of the Apple iPod and, more recently, the founder of NEST Labs – a start-up famous for its "smart" thermostat that had just been bought by Google for $3.2 billion – for a public discussion on architecture and digital technology. For Fadell, the symbiosis was an extraordinary opportunity and, detecting Koolhaas's palpable suspicion about the threats these objects represented, attempted to convince the architect on a number of fronts. Besides a strong firewall separating the data gathered by NEST from its host organism, Fadell reassured his audience that this technology was not about wresting control from either the designer or dweller; instead the opposite was the case.

> You are always in control, so these products don't take control away from you, all we're doing is learning from your habits, so we're not imposing anything on anyone. In fact in most cases, we're just educating and giving you feedback on what your abilities are. . . . [A]t the end of the day people don't know how much energy is being consumed, they don't understand how much heating and cooling does actually consume all of your dollars. So all we're doing is giving you a feedback loop to allow you to adapt, if you so choose.
>
> (Biennale Channel, 2014)

Koolhaas grimaced. Unimpressed by the reassurance of a corporate separation of company from state, let alone company from parent company, the architect argued that what these apparatuses threatened was the annihilation of privacy. Not wanting to dodge the question, Fadell responded by putting it in context of the seemingly limitless scale of connectivity that new technology could provide. Hanging in the balance was the trade-off human beings make between convenience and freedom. Here the engineer channeled the pragmatism of the Scottish Enlightenment. If, as Adam Smith said, "the utility of any object pleases the master by perpetually suggesting to him the pleasure or convenience which it is filled to promote" (Skinner, 1992, p. 391), Fadell argued that what companies like NEST offered was simply a digital update of liberalism's fundamental principle. "There is no difference", Fadell said, "between freedom and convenience; you are always in control, but in order to have this convenience, you need to have some connectivity in order to control them".

At which point the conversation reached an impasse. Recognizing that the technological intensification of social connectivity was warping the human fabric, Fadell outlined a new kind of partnership. If social life, economic activity, and policy-making were now path dependent on digital connectivity, then this did not mean the end but a new beginning for architecture's social project. Architecture could provide something that social networking companies were, as yet, unable to give society: namely, the environment necessary to collectively educate and discuss changes happening in and through digitalization. Koolhaas, however, shook his head; it was too late. And with a peculiar turn of phrase, he explained that this scenario would only have been possible if they had met many decades ago, before digital engineers began to adapt so many "unloved products" – like walls, ceilings, doors, and thermostats – harnessing them to an infinitely expandable digital surface area, controlled and operated by private companies. Before, in Koolhaas's words, a cadre of digital engineers "planted a device in my element".

## The chip and the bubble

At the end of the 20th century, Negroponte's text *Being Digital* spun benign speculations about liquor stores that would automatically remember your preference for Sancerre over Chardonnay. Some 20 years later, such anticipations soured amid an inundation of information, social media, and smartphones. And as a one-time screenwriter of exploitation films, Koolhaas seemed to channel the "home invasion" genre when he described the smart home's dark future. We are on the threshold, Koolhaas said in an interview, of sleepwalking into the "potentially sinister" situation of "being surrounded by a house full of sensors that can follow you on the moment of entry, to the moment you set your bedroom temperature, to the moment you set your likely return to your house" (Frearson, 2015).

The fear of a building that knows you better than you know yourself can be traced back to the genre of the ghost-story and the haunted house, though the poltergeist that Koolhaas had in mind was a very different kind of specter. In the wake of Edward Snowden's disclosure about the collusion between Silicon Valley and the American state, Koolhaas's diagnosis channeled a wider cultural pessimism about the end of privacy. However, there is another way of interpreting Koolhaas's unease: one that requires us to remain at the level of the built environment and to consider how architecture mediated the spatiotemporal volatility of financial speculation. In this respect, when considering the processes that had led to an installation of sensory equipment in the home, it could also be read as a symptom of another phenomenon, what the cultural critic Fredric Jameson called "the last symptom of that dissociation of the private and public, the subject and the object, the personal and the political, which has characterized the social life of capitalism" (1982, p. 148).

Jameson's analysis of the spatial logic of late capitalism represented a synthesis of the Marxian critique of urbanism developed by Henri Lefebvre and the geographer David Harvey. Building on Lefebvre's apprehension that urbanism was providing financial capital with a medium of survival, Jameson argued that the symptoms of spatial liquidity – the dissolving of the private and public, the dominance of currency flows over social planning, etc. – was the result of a specifically spatial cause (Jameson,1998). As for all the discussion of the de-territorializing powers of financial capitalism, this abstract machine was nothing unless its logic was able to influence the circumstances that determine what economists once called the "ordinary business of life". What the Marxian critique of urban space demonstrated was that capitalists needed to build an environment in order for financial capitalism to become second nature.

Which was why urbanism or, more specifically for Jameson, Koolhaas's theorization of urban architecture seemed to offer a privileged perspective on this new phenomenon. Not because it was able to reconcile the global with the local or assert some control over the volatile rhythms of financial speculation, but precisely the opposite. What Koolhaas argued in texts like *Delirious New York* was that architecture was an instrument enabling the spatial reconfiguration of capitalism. And it was instrumental because the restructuring was guided by an urban mode of decision-making – real estate – whose calculus ruled the design process. Empowered by the politically and technologically enabled deregulation of financial markets in the 1970s and 1980s, the estimation of the urban environment's asset value took on a new autonomy in the planning process. Thus, real estate became a channel through which financial capital was able to subsume to its logic the practices of everyday life, market exchange, and political decision-making, immersing the spatial apparatuses and social infrastructures that people need to live in a debt-based system of dependency.

Of course, the totally corrosive effects of "financial deepening" and its urban cause (speculation on real estate markets) would only become clear in the aftermath of the 2008 global banking crisis. Nonetheless, in the early 90s, Koolhaas had already mapped a four-story "mutation" in built form caused by the changing scale of urban investment, with each level highlighting how architecture was transcoding the logic of financial systems into the fabric of social life. First, with the emergence of structures of such massive scale and mass, the exterior and interior of buildings separate where "the two [become] completely autonomous, separate projects . . . to be pursued independently, with no apparent connection". Second, "within such a building, the distances between one component and another . . . become so enormous that there is an autonomy or independence of spatial elements". Third, the functional problems of managing social life and human functions mean that logistical imperatives take over such that "the role the elevator plays in such a building" overwhelms all other concerns. Fourth, as scale and mass become their own aesthetic, "the building is impressive simply through its mass . . . the dumb fact of its own existence . . . the effect of the scale alone and its intimidating volume, is something that is very disturbing" (Koolhaas, 1996, pp. 15–18).

## Regressive utopia

The spatial innovations of the late 19th century – the skyscraper and the central business district – had, in the space of a century, become the "pattern language" of global capitalism (Moreno, 2014). This was the assessment of the postmodern critique of capitalist urbanism. Wrapped in a curtain-wall system, the multinational corporation was coded by an architectural formula whose iconology was at once universally understood and geographically mobile, but whose practical significance was totally opaque to those uninitiated in the stock market. What, though, did this critique say about spatial products that slipped through Koolhaas's S, M, L, XL metric? Where, then, did the emergence of microscopic devices like "sensors" fit in the macroeconomic logic of finance capital?

Given that Koolhaas formed the bulk of this analysis in the early stages of global capitalism's spatial reconfiguration, it would be wrong to characterize the rejection of technology like NEST as reactionary. Instead, Koolhaas's response seemed to reinstate the notion of a "crisis of design" first formulated in 1969 by the architectural historian Manfredo Tafuri (1979, 2000). Tafuri argued that as technological modernization developed new instruments to divide labor and accumulate capital, the social question of urban development – designing cities that fulfill the individual needs and desires of a human multiplicity – was increasingly referred to an algorithmic solution: a black box that computed social progress with the convergence of "economic growth" and "technological change". Thus, having equipped multinational capital with a world-building system that could urbanize the planet, but unable to solve basic questions about how to administer the welfare of the urban body, the role of the design process had been reduced. The avant-garde role of architecture was to craft "regressive utopias", Tafuri's term for spatial products that decorate capitalism's self-replicating superstructure. And where Koolhaas's practice OMA was once able to extract psychedelia from the symbolic overflow of capitalist urbanism, by 2014 the architect now seemed to find nothing but a joyless science directed by financial logic, construction management, and digital engineering.

In an interview for the Biennale, Koolhaas channeled Tafuri's downbeat outlook. As "a result of neo-liberalism or globalization, which should have [produced] a fantastic playground for architecture, assuming many more roles and many more opportunities . . . the effect is the killing of creativity and of innovation" (Oosterman and Cormier, 2014). Technological opacity neutralized understanding, monumentality overpowered political imagination, and the modernist problematic – how to design cities that released human beings from subordination to tradition – was sucked into a vacuum called utopia. So goes the pessimism of Tafuri-Koolhaas.

But here we reach a limit in the architectural critique of capitalism. Although it was possible to grasp how commercial architecture made possible the urban integration of the global market – a geographic shift manifesting not only a monumental aesthetic but also a suite of spatial techniques to mold urbanity according to the rhythms of capital accumulation and technological change – when extended to the realm of the sensor, this critique still assumed what needed to be explained: namely, what was the process that planted information technology in the practice of architecture? On this point, the Marxist analysis of urbanism was silent, as although the structural focus indicated the concentration of financial capital in the real estate and construction sector, the critique left untouched the practical role of architecture in mediating a reflexive, multi-dimensional, scalable relationship between economy, law, and culture – or, as Jameson might say, a mediation that related infrastructure to superstructure.

## Habitable circulation

A clue lay in another critique of design history, appearing in the same year as *Architecture and Utopia*. In *The Architecture of the Well-Tempered Environment*, Reyner Banham (1984) argued that to comprehend the overall conditions that produced a "modern" habitat, it was necessary to bypass an architectural preoccupation with aesthetic problems (and by extension the preoccupation with individual architectural genius) and instead get into the guts of the building. Because, once one began to appreciate that the driver of modern architecture was not the brilliance of individual architects but the need for buildings that distribute an even flow of heat, light, and water, then the whole concept of architecture was radically transformed.

According to Banham, loaded with a "complex of piping, flues, ducts, wires, lights, inlets, outlets, ovens, sink, refuse disposers, hi-fi reverberators, conduits, freezers, heaters" (1965, p. 70), the primary problem of architectural design was to produce structures capable of integrating all these services. More than this, however, Banham suggested that architects, threatened by the formlessness of mechanical services and the invasion of engineering into their domain, formulated a set of conditions which gave their practice an aesthetic distinction. Thus, in making the history of modern architecture a byproduct of the history of environmental services – the development of heating, cooling, lighting, air conditioning, and latterly information services – the development of modern buildings was cast in a new light. Modern architecture was far more than just the symbolic expression of the way technology was put to social use. What distinguished the aesthetic form of a modern building was the success with which the structure concealed a growth of service systems. The design function was, in short, to *disappear* the entire network of services that produced urban space.

Banham's argument helps explain the nature of Koolhaas and Fadell's dispute. The architect's irritation with the need to accommodate a newfangled thermostat was a reaction that itself had a history, stretching back at least as far as Le Corbusier's fatigue at having to allocate space to pipes and plumbers. As Banham said, the need for devices and services was a "fact" that architects had long sensed was a "cultural threat to their position in the world" (ibid). What had changed since Banham's time was the nature of the threat. As soon as WiFi became a requirement as basic as the provision of hot running water, then the design problem, not to mention the experience of the city, was transformed. Building design was an adjunct to a distributional problem concerning the personal and interpersonal consumption of flowing water, heating, electricity, and information. Thus, priming Koolhaas's discomfort about domestic surveillance was an older dilemma relating to who, or what, was responsible for giving the environment form. And according to Banham, the occupation of architect did not have a privileged relationship to the practice of architecture. What architecture designated was a protocol, one that facilitated the interoperation of all those services that made technology a lived experience, a built environment.

Equipped with Banham's formulation – of architecture as a spatial protocol that makes the circulation of information an inhabitable, adaptable, urban phenomenon – we can reboot the architectural critique of urban economy. The emergence of a sensory architecture manifests a new phase in the architectural history of environmental control, a phase that brings with it what Tafuri would have called a "redimensioning" of urban economic opportunity. Because, as well as accumulating capital along a vertical axis, now the horizontal field could be scraped for value, as buildings formed a disjunctive network sifting the socius for particles of capital floating like pollen in the atmosphere.

Though we need to be careful not to just assume total financial control over the spatialization of information technology, which would present the built environment as simply a container of data in which technology companies compete for corporate dominance. Aesthetic ideas, cultural qualities, and the contingent flow of social desire have to be part of the itinerary, something which is particularly crucial if we are to explain how, for example, the emergence of a sensory architecture maps onto an appreciably spatial change in the tastes, behaviors, and values of the social environment.

## Parallel of life and computation

The difficulty, however, is the tendency of cultural theorists to view the automation of sensation, perception, and cognition as the end of political agency. As the philosopher of cybernetics Luciana Parisi (2017) argues, a general mistrust of the "technosciences of communication and control" pervades the tradition of critical philosophy, and this is because "the forms of instrumental reason embedded in cybernetic and computational communication continue" to be treated as "a black box that has no aims . . . unless these are politically orchestrated". Which constitutes a problem, since the assumption – automated cognition equals social control – blocks the ability to explain the conditions that underpin thinking as an activity.

Black boxing the politics of technoscience in a container marked either "Neoliberal", "Control Society", or "Designed in California" also does not shed much light on what precipitates a transformation of the aesthetic and moral systems of evaluation that gives capitalism a recognizable economic structure. For instance, let us assume that technology companies, like Google or Amazon, which have mastered the everyday use of the internet, are now investing in sensors to fold the fabric of space in the digital networks they control. Rather than just assume this follows a capitalist logic, we should ask, "How does the automation of sensing and cognition affect the pattern of perception which enables a capitalist to minimize costs and maximize profits?" What, in other words, are the tendencies that allow us to track the adaptation and, therefore, the survival of capitalism not simply as a system of cognition but the aesthetic systems that underpin decision-making? Here, the essay "Reprogramming Decisionism" is suggestive (Parisi, 2017). Though primarily concerned with the relationship of machine learning to contemporary politics, Parisi's critique culminates in a hypothesis that dovetails with Banham's architectural radicalism.

Parisi's first move is to undercut the assumption that the digital modality of contemporary capitalism tells us anything about how machines intervene in political decision-making. Take, for example, the rise of so called "post-truth" politics and the attribution of this new irrationality and brutality in social discourse to new technology. Parisi suggests that it is a misnomer to explain this phenomenon purely in terms of the digitalization of social networks and intellectual activity. It is a misnomer because when one looks closely at how contemporary algorithms of search and networking function, automated intelligence "does not follow its own internal binary logic of either/or but follows instead whatever logic we leave enclosed within our random selections" (Parisi, 2017). Machines, therefore, are trained not to make *sense* of what humans think, but to learn to know how to deal with the sheer weight of *non-sense* that their search queries produce. In this respect, computation has, Parisi says, gone "meta-digital" insofar as the algorithms that make Google essential to web navigation (like the RankBrain interpreter algorithm) are indifferent to "verifying and explaining problems"; instead, they survey the blooming, buzzing consumption of search results in order to recognize patterns amid the confusion of real-world activity.

The second point is that this meta-digital approach to computation augments social reactivity. What Parisi, therefore, calls the "new brutality" of online discourse – the virulent communication of racism and sexism, often attributed to big data, predictive analytics, machine learning, etc. – is, in effect, an artifact of the inclusion of habits, prejudices, intentions, actions, and behaviors that machine intelligence amplifies. As what machine learning amplifies are "affective predispositions or reactions . . . agencies or action patterns", the problem of needing to decide what is right rather than wrong, true rather than false, is replaced by simply *the need to decide*. Parisi calls this new meta-digital order of things "technological decisionism, which values making a clear decision more quickly than it does making the correct one. For decisionism what is most decisive is what is most correct" when dealing with an indeterminate torrent of information. This helps to explain what Fadell meant when he said this form of information technology is meant to provide a medium to augment human decision-making. "We are not taking control away from you; we're just educating and giving you feedback on what your abilities are".

The third point is that the increasing capacity of machines to intuit social patterns in a storm of communication indicates a new political environment. Whereas before the institutions of the state, the market, the media, and organized labor would struggle over the technological structure of society, now politics is inflected by waves of feeling whose memetic spread can influence the direction of political discussion and cultural consciousness. And while, Parisi says, "one can assume that this inclusion of indeterminacy – or irrationality or non-conscious activity – within the computational process is but another manifestation of the ultimate techno-mastery of reality", these results are contingent on racialized and sexualized patterns of activity already "baked" into the architecture of civil society. The question then is not the way systems of machine learning can be gamed for political advantage. After all the stimulation of resentment for gain is hardly peculiar to techno-politics. Rather, the role of critique is to explain how the internet has come to acquire racist and sexist patterns of cognition, based on analyzing and emulating the forms of "conduct" emerging from the enormous traffic of interpersonal communication.

## Near present

Parisi's essay does not discuss the economic ramifications of machine learning, but it is clear that the ability to follow "evolving variations in the data" has been instrumental to the internet's monetization. Google's chief economist Hal Varian has made no secret of how machine learning has augmented Google's core business – Adwords (now known as GoogleAds) – an auction process that sifts search queries for keywords that match consumers to products (Varian, 2011).

Moreover, the monetization of automated cognition has also begun to influence the way governments sense change in the socio-economic atmosphere. For example, treasury departments traditionally estimate the future state of the economy by measuring numbers of people registering unemployment, consumer consumption, business sentiment, etc. But because the collection, processing, and verification of data is so time consuming, the estimation of the economic future is based on analysis of what happened two or three months ago. Google's method of economic prediction is quite different. Because the search engine records and analyzes contemporary trends in "people's interests, intentions, and future actions" through analysis of search queries and keywords, it becomes possible to follow the state of unemployment in real time based on the correlation of widely disassociated searches. "Google found", the *Washington Post* reported in 2014, "that rising unemployment was not only linked to phrases such as 'companies that are hiring'. It was also closely correlated to searches for new technology ('free apps'), entertainment ('guitar scales beginner') and adult content ('jailbait teen')" (Mui, 2014).

So as well as converting the "free gift" of search into a technology that enables businesses to know their audience at a personal level, Varian argues that Google offers a "database of intentions" that provides society with a window: a portal looking not into the near future, but the space of the near now (2011). Instead, then, of speculating on what may happen, Varian talks of a new microeconomic capability, which he calls "nowcasting": predicting the present from real-time patterns of information that emerge from random selections of microeconomic data.

Which leads to a practical question: What kind of present do we wish to inhabit? Updating Banham's notion of "new brutalism",[1] Parisi suggests that architecture manifests a mode of spatial intervention. And this is because, as Banham said, architecture manifests the spatial programming of all those instruments that make life "viable and valuable" and therefore predictable (Banham, 1984, p. 11). As a result, Parisi argues there is an opportunity to reprogram how cognition literally takes place in and through the machinic environment. "Since instruments are already doing politics", Parisi says, "one question to ask is how to reorient the brutality of instrumentality away from the senseless stirring of beliefs and desires, and towards a dynamic of reasoning that affords the re-articulation – rather than the elimination – of aims" (Parisi, 2017). In some ways, this echoes Fadell's appeal to Koolhaas. Since people enjoy the freedom and pleasure that information technology provides but find it difficult to live with the intense demands of continuous sociality (and being continuously connected to devices), then this generates a brand new urban question for architecture to solve: how to produce cities which enable society to learn to collectively think with (and live within) autonomous systems that think on society's behalf.

Parisi, however, reverses Fadell's position. Instead of some new human balance between brain, body, computer, and environment, Parisi argues that the disclosure of violence as a system of decision-making indicates a need to confront the "inhumanness of instrumentality". Like Banham and the New Brutalists, who rejected the idea that architecture should civilize the technological institutions of modernity, Parisi therefore argues for an architecture whose aesthetic produces "an awareness of alienness within reasoning, that could be the starting point for envisioning a techno-philosophy, the reprogramming of thinking through and with machines". So unlike Koolhaas, who found nothing left in the history of architecture to confront the invasive influence of digital power, Parisi argues that the idea of "concrete, mass modular, interconnected blocks and self-contained individual cells, elevated above the local territory, united by streets in the sky or networks of corridors across discrete parts of building" still provide a blueprint to revivify the social relationship to technology, one that can disclose the disturbingly real and properly *surreal* sense of what machines can do with (or without) the faculty of human cognition.

The recuperation of New Brutalism is fascinating because it provides a vantage point to survey the principles that modulate the architecture of urban and electronic social systems. Though as soon as we begin to consider its application to reprogram sociality, we are faced with the instrumentalization of its aesthetic. For example, think of how the "warehouse aesthetic", which Alison and Peter Smithson used for their own office in the 1950s – an approach that itself caused a sensation in post-war design – now provides a template for the mixing of commercial and residential real estate in a post-industrial environment. The stripping back of walls and ceilings to expose both structure and service has become more than just a design cliché; it is an environmental format. Which is to say, it has become the interior design equivalent of the curtain-wall system, the default setting for the inhabitation of urban networks. And if the idea that "exposed services" is now an accumulation strategy seems a stretch, then we need only consider the way other pioneering aspects of New Brutalism – the utilization of "as found" materials (existing buildings) and the fascination with urban image (the Instagram fetish for concrete architecture) – have all been adopted as essential components of the "regeneration" aesthetic of commercial and residential real estate companies.

I make the point not to castigate the Smithsons and Banham for the integration of their design ideas into the strategies of gentrification, which, as a critique, would be as trivial as attributing the delirium administered by Google to the psychology of Sergey Brin and Larry Page. Instead, the commercial applications of New Brutalism compel us to examine the renewal of a protocol which made possible the mutual modification of the internet and inner city. This is the protocol of real estate – a mode of capitalization that Banham recognized to be an American device that generated suburbia (Banham, 1965, p. 78) but never envisaged as something that could acquire a cybernetic form.

## WeWork's New Brutalism

The textbook definition of the real estate market is an auction system that decides the spatial distribution of capital in land and buildings. Though in a report exploring "the shape of urban trends to come", MIT's Center for Real Estate says it is important not to limit the definition of this market to "buildings – such as homes, apartments, hotels, retail malls, offices, factories, and warehouses. Our definition also includes the social relationships that are formed and take place therein" (Saiz and Salazar, 2017). The reason for such an expansive definition is that internet technologies that make social communication so financially attractive are not just beginning to affect real estate as an asset class. The MIT report argues that the automation of perception and cognition is beginning to transform the accumulation of capital in and through a renewal of the experience and inhabitation of urban space.

The paradigmatic case study of this shift is the company WeWork. Following the opening of its first workspace in New York in 2010, WeWork was promoted as more than just collaborative office space; WeWork was

*Figure 7.2* WeWork co-working space, 333 Seymour Street, Vancouver

nothing less than the spatialization of the social network, whose capacity to perfect urban creativity was matched only by its capacity to disrupt the office market. But beneath the Californian ideology of community building and consciousness raising, WeWork's disruptive power lay in the application of internet-based technology to redesign the social environment. Extracting a few details from the literature covering WeWork's design strategy, we can trace the outline of a new kind of Brutalism crystallizing out of a desire to infuse social computation, inhabitation, and collaboration with financialization.

Starting at the level of the city, WeWork picked leases on existing buildings through analysis of data sets that rated the viability of locations "based on proximity to amenities and businesses, including coffee shops, restaurants, bars, hotels and gyms" (CB Insights, 2019, p. 12). Having identified an environment attractive to members, building interiors were then put through a Building Information Modelling process scanning the total "square footage, window mullions, door sizes, slab flatness/thickness, and ductwork and piping" to ensure the provision of "ample common space, meeting rooms and natural light" (p. 14). The map was then tested against data on space consumption harvested, via a sensor array, "from prior offic[e]" fit outs. When a fully layered three-dimensional image of the entire building had been produced, the architecture was pulled through a neural net, – which analyzed time series data of human circulation and interaction throughout the WeWork estate – to generate a plan of "private offices, meeting rooms, single person rooms, open desks, and common areas" (p. 16).

Conceiving their buildings as "giant computers", the company's product service team treated the consumption of their estate as valuable data that would extract value from the most basic elements. "After all", as a glowing Forbes report put it, "one extra desk can add up to $80,000 in sales over 10 years" (p. 8). Moreover, socio-spatial data provided the company with a plan to shape social contact, with their product teams envisaging the use of "heat maps" to create "areas of 'intentional congestion' to encourage WeWorkers" to interact with each other (McCorvey, 2016). It was this recombination of locational analysis, architectural design, construction management, machine learning, and social engineering that WeWork claimed made its spatial products exceptional. WeWork's space was not only honed to squeeze as much rent as possible from the floor space of the building; the cultural tastes, psychological profiles, and social desires of high-end urban individuals were all seen as exploitable income streams. The use of technology "to uncover patterns in the interactions between people and space" was, as a machine learning researcher for WeWork concluded, "information that can make better design and programming decisions" (Phelan, 2016).

For the financial markets, the image of a members-only city, programmed, designed, and curated by WeWork proved irresistible. In January 2019, following an earlier injection of $10 billion from the Japanese multinational tech investment company SoftBank, WeWork was given a $47 billion market valuation. This quotation, based on an estate covering 100 cities in 28 countries with 466,000 members, indicated a company able to command revenue "growth", which, according to the *Financial Times* (2019), "even Facebook and Google would envy". But such an unprecedented valuation indicated something else: a financial bubble. Well in advance of WeWork's fall, skeptics pointed out that the concentration of investment in one company represented a mutual intensification in the financial volatility of both real estate and tech sectors. Because "if WeWork were to fail its sudden departure would cause commercial real estate prices in key markets such as London and New York to plunge" (CB Insights, 2019). Thus with "more than 5.2 million square feet" of New York City under management, WeWork was in danger of becoming another type of business: a financial service that was becoming "too big to fail".

Since the dramatic collapse of the company's value in October 2019 – losing $40 billion in just one week – the WeWork story has been presented as a cautionary tale for business schools to mull over: a case study about how a charismatic individual was able to market a mundane business for a cosmic price (Levine, 2019). But this story misses a larger point. Internet technology has provided an age-old practice with a high-tech form. WeWork's business model, which dazzled the financial world, was little more than the dirty business of "rent arbitrage: charging its members more than it has to pay its landlords" (CB Insights, 2019, p. 6). More generally, then, what the bursting of WeWork's bubble highlighted was the renewal of a tradition: the use of computational power and social networks to revitalize real estate's core function – to clear space and divide life in order to escalate the financial price of land.

*

Of course, back in the mid-90s, Brian Carpenter's metaphor of "urban renewal" was wholly innocent of the machinations of 21st-century real estate. Nonetheless, the growth of sensory architectures that deepen the spatial reach of financial capital requires us to consider the roots of a "tradition" that identifies cultural progress with the technological extraction of rent from land and human capital. Such a development even has a name – "real estate fracking" – a term coined by MIT's Center of Real Estate to describe the application of "AI, big data, wide data, machine learning, neurolearning", in order to break space into

> smaller bits and reconfigured in higher values . . . taking under or unutilized real estate and monetizing it on three different axis and in four to five different dimensions – monetizing the use of assets in ways we never thought were possible – all because of tech.
>
> (Sullivan, 2018)

And to be clear, the fracking of the geography, ecology, and sociology of cities is presented not as a threat but an opportunity for market expansion. For the economists and planners at MIT, machine learning enables the regeneration of the real estate protocol, drilling into a stratum of psycho-geographic life hitherto unimagined.

## Note

1  In a famous 1955 essay, Banham described the social architecture of Alison and Peter Smithson as a "New Brutalism" in defiance of a post-war attempt to salvage modern architecture as a humanist project. Rejecting modernism's attempt to "civilize" technology (Banham, 1984, p. 122), Banham conceptualized New Brutalism as an architectural attempt to feed back the materiality of the world "as found", to disclose the technologies concealed in structure, in order to generate a dynamic image of social life that short-circuited the classical requirement for human proportion, symmetry, and utility.

## References

Banham, R. (1965), 'A home is not a house', *Art in America*, 2, pp. 70–79.
Banham, R. (1984), *The Architecture of the Well-Tempered Environment*. London: Architectural Press.
Baum, A. (2017), *PropTech 3.0: The Future of Real Estate*. Oxford: University of Oxford.

Baynes, C. (2018), 'Uber Eats couriers shut down major London roads in protest demanding £5 minimum per delivery', *The Independent* [Online]. Available at: www.independent.co.uk/news/uk/home-news/uber-eats-couriers-shut-down-major-london-junctions-in-protest-demanding-5-minimum-per-delivery-a8547616.html. [Accessed 31 July 2019].

Biennale Channel (2014), 'Biennale Architettura 2014 – Conversazioni/talks (architecture and technology)', *Biennale Channel* [Online]. Available at: www.youtube.com/watch?v=dxqFqbAp2Fo [Accessed 31 July 2019].

Castells, M. (1989), *The Informational City: Information Technology, Economic Restructuring, and the Urban-Regional Process*. Oxford: Blackwell.

CB Insights (2019), "WeWork's $47 Billion Dream: The Lavishly Funded Startup That Could Disrupt Commercial Real Estate". Available at: https://www.cbinsights.com/research/report/wework-strategy-teardown/ [Accessed 5 July 2019].

Frearson, A. (2015), 'Rem Koolhaas: Smart home technologies "potentially sinister"', *Dezeen* [Online]. Available at: www.dezeen.com/2015/05/27/rem-koolhaas-interview-technology-smart-systems-peoples-eagerness-sacrifice-privacy-totally-astonishing/ [Accessed 5 July 2019].

Google (2015), 'Google's proposal for North Bayshore', *YouTube* [Online]. Available at: www.youtube.com/watch?v=z3v4rIG8kQA [Accessed 31 July 2019].

Jameson, F. (1982), 'Progress versus Utopia; Or, can we imagine the future?', *Science Fiction Studies*, pp. 147–158.

Jameson, F. (1998), 'The brick and the balloon: Architecture, idealism and land speculation', *New Left Review*, 1, pp. 25–46.

Koolhaas, R. (1996), *Rem Koolhaas: Conversations with Students*. New York: Princeton Architectural Press.

Levine, M. (2019), 'How do you like we now', *Bloomberg.com*, October 23 [Online]. Available at: www.bloomberg.com/opinion/articles/2019-10-23/how-do-you-like-we-now.

Martin, R. (2005), *The Organizational Complex: Architecture, Media, and Corporate Space*. Cambridge, MA: MIT Press.

McCorvey, J.J. (2016), 'At WeWork, humans supply data for its "giant computers"', *Fast Company* [Online]. Available at: www.fastcompany.com/3062701/at-wework-humans-supply-data-for-its-giant-computers.

Moreno, L. (2014), 'The urban process under financialised capitalism', *CITY*, pp. 244–268.

Mui, Y.Q. (2014), 'The weird Google searches of the unemployed and what they say about the economy', *Washington Post* [Online]. Available at: www.washingtonpost.com/news/wonk/wp/2014/05/30/the-weird-google-searches-of-the-unemployed-and-what-they-say-about-the-economy/ [Accessed 5 July 2019].

Negroponte, N. (1995), *Being Digital*. New York: Vintage Books.

Oosterman, A. and Cormier, B. (2014), 'Critical Globalism: Rem Koolhaas, Interviewed by Brendan Cormier and Arjen Oosterman', *Volume* [Online]. Available at: http://volumeproject.org/critical-globalism-rem-koolhaas-interviewed-by-brendan-cormier-and-arjen-oosterman/ [Accessed 5 July 2019].

Parisi, L. (2017), 'Reprogramming decisionism', *e-flux Journal* #85 [Online]. Available at: www.e-flux.com/journal/85/155472/reprogramming-decisionism/.

Phelan, N. (2016), 'Designing offices with machine learning – Newsroom', *WeWork* [Online]. Available at: www.wework.com/newsroom/posts/designing-with-machine-learning.

Platt, E. (2019), 'WeWork: The "hypothetical" company at the heart of the property market', *Financial Times* [Online]. Available at: www.ft.com/content/0e426c90-8c45-11e9-a1c1-51bf8f989972.

Saiz, A. and Salazar, A. (2017), *Real Trends: The Future of Real Estate in the United States*. Cambridge, MA: MIT Center for Real Estate.

Skinner, A. (1992), 'Adam Smith: Self-love', *Revue européenne des sciences sociales*, 30, pp. 389–402.

Streitfeld, D. (2018), 'Protesters block Google buses in San Francisco, citing "techsploitation"', *New York Times* [Online]. Available at: www.nytimes.com/2018/05/31/us/google-bus-protest.html [Accessed 5 July 2019).

Sullivan, K. (2018), 'PropTalk: 5 questions with Steve Weikal of the MIT center for real estate', *HQO*, July 19. [Online]. Available at: www.hqo.co/blog/proptalk-5-questions-with-steve-weikal-of-the-mit-center-for-real-estate [Accessed 5 July 2019].

Szacka, L.C. (2016), *Exhibiting the Postmodern – The 1980 Architecture Biennale*. Venice: Marsilo.

Tafuri, M. (1979), *Architecture and Utopia: Design and Capitalist Development*. Cambridge, MA: MIT Press.

Tafuri, M. (2000), 'Towards a critique of architectural ideology', in K.M. Hays (ed.), *Architecture Theory since 1968*. Cambridge, MA: MIT Press.

Turk, V. (2018), 'How protestors stopped the Berlin Google Campus', *WIRED* [Online]. Available at: www.wired.co.uk/article/google-campus-berlin-protests [Accessed 5 July 2019].

Umoja Noble, S. (2017), *Algorithms of Oppression: How Search Engines Reinforce Racism*. New York: New York University Press.

Varian, H. (2011), "Predicting the Present", *Think with Google* [Online]. Available at: https://www.thinkwithgoogle.com/marketing-resources/predicting-the-present/ [Accessed 5 July 2019].

Vincent, J. (2017), 'Former Facebook exec says social media is ripping apart society', *The Verge* [Online]. Available at: www.theverge.com/2017/12/11/16761016/former-facebook-exec-ripping-apart-society [Accessed 5 July 2019].

# Part III
# Platforms

# 8    Platform urbanism

## City-making in the age of platforms

*Peter Mörtenböck and Helge Mooshammer*

Since the beginning of industrial production, the utilization of technological innovation has been a major factor propelling economic growth. New forms of land use and the expansion of cities into their peripheries have reflected these changes in many different ways. A common strategy of expediting the spread of technological changes has been the implementation of new types of urbanization that help push productivity. This could be seen in the era of industrial paternalism, when companies embarked on a program of building boarding houses to accommodate and retain the growing numbers of workers within tightly controlled urban environments. From the early to mid-20th century onward, this interaction between technological and urban changes has also become apparent in the rise of suburbs that both echo and fuel the proliferation and accessibility of mass-produced commodities. But what we are seeing now, in our age of digital knowledge production and data processing, is less an integration of urban development into technological changes than the transformation of the process of city-making itself into a vehicle for steering technological advancements and, by extension, channeling massive profits towards the highest strata of society (Piketty, 2014).[1]

The rise of urban metropolises during the capitalist era was a secondary albeit sometimes momentous effect, one initially determined by the aggregation of factories along specific supply chains and, later on, by the concentration of office spaces around the demands of service industries. But in recent years the expansion of new data-recording technologies and the rise of platform applications that promise ways of capitalizing on these data have brought a profound shift in focus. Now urban life itself has been identified as the prime mechanism for inducing economic growth and wealth generation. That is to say, cities, both as physical structures and cultural and social fabrics, have become the primary target when it comes to accessing and controlling data as a key ingredient for the success of novel platform economies. In addressing this change, consideration needs to be given to data extraction not only in terms of media platforms that capture urban activity, but also with regard to the emerging platform of the urban itself as a medium of capture (Krivý, 2018).

From the point of view of interface design, the routine business of urban life offers the dual benefit of being a data source that can be mined and a channel that can be utilized to sell services based on the exploitation of that very data. As such, cities have become the perfect lubricant for the global distribution of technologies that attract investment in change. There is an urgent need to better understand how these processes have transformed not only the built environment but also urban social life and politics, engendering a new art of city-making in which "today's movements from below might be potentially constituted *in and through* finance" (Wissoker et al., 2014, p. 2792). A clear indication for this is the shifting composition of capitalist expansion toward knowledge-based creative ventures, be they cloud-based software, social media, mobile applications, or similar devices. Cities around the world are outcompeting each other to attract a strong talent pool of young creatives and innovators in the hope that venture capital will follow in their wake, resulting in crops of fast-growing companies. A case in point for this significant development is the phenomenal rise of WeWork, a real estate company valued like a tech company to become a USD 47 billion company in just ten years, managing around 10,000,000 square feet (approximately 930,000 square meters) of office space in more than 100 cities worldwide and its subsequent rebranding as the We Company in 2019.[2] WeWork has become the world's single largest operator of temporary workspaces and has taken the venture-capital market by storm. As the leading

*Figure 8.1* WeWork, West Hollywood, CA, USA

*Source*: Photo by Peter Mörtenböck and Helge Mooshammer, 2017

provider of enticingly new "urban socio-material infrastructures" (Merkel, 2015, p. 136), and thus in possession of enormously attractive know-how about changing work patterns, as well as a highly successful start-up in its own right, the company has established itself as the much-courted darling of city mayors and planning directors.[3] Getting WeWork to expand its reach into their cities is viewed as a proven way to capture the zeitgeist and to jump-start regeneration by hip entrepreneurialism in their locales too.

However, in order for a city to be considered fertile ground for generating new profit streams through the clustering of a highly skilled young demo-graphic, it has to be perceived as matching the expectations of that particular target group. Consequently, new types of city-making have arisen to create a better fit with the millennial mind-set: urban development centered on innovation hubs that cater to millennials' quest to access global networks, co-working and co-living spaces that meet their desire for collaboration and communication, crowdfunded civic projects that reflect their pursuit of a unique contribution to urban neighborhoods, environmentally conscious and playful urban schemes that acknowledge how important purpose and passion are for digital nomads, and innovative modes of urban infrastructure available at one's fingertips that echo their penchant for enriched experiences and an enhanced life-work balance. A roundup of quotes from high-profile investment managers in a Reuters news article seeking to analyze the global real estate market's mounting envy of WeWork's appeal highlights how these once-niche sentiments have become accepted as the guiding rationale for urban economic development: no longer simply the domain of wage-earning labor, urban workplaces are now framed as cultural hubs triggering and serving the formation of communities – "we want everything, everywhere, all the time" because "talent is calling the shots" and "culture is the new capital" (Lash, 2019). These patterns of city-making perform like sets of competing asset classes, offering different opportunities for engagement for different investors and contributing to the emergence of highly volatile and complex "financescapes" (Appadurai, 1996). A willingness to invest oneself in this volatile "financescape", destabilizing the boundary that separates life from "reliable" work, relates to what Gina Neff has identified as the growth of "venture labor" in the "Dot-Com Era" or Internet Boom in New York's "Silicon Alley" in the late 1990s. This is a labor she defines as

> the investment, time, energy, human capital and other personal resources that ordinary employees make in the companies where they work . . . people taking risk for their jobs, as much as it is about their subjective embrace of that risk.
>
> (2012, pp. 16–17)

In this chapter we explore some of the civic, social, and cultural implica-tions of this speculative approach to city-making. How is the neoliberal imperative of "city" as "platform" enlisted in shaping new subjective and collective experiences, attitudes, and expectations? How do experimentations in architectural design and urban planning interfere in the political, economic, and cultural conditions of data generation, data analytics, and dataveillance? Can the urban realm facilitate new forms of publics emerging beyond the techno-capitalist vision of an information society? In order to address these interrelated questions, we will first examine the spatial and social dynamics fostered by emergent types of platform urbanism. Drawing on these reflections, we will then interrogate the complex entanglement of contemporary subject formations with the imperatives of investment-driven expansionist urban politics – what is it that makes us participate so extensively, and seemingly voluntarily, in these enterprises? By way of an open-ended conclusion, we will seek to employ these insights as a framework for delineating alternative perspectives on our involvement in the platform city. What would be required, for instance, to recuperate the social in social media–based urban infrastructures, both conceptually and practically? What other "networked cultures" can be envisaged to engage with the opportunities of platform structures so that the concept of unbounded connectivity is not reduced to a convenient way of distributing risk and precariousness across a wider spectrum but is rather elevated to a forum of diversity and exploration?

## The ambitious new urban spirit

The urban emerged in the 19th century as a cohesive and transferable solution for organizing a range of new social relations, and there is hardly any aspect to be found in this historically contingent restructuring that is not a matter of dissemination in space and time, involving infrastructure and its logic of circulation (Adams, 2018, p. 3), whether this has to do with how we participate in the world of work (how labor is split into different sectors and grouped accordingly); how we go about the reproductive side of life (how we dwell and take care of ourselves and the environment); how we interact in social and cultural communities (how coexistence is organized through political and administrative institutions, how we engage in leisure activities, etc.); and, last but not least, how these spheres are connected and how we move between them (how we commute between different places of work, home, and leisure; how resources and goods are shifted around; etc.). Over the last years, all these spheres of activity have become the subject of platform operations. And in most of these instances – whether they involve city services, urban space, or everyday life – the impetus has been to disrupt the way things are commonly done in favor of an alternative form of organization that gives the impression of providing a more efficient service for the population and helping improve lives. Disruptive innovation (Christensen et al., 2015) has replaced the allure of technological utopianism and liberation, gesturing at the technological promise that lies in the act of disruption itself. "Making the world a better place to live in" has since become the camouflaging mantra of any such act. Mark Zuckerberg's "The Hacker Way"–dubbed letter to investors published ahead of Facebook's initial public offering (IPO) in early 2012 illustriously opened with the statement that "Facebook was not originally created to be a company. It was built to accomplish a social mission – to make the world more open and connected" (Letter from Mark Zuckerberg, 2012). Similarly, WeWork, the global leader in developing co-working office spaces, stated in its own prospectus summary (filed on 14 August 2019, ahead of its IPO initially planned for the third quarter of 2019), "We are a community company committed to maximum global impact. Our mission is to elevate the world's consciousness" ("Our Story", 2019).

There is virtually no sector of the urban realm and no aspect of urban life left that has not been targeted by an investor-backed start-up company boasting that it has found a "smarter" way of living and working in cities. At the heart of these disruptive ambitions lies a platform-based digital app promising to allow for things to be organized differently by bypassing established conventions, which are perceived as being over-determined by centralized, hierarchical, and inflexible institutional frameworks. Digital platforms are presented as alternatives that offer direct and unrestricted contact between numerous entities based on choice, voluntary participation, and mutual interest. Thus, organizing specific interactions via a platform technology is advertised as being not only much more efficient but also much more beneficial to all partners concerned, whether it is about searching for a place to stay, sourcing the most sustainable form of energy supply, or wishing to hook up with one's neighbors to form a local care and support network. The big advantage of platform organization, so the spin goes, is that it allows users to cut out the malicious middleman, often depicted as a greedy monopoly business or suppressive public bureaucracy. Technologies of platform organization, it is often claimed, allow for much more open, more horizontal, and, in effect, more democratic interactions between fellow human beings, turning the urban realm from an experience of limitations into a space of opportunity (Barns, 2020).

But in actual fact, as we and many others have pointed out before (Cardoso Llach, 2015; Mooshammer and Mörtenböck, 2016; Srnicek, 2017), platforms do not cut out the middlemen; they simply replace them. This is most evident in the track record of successful platform companies: whenever such platform-based initiatives take on a particular area of life and begin to intervene in its orthodox mode of operation, more often than not the new operational paradigm is quickly channeled into a commercially minded service. Whether that service has to be purchased with money or not, there is always a price to be paid for its usage. Even though the exposure of the murky means by which some of the most powerful global players in this market extract the "price" they want from their users has led to a heightened public sensibility resonating in more news coverage and a multitude of political statements,[4] what is still lacking is a firm grasp of the impact

174 *Peter Mörtenböck and Helge Mooshammer*

the pervasiveness and scale of these technologies will have on the shape and quality of future urban life.

What makes the task of tackling these shortcomings so challenging is the inherent invisibility of the core operations of platform technologies. In most cases, their immediate visual presence consists of nothing more than an app interface, which can be accessed via smartphones or similar digital devices.[5] When not in use, nothing remains to remind us of the functionality of the infrastructures in the background. A smartphone might leave an unsightly bulge in one's trouser pocket, but other than that, these services quickly slip out of sight and out of mind. Yet the rapid expansion and ubiquity of platform-based services has triggered a cascade of effects that are leaving clearly noticeable marks on everyday urban life. Most notably, they have begun to encroach on a wide range of domains determining the focus, priorities and direction of many societies across the world: whether it is the question of labor, as seen in the rise of a new class of precarious workers required for the provision of new on-demand urban services; whether it is the question of aspiration and imagination, which is increasingly being shaped by the rapid consumption of visual information and influenced by the speed of circulation of new services and commodities; whether it is the question of civic responsibility that arises in the wake of a new gold-rush mentality surrounding platform industries, where the pack at the front reaps all the rewards regardless of the damage left behind; or whether it is the question of individual liberties, when even the most basic forms of social participation, such as buying a bus ticket or checking the weather forecast, become impossible unless one subscribes to the services, and demands, of a platform that handles the entire process.

We should not, of course, forget that the use of the term "platform" in this context represents the result of quite deliberate discursive work serving specific aims (Gillespie, 2010, p. 359) and that these new technologies are appearing in all shapes and sizes, ranging from small-scale local initiatives that rely on volunteers to big global corporations backed by billions of dollars of venture capital. What has been emerging as a new constant under the guise of the non-partisan notion of "platform", however, is the proliferation of a "platform mentality" through which certain demands – the quest for instant gratification; the prioritization of aesthetic appeal; the activation and management of cultural and social capital for other, increasingly financial, gains – are embraced as guiding principles and implemented as a sensitizing narrative in the urban imagination. In doing so, platforms are all contributing to a fundamental shift in terms of actors when it comes to who determines urban development: a shift away from politicians and professionals toward citizens and entrepreneurs, with the domains of the latter two progressively merging under programs that enforce concepts of citizen-entrepreneurs.[6] It is this shift in power that has become one of the most defining experiences of the rise of what we might term "platform urbanism".[7]

## Campus life

One of the key questions raised by platform urbanism is how to respond to the shift of power from the public domains of politics and paid work to the private spheres of investors and innovators. Clearly, this can no longer be the task of institutional politics as such, given its increasing dependency on the capriciousness of platform media. Rather it has to be a matter of public engagement. We will come back to this when discussing the critical role of civic participation in the performance of platform economies, in their future development, and in the debate on platform urbanism. But first we want to take a closer look at the range of novel spatial typologies and socio-urban concepts that have begun to form the building blocks of platform urbanism.

While it may be desirable for users that urban platform operations emerge in many different shapes and sizes, it is the big global players such as Google, Amazon, and Facebook who wield the greatest power over the underlying technologies and thus over the direction of the future imperatives of urban life. With regard to these tech giants' impact on novel modes of spatial production, we can distinguish between two distinct arenas of engagement: first, most of them have been designing their headquarters as pioneering examples of what, in their view, the world of work should look like in the future. Seen as having to be particularly attractive for the much-sought-after millennial generation of tech-innovators, their enthusiastically hyped "campuses" don't just comprise office spaces but attempt to showcase a new breed of hybrid urban spaces which have the capacity to simultaneously satisfy numerous needs, ranging from their staff's desire for inspiring environments and a sense of community to a commitment to design that helps tackle climate change. Second, a key growth model for many leading tech companies (e.g., manufacturers of phones or other interface devices, developers of sensors, or providers of cloud computing) now centers on the search for ways of expanding their primary product line and market reach by encroaching on other areas where it might be possible to apply know-how gained through data gathering in previous core operations. Even if we consider "classic" platform companies such as AirBnB, WeWork and Uber as characterized by their focus on providing a highly specified service, it is easy to imagine how the accumulation of "disruption experience" can be turned into a competitive advantage and allow for the duplication of earlier successes by disrupting other fields as well.

Indeed, many technology corporations are increasingly setting their sights not just on the provision of goods or services but on the production of worlds to live in. The urban realm, with its rich entanglement of social encounters and economic exchanges, has become a preferred target in these endeavors. It is in this context that we have to locate the growing investment of big tech players in the establishment of subdivisions specifically dedicated to providing access to the arena of urban development. Market-oriented real estate has a long history as an economic domain particularly prone to the excesses of capitalist speculation,[8] and, as in other sectors such as finance and global trade, there is immense appetite for the opportunities the integration of technology – as in the case of PropTech – might hold. It will be important to keep both these perspectives – campus experiments and encroachments on the urban landscape – in mind when examining how the leading global tech corporations have entered the field of urban development and have begun to purposefully intervene in how future urban life is imagined.

First, let's take a closer look at the scenarios emerging from the showcase campuses of these companies. California's Silicon Valley has become the epicenter of attempts to structure not only global communication but also global communities. Facebook and its social network are a case in point: the company's increased focus on Facebook groups as a unit of meaningful interaction is not primarily driven by economic valorization based on likes of individual pages and the value generated by its own social network. Rather, the new engine powering the rhetoric of Facebook's "global community" is the formulation of a model of society based on "meaningful" social interaction, and groups are the starting point for such a model (Terranova, 2015).[9] Much has been written in architecture books and journals about the fusion of life and work on the corporate campuses of Facebook, Apple, and Google and the particular value systems they project in terms of design: sketching a relaxed but professionally polished setting for like-minded people, the trope of the (post-university) campus suggests a place of encounters and innovation, a feel-good environment for an idealized community of knowledge workers who, in return for their willingness to spend endless hours working on campus, are being pampered with numerous perks such as unlimited food and drink supplies, fitness studios, onsite health care, social programs, and all kinds of other conveniences (Lange, 2012; Borries, 2017; Galloway, 2017).

Two significant planning characteristics distinguish the *campus* (Latin: plain or open field providing opportunities for action, gatherings, and debates) from other urban quartiers and explain why it has become the favored model for big employers in the new creative tech industries. One of its advantages is the ease with which large-scale workforces can be distributed across different buildings embedded in airy and welcoming surroundings. Yet while these settings play with the illusion of openness and transparency, they are most strongly defined by clearly set boundaries that separate life on campus from a very different world outside. This "bubble" effect of the campus is the foundation of its surge in popularity among investors in the technological frontier. Its elasticity is used as a safeguard to keep at bay unwelcome interruptions from the outside (whether uncontrolled intrusions, noise emissions, or having to queue alongside "strangers") without obstructing the potential for innovation-sparking chance encounters between employees.

Admittedly, Facebook's Menlo Park campus on 1 Hacker Way has proved far from ideal in that respect, with one of its most apparent shortcomings lying precisely in the lack of a smooth (i.e., unnoticeable) management of the thresholds between inside and outside worlds. The bizarre positioning of a white billboard showing Facebook's "Like" icon – the company's only accessible onsite visitor attraction – in shades of blue at the intersection of Hacker Way and Bayfront Expressway has become a much-derided symbol of inaccessibility. The fact that Facebook fans, who might have travelled from afar, have to scramble through a thicket of overgrown vegetation to reach this much-coveted signage, hoping to produce an Instagrammable selfie "at Facebook" while heavy trucks thunder past them on a nine-lane traffic corridor, makes it challenging to enact complicity with the company ethos. Just a few yards away from the Like sign, Facebook's private traffic wardens try to keep on top of the daily commuter chaos, turning unauthorized people away and directing employees to secure parking lots. Like other major Silicon Valley employers, Facebook has chartered a large fleet of unmarked black coaches, which shuttle staff from numerous locations across the Bay Area to Menlo Park in the morning and back again in the evening in order to soften the friction created by lengthy commutes and encourage employees to lose no time generating fresh ideas. However, the interaction between these private transport systems and the urban landscape surrounding Silicon Valley's flagship campuses does not match the happy picture of an elevated work experience. Waiting between shifts, countless coaches can be seen parked up in the dusty no man's land of disused byways, along the fences of electric substations and next to the ditches of irrigation canals, with only a few of them managing to catch some shade under the canopies of rustling eucalyptus trees.

*Figure 8.2* Facebook, 1 Hacker Way, Menlo Park, CA, USA

*Source*: Photo by Peter Mörtenböck and Helge Mooshammer, 2018

Camouflaging such frictions is the mission of a new breed of colossal campuses erected in Silicon Valley and other top tech locations from 2015 onward. Seen together, these commissions of high-impact architectural design have triggered a wave of competitive image production targeting both the company's employees and the outside world. Facebook's MPK 20 and MPK 21 complexes opened in 2015 and 2018, respectively, and are situated just across the Bayfront Expressway from the original campus. The design by Frank Gehry includes ample open space, cycling tracks, roof gardens, and elevated walkways, which have often been compared to New York's High Line. Connected to the existing MPK 20 structure via a sunken garden, the MPK 21 extension is meant to manifest a new kind of architecture within Facebook culture. There are tropical plants as well as maturing redwood trees, flexible workspaces, a sort of town square, numerous restaurants, "green" features such as photovoltaic solar panels and a water recycling system – everything one might wish to find in a well-equipped city. Clearly, the goal here is to create an atmosphere of vibrant sociality, a scenario required to address the peak millennial goal: happiness and a good life. In keeping with this ambition, Facebook aims to expand its operations with plans for a mixed-use village for its 30,000 employees, called Willow Campus.[10] With this scheme, Facebook seeks to take on a more sovereign role than it has so far. The company plans to set its own policies to design village life from the bottom up, including housing provision, transport infrastructure, services, and regulations pertaining to social life. Under the slogan of "All those in favor of the future, raise your hands", the PR campaign accompanying Facebook's revised 2019 planning application, entitled "Willow Village – Picture the Possibilities" and led by real estate developer Signature Development Group, promises "vibrancy, excitement, and opportunity for the entire community".[11]

Among Silicon Valley's high-tech leaders, all of whom have ambitions to increase investment in the integration of their hardware product lines into all kinds of platform applications, Apple has developed a very distinctive approach to image management. It centers its activities on the skillful mediation of ideas, to such a degree that it is often difficult to tell fiction from reality. It is a characteristic of the company that seems to be symbolized by Apple Park, Apple's gigantic headquarters in Cupertino. Designed by Norman Foster, the structure's perfect closed-ring shape, which has a circumference of one mile and a diameter of 1,512 feet, combined with its strict separation from the outside world, seems to have been deliberately made to look alien. Everything is meticulously crafted and designed, but all value seems to hinge on the perfection of mediation. Hidden behind rows of grand conifers, landscaped mounds, and a steel-rod perimeter fence reminiscent of the US-Mexican border wall, the site is only accessible via highly secured entrance points, again artfully screened by vegetation and an expansive use of glass, which blocks all views into campus life by perfectly reflecting its surroundings. There appears to be no face to the outside world, no contact or stimulation. Instead, Apple has commissioned a state-of-the-art visitor center across the road. Here, Apple fans are greeted by well-informed hosts and directed to look at a range of design artifacts ranging from an exclusive selection of Apple merchandise to architectural models standing in for the real thing. Visitors are handed iPads that can be pointed at an immaculately detailed scale model of Apple Park in solid wood, and if one catches the right angle, the iPad screen discloses for a brief moment the secret interior of the Apple mothership. Although the real Apple Park headquarters building can be glimpsed through the windows directly behind the model, it is the computer-generated images that draw the attention of and reassure the center's visitors. This decoy strategy may contribute to an experience of apparent privilege and access. Yet it is precisely the strictly choreographed set of operations – being guided to enter selected parts of the curated megastructure while avoiding the impenetrable space of the vast closed ring that is walled off for Apple employees – that makes visitors feel a sense of closure and exposes the total interiority of the habitat created by the platform (Bratton, 2015, p. 187). What becomes tangible is that the real privilege is afforded only to Apple citizens. Armed with permission to cross the threshold between outside and inside, they are entitled to join an elect community whose Elysian perk-rich campus life remains out of reach for outsiders.

At the other end of this spectrum of image strategies we find Google, a tech corporation that strives to project the virtues of openness and playfulness,

*Figure 8.3* Apple Park, Visitor Center, Cupertino, CA, USA

*Source*: Photo by Peter Mörtenböck and Helge Mooshammer, 2018

not least when it comes to its campus in suburban Mountain View. Google has expanded its headquarters in the same neighborhood several times, and there are various relicts of an earlier period, when a peripheral location with a group of human-sized android characters, such as Bugdroid, the green robot, or Donut and Eclair,[12] was all that was needed to create an immersive visitor experience. What we see when walking across the old Google campus is first and foremost the ambition to provide a relaxed work environment permeated with various offers of leisurely activities so as to allow for breaks from tiring routines. The design for a new Google headquarters next to the current site by Thomas Heatherwick and Bjarke Ingels (BIG) seeks to radically advance the old idea of the campus. Resembling a giant tent covering an area of close to 410,000 square feet (38,000 square meters) and rising to a height of 111 feet (34 meters), their design focuses not on the idea of an environment for knowledge workers but on curating the diversity and liveliness one would find in an urban neighborhood.

Presenting "a bold architecture" that reflects Google's "culture of innovation", the ambition here is to design the prototype of an urban neighborhood around the Google ethos, one that is full of wildflower meadows and bicycle paths, yoga classes, pop-up entertainment, sculpture gardens, and lots of other community-building activities. Architecturally, BIG's design looks like a hybrid of Facebook's plans for Willow Campus and the new Apple Park in Cupertino. On the one hand, it claims to aim for a village-like

*Figure 8.4* Googleplex, Google HQ, Mountain View, CA, USA

*Source*: Photo by Peter Mörtenböck and Helge Mooshammer, 2019

composition where business blends organically into the natural environment, with pavilions nestled together and a public artery replete with shops and cafes on the ground floor level, creating a "bustling social and retail destination".[13] On the other, all these possibilities are aggregated within one monumental form that keeps everyone together under one roof and evokes something akin to the realm of the sacred. At the core of this design is the dream of ultimate flexibility, with architecture as a software that can be updated anytime on demand. Given the scale of its ambition and the references to values that are in many ways reminiscent of 1960s countercultural movements – freedom, sharing, equality – it is no surprise that the design has been compared with utopian visions of architecture from that period, such as Buckminster Fuller's geodesic dome designed to cover Manhattan (1964), Cedric Price and Joan Littlewood's Fun Palace (1961), Archigram's Plug-in City (1964), and similar visionary plans that aimed for a unique adaptability and openness. Like these schemes, the panoptical worlds of Silicon Valley's tech giants promise to reorganize production and labor by breaking down the barriers of bureaucracy in search of new frontiers on which non-hierarchical communities can apparently explore their collective possibilities (Turner, 2008; Spencer, 2016). What is striking is the similarity between the marketing slogans of today's platforms and the demands of the countercultural movements of the 1960s and 1970s. As the 1964 Fun Palace promotional brochure suggests:

> Choose what you want to do – or watch someone else doing it. Learn how to handle tools, paint, babies, machinery, or just listen to your favourite tune. Dance, talk or be lifted up to where you can see how other people make things work. Sit out over space with a drink and tune in to what's happening elsewhere in the city. Try starting a riot or beginning a painting – or just lie back and stare at the sky.
>
> (Price and Littlewood, 1964)

## From campus to urbs

What the current wave of planning initiatives by the big players in the sector – Facebook, Apple, and Google – demonstrates is that the public appeal of their designs is crafted in such a way as to present carefully curated narratives about a quasi-magical environment based on principles of freedom, harmony, and equality. These schemes aim to be opening up a new frontier of political and cultural change that renders possible the liberation of both individuals and society. The primary purpose of these beautiful new worlds, we are supposed to believe, lies solely in liberating and activating the resident population in the most effective way possible – a paradisiac universe fulfilling millennials' every wish, albeit one that is becoming increasingly closed in on itself. But the urban design ambitions of global tech corporations don't stop with the development of their own headquarters and sites of direct production. Google's sister companies, in particular, are at the forefront of exploring novel ways of creating environments that can function both as outlets and laboratories for their products and services. In these quasi-holistic worlds, where all needs are catered for "under one roof", spheres of work and leisure merge in a sensual experience of membership and belonging. It becomes virtually impossible for inhabitants of these quarters to maintain control over and distinguish between different segments of their lives. In order to enjoy the benefits of having access to these worlds, one has to subscribe to various packages of surrendering sovereignty. It is not just the profits of labor that are handed over. Many more aspects of human subjectivity have to be made available for extraction – most notably in the form of data, the tracking of movements, and the harvesting of emotions – if one does not want to risk exclusion from these zones of progress and prosperity.

The case that has attracted the most widespread attention in recent years has been a proposal by Sidewalk Labs, the urban innovation subsidiary of Google's parent company Alphabet, for the development of a major slice of Toronto prime real estate by planning communities from "the internet up" with the help of smart technologies, materials, and processes.[14] Following an agreement with the tri-government agency Waterfront Toronto in October 2017, Sidewalk Labs began work on the Master and Innovation Development Plan (MIDP) for Quayside, a five-hectare site in Toronto's East Bayfront neighborhood. Describing the process as "creating a new type of place to accelerate urban innovation and serve as a beacon for cities around the world", Sidewalk Labs presented staggering figures to support the assertion that its plans for Quayside would bring significant economic benefits to Toronto, from a USD 2.1 billion increase in annual tax revenue and an additional 27,000 jobs to the unlocking of USD 22 billion in third-party real estate investment. Wrapped in the language of public consultations, Sidewalk Labs proudly stated that "at the core of a future city is a layer of digital infrastructure that provides ubiquitous connectivity for all, offers new insights on the urban environment, and encourages creation and collaboration to address local challenges" (Sidewalk Labs, 2019c, pp. 31, 151).

Looking for ways to "scale digital innovation" and "catalyze the growth of an urban innovation cluster" (Sidewalk Labs, 2019a, p. 405), Sidewalk Labs' primary target was urban data defined as "information gathered in the city's physical environment, including the public realm, publicly accessible spaces, and even some private buildings" (Sidewalk Labs, 2019b, p. 377). As it stated in its Digital Innovation Plan,

> Sidewalk Labs proposes to launch a minimal set of digital services that would catalyze this ecosystem of urban innovation. These services and applications . . . represent innovations currently not being pursued by the market but that remain essential to achieving Waterfront Toronto's quality-of-life objectives.
>
> (Sidewalk Labs, 2019b, p. 378)

Designing new urban enclaves in line with the requirements of data-driven services, such as embedded sensors that direct self-driving cars, AI-enhanced metadata schemes for buildings, and tracking devices that record and monitor environmental changes, is like a dream come true for companies focusing their business operations on data – the dream of purpose-designed communities happily serving as data-generating subjects on which to test and deploy not only novel products and technologies but also "geographically targeted" governance structures (Sidewalk Labs, 2019c, pp. 44, 68). These new developments are testament to Fredric Jameson's critique of the mesmerizing spell of enclave life in societies of high productivity (Jameson, 2005) and its encouragement of unsustainable fantasies of sharing, equality, and freedom within capitalist affluence.

One of the most controversial ideas raised by Sidewalk Labs in the MIDP related to its proposal that in addition to a range of revenue streams such as real estate sales and charges for advisory services, it would receive performance payments from Toronto's public bodies "to compensate the company for its role in accelerating development". These payments were supposed to recognize the risks assumed by Sidewalk Labs in its efforts to help "generating billions of dollars of economic activity" and "producing substantial revenues for the governments that would otherwise go unrealised" (Sidewalk Labs, 2019c, pp. 174–179). While adding further to the outrage of local initiatives about what they see as an undemocratic capture of a public process by a private corporation,[15] such disruption of the common understanding of what urban planning is meant to achieve is intrinsic to platform urbanism, for which every aspect of urban metabolism can be turned into a chargeable service, even the genesis of the city itself. Speculative profits are generated not only through real estate sales, leasing contracts, and loan repayments; the mere "success" of an urban neighborhood – the fact that a city manages to "persist" – becomes an object of speculation. Public authorities (and, by extension, citizens) are forced to pay for the sheer fact of their survival in a global, competitive environment. The partnership model presented in this proposal is doomed to provide the template for the terms and conditions regulating such partnerships in many regions across the world. In more and more cities, sections of publicly administered urban services are being snapped up by tech companies, which subsequently implement their own kind of sovereignty.

What does investing in a city mean exactly from the viewpoint of a platform enterprise? For years, platforms such as Amazon, Facebook, Google, and WeWork have been looking beyond their original business models and striving to penetrate as many spheres of social production and reproduction as possible in order to extend their market dominance and embed their speculative investment model in the structure of finance-capitalist bank lending. Amazon has developed from a virtual bookshop into a world-leading retailer of material goods and is now seeking to exploit its access to billions of customer reviews to tailor a range of product offerings in physical retailing outlets within urban space. AirBnB is not only a global rental agency for short-term accommodation but is also using its specific know-how about managing vast quantities of urban data to strategically link up with other rapidly growing data-driven economic arenas such as the internet of things (e.g., by providing open access to its workflow management platform Airflow). Alphabet, as already mentioned, is using its supremacy in the realm of the organization of information for the development of entire city districts (Sidewalk Labs). WeWork has rebranded itself as We Company as part of an attempt to extend its know-how regarding space optimization and people's desires for communality from co-working to co-everything, beginning with housing and education. And Uber is using the data it has recorded about the movement of people in urban space to establish strategic partnerships with urban planners (Uber Movement).

For platforms, increasing the scale of their operations thus does not mean simply recasting the dimension of their field of activity but is also an important step in opening up new fields that seem destined to assume a far greater economic significance. The associated potential is, in turn, a decisive mechanism for increasing the financial value of the enterprise and user numbers. Due to the network effects typical for platforms, changes in scale can be utilized as growth drivers but require an appropriately prepared environment for further expansion. Growing metropolitan regions and their inexhaustible supply of willing economic agents offer an ideal arena for sounding out new facets of market expansion. Decisive here is the factual capacity of platform enterprises to select from a wide range of options the city that seems worthy of investment. Being able to decide which city is worth investing in alters not only the previous balance of power between city governments and corporate businesses. The lever of financial speculation that platform enterprises are able to deploy in their selection of investment recipients affects the preparedness of cities to meet the expectations of these investors. The investment-worthy city has thus become the objective of contemporary urban development, as opposed to the city in which citizens are free to develop their lives, talents, and abilities. Such freedom to develop has been replaced by pleasure and enjoyment, two components that, in current planning policies, are increasingly serving as both inducement and driving force in the effort to keep pace with economic competitors.

Ultimately, the real battle will be about how far cities are willing to go in allowing the mobilization of urban data for building and advancing artificial intelligence and machine learning, which can then be fed back into plans for even more advanced urban schemes. As it moves in this direction, urban life and its capture is turning into a pawn in the race between the world's most powerful platforms to achieve market leadership. In such data-driven environments, our personal data is not only mined and exploited for the purposes of platform industries; a key aspect of this development is the valorization of our individual performances as human subjects. As a result, access to these new cities is not only a question of individual wealth and class, but also a question of personal collateral based on reputation, and, as a consequence, these cities won't be open to everyone. If our social graph/credit is not up to scratch, access to these brave new worlds might be denied to us.

## Access is the new capital

According to French economist Thomas Piketty, the sharp rise in inequality since the 1980s, which can only be reversed by strong economic growth and the taxation of wealth, is due to particular distributional failures (Piketty, 2014). Taking for granted the key role of knowledge and skills in the distribution of wealth in society, one of the most harmful failures today has to do with distributional issues around the use of new data technologies. Many technologies of data gathering and data extraction that are in use are inaccessible to most people, making it easy for the accumulation and absorption of the profit they enable to benefit the few, not the many. What is even worse is that these inequalities are increasingly being planned, realized, and regulated by means of structural interventions into urban space: that is, into the space meant to be shared by all of us. The ensuing problem is that we have now arrived at a point where city-making has become an important domain for the consolidation of wealth concentration and not a domain for wealth distribution.

One of the key questions that needs to be raised in response to this situation is how to make sure that it is not just an elite of stakeholders but every citizen who is involved in urban decision-making and that all stakeholders have equal power in this respect. To achieve this, we need to take into account two things: first, our cities are increasingly data-driven environments, and this means that we need to consider how the forces of change unleashed by digital technologies and big data can be used to extend access to opportunities for engagement in the urban realm. And second, calling for meaningful civic engagement in a Lefebvrian sense is not just about the utilization of a right to the city. It is about not being excluded from urban form (Lefebvre, 2003) or, in other words, about collectively redefining the terms underlying the production of urban space. As Evgeny Morozov argues in a commentary for the *Financial Times* (Morozov, 2018, p. 11), claiming one's right to the city under the reign of data capitalism needs to include demands for our right to data. What is therefore at stake in data-driven environments is a better understanding of the way citizen-data interaction constitutes acts of production and how access to decision-making about new modes of urban mediation can be distributed evenly in these ecologies.[16]

Although in the ecologies generated by platform urbanism the city is being increasingly reduced to its infrastructural capacity with the help of algorithmic processes, representation and mediation play an important role. As in the avant-garde designs produced by Archizoom and Superstudio in the 1960s and 1970s (Aureli, 2008), for platform urbanism, the city no longer *represents* the system but rather *becomes* the system. The mediation of interests is replaced by a belief in an urban existence free of politics, which is expressed in an infrastructure that takes on the character of a fetish. The envisaged efficiency, optimization, and development of new markets based on the utilization of data are the central specifications of the requirement profiles of these urban designs. Here, representation is accorded a different function. Rather than simply disappearing into the background, it is supposed to support the system, just as under neoliberalism the state is supposed to have the task of actively paving the way for the unfolding of free-market forces. In this contest, representation thus has a moderating, propitiatory, and palliative function that is supposed to enable the system, in the guise of urban form, to function without restrictions, rather than the task of giving expression to specific interests, of representing and mediating them in visual or spatial terms.

Returning to our initial question of what makes us participate in these processes of profound transformation, we believe it is crucial to acknowledge this "networking" effect of representation in order to gain a better understanding of our own role as protean subjects of interest in the proliferation of platform urbanism. Echoing the pervasive capacity of platform environments to act as an exchange for trading different sets of values (financial, social, aesthetic, etc.), our interest in creating these new urban worlds is also undergoing numerous reframings as it is communicated back and forth between different platform participants: from desire to expectation and from reward to profit. Both platforms and interest (from Latin: *inter-esse*) denote situations of "in-between". With platform environments employed to direct interest to the socio-aesthetic performance of interest itself, speculative operations become decoupled from their contexts and risks externalized to somewhere else (i.e., outside the platform).

Skillfully manipulating the spectacle of interest becomes the preferred way of managing a collective belief in speculative investments and expanding the reach of what Franco (Bifo) Berardi has conceptualized as the reign of semio-capitalism in which "semio-capital is capital-flux that coagulates in semiotic artefacts without materializing itself" (Berardi, 2007, p. 76). Functioning as a derivative, representations of interest might propel the rise of platform urbanism through the logics and inclinations of semio-capital, but signification alone does not fully account for the complexities of urban life. The current boom of e-scooters and other novel forms of mobility, for instance, might help imagine a global market around innovative individual transport systems and contribute to the rise of a gold-rush mentality, with numerous competitors hoping to benefit from this investment bonanza, but realities on the ground pose rather different challenges.

Indeed, many cities have begun to embark on defensive actions, seeking to end a situation in which nobody appears to be accountable for unresolved legal issues, rising tensions among urban populations, and mounting environmental costs. The increase of digitally mediated informal practices in the urban realm (unregulated private transport, short-term urban sharing, co-living and co-working schemes) that goes hand in hand with such developments (Ferreri and Sanyal, 2018) is backed by what Manuel Aalbers has termed "regulated deregulation" (Aalbers, 2016) – a systematic approach ensuring that greater freedom from state control is given to some economic agents at the expense of others. In the case of digital-platform economies, this approach has often led to an undermining of city authorities' ability to use data for public benefit, because data is often deemed to be part of a commercial relationship between the city's (human and non-human) infrastructure and companies whose business model relies on exploiting the potential of big data techniques.

Key to all these frictions that are increasingly configured and played out in the urban environment is the question of access. Access has become the new capital, not just for the majority of millennials who are purported to prefer access over ownership, but for everyone wishing to be part of the experience and possibilities of urban life. Organizing access to the material, social, and symbolic dimension of the city has long been a form of the social and political order, whose features are orientated to the configuration of political participation and the exercise of power and, in many cases, result in discrimination in terms of class, gender, and ethnicity. By contrast, platforms represent a technology with which this access can be transformed into a tradable commodity. Access is no longer something that is granted or denied in a political sense, but becomes a purchasable product, measurable and exchangeable in accordance with its monetary equivalent. In conjunction with platform technologies, access is traded as a form of capital that is bound up with other novel currencies, such as social esteem, trust, value orientation, friendship networks, and lifestyle attributes.

The notion of "platform" is usually relative to its design, utility, and environment, but can be represented by a spatial analogy, as a "raised structure" or literally "levelled shape", an idea echoed in the way digital platforms provide improved access to people, goods, and services. Platforms are often promoted as a kind of superimposed infrastructure that offers an improved range of access or more efficient way of connecting, but they do so by excluding that which is seen as an obstacle or potential interference to the desired action. As an elevated structure, platforms provide better service by leaving something else behind or below. Structurally, then, the promise of platforms to offer improved access is thus inherently bound up with acts of exclusion. They exclude what could impinge on the desired service, and they exclude those who do not happen to be on the platform concerned. In other words, platforms do not just provide access but, by way of this process, gain control over access as such, turning it into an experience of privilege. By not only controlling access (in the most direct sense) to consumer goods and services but by fundamentally reorganizing access to a wide spectrum of fundamental domains, such as education, housing, health care, or even political information, platforms are destined to become the most powerful players regulating the way we live in cities. And consequently, some of the fiercest political struggles that are going to arise in cities around the world will inevitably revolve around questions of digital access control.

In bringing these different lines of thinking together and concluding here, we propose reflecting on access in the urban realm as the critical moment in the process of defining the terms of co-producing the cities we live in, rather than as the moment of accepting the terms presented to us. In Irit Rogoff's words, access is "the ability to formulate one's own questions, as opposed to simply answering those that are posed to you in the name of an open and participatory democratic process" (Rogoff, 2008). Sharing resources across different members of society is never a level playing field. In platform economies, it is very clear that those who formulate the questions produce the playing field, while everyone else is supposed to play along. So as long as access is designed as something that can be granted or sold to people acting in the role of users, subscribers, or followers, there will always be an alienating tension between the images projected by service providers and the substance at the core of urban life. In keeping with Neil Brenner's insistence that "the world economy is a design problem" (Brenner, 2014, p. 22), the consequential demand can only be to deny platforms unrestricted control over access. Rather than simply accepting the prevailing design monoculture of platform urbanism, it is in the public interest to give democratically legitimate organs the opportunity to design access to access – whether in the form of digital access portals that regulate central elements of urban life or in the form of digital communication that can provide a framework for a diversity of social being. As long as access is traded as an investment-worthy sort of capital on the free market, the design of new urban forms will be determined by a matrix of privileges and exclusions, scarcity and pricing. We require ways of deploying and further developing technologies that provide equal access to the city for everybody.

## Notes

1 In his book *Capital in the Twenty-First Century*, Thomas Piketty also points to the key role of knowledge and skills for an even distribution of prosperity in society.
2 Less than ten years after its founding in 2010, WeWork's valuation at the beginning of May 2019 was stated as being USD 47 billion. In comparison, the valuation of Uber – another high-flying unicorn, which at that time had just had its stock market debut – was USD 84.2 billion (Lash, 2019). It is worth noting that while the market valuations of the companies ranked as the world's top four in most global league tables – Apple, Microsoft, Amazon, and Alphabet – were repeatedly reported to have scratched the USD 1 trillion mark during the first half of 2019, companies ranked 50 or below were valued at USD 150 billion or less, which underscores the massive influence businesses like WeWork or Uber have gained within a very short period of time.

In September 2019, reports about revised valuation figures began to circulate, suggesting that WeWork expected to be valued at about USD 20 billion in its forthcoming IPO. The sharp discrepancy between this figure and the USD 47 billion valuation quoted in Japan's SoftBank funding round highlights the extreme volatility inherent in these primarily investment-fueled, rather than policy-led, urban development projects. One factor contributing to this decline in valuation has been the persistent refusal by financial market analysts to regard WeWork as one of the new breed of disruptive technology companies, insisting instead on portraying it as a loss-making real estate company. See, for instance, Davis et al. (2019).

3 Having started with the renting of one building in Soho, New York, in 2010, WeWork's worldwide expansion has since accelerated from locations in 16 different cities in 2015 to 120 cities by the second quarter of 2019 (Platt and Edgecliffe-Johnson, 2019).

4 One of the most telling examples in this context is the 2018 Facebook-Cambridge Analytica data scandal that triggered a huge public outcry and led to Mark Zuckerberg testifying before the United States Congress.

5 The question of urban interfaces has been explored critically by media scholar Shannon Mattern in her articles for *Places,* including "Interfacing Urban Intelligence" (2014), as well as in her book *Code and Clay, Data and Dirt: Five Thousand Years of Urban Media* (2017).

6 See, for instance, Lilly Irani's (2019) analysis of policy paradigms hinging social and economic development on disruptive technologies in the context of India.

7 This argument resonates with architecture historian Keller Easterling's argument in *Extrastatescraft* (2014), which identifies the production of the urban with software logics.

8 See, for instance, Harvey (2006), Smith (2010), Sassen (2014).

9 See also the open letter from Mark Zuckerberg, "Building Global Community", published on 16 February 2017. Available at: www.facebook.com/notes/mark-zuckerberg/building-global-community/10154544292806634/.

10 Adding a further 1.75 million square feet of offices, this would push Facebook's total office space in the Bay Area past the 6-million-square-foot mark.

11 Available at www.willowvillage.com/.

12 These various "desserts" are code names of versions of Google's Android mobile operating system.

13 67-page planning document submitted for "Google Charleston East", Formal Review, 23 January 2017, Mountain View, California.

14 In May 2020, Sidewalk Labs announced that it would no longer pursue the Quayside project due to the anticipated economic fall-out of the COVID-19 pandemic: "As unprecedented economic uncertainty has set in around the world and in the Toronto real estate market, it has become too difficult to make the 12-acre project financially viable without sacrificing core parts of the plan we had developed together with Waterfront Toronto to build a truly inclusive, sustainable community." Daniel L. Doctoroff, "Why we're no longer pursuing the Quayside project — and what's next for Sidewalk Labs", published on 7 May 2020. Available at: https://medium.com/sidewalk-talk/why-were-no-longer-pursuing-the-quayside-project-and-what-s-next-for-sidewalk-labs-9a61de3fee3a.

15 See, for instance, the campaign #BlockSidewalk, which under the heading "Campaign Values" states that "Urban planning is something that happens between Torontonians and the City, focused on the public interest". Available at: www.blocksidewalk.ca/about.

16 See, for instance, Shannon Mattern's "Interfacing Urban Intelligence" (2014), which argues for a specific kind of transparency in response to the privatization of urban data and its interfaces.

# References

Aalbers, M. (2016), 'Regulated deregulation', in S. Springer, J. MacLeavy and K. Birch (eds.), *Handbook of Neoliberalism.* London: Routledge.

Adams, R.E. (2019), *Circulation and Urbanization*. London: Sage.

Appadurai, A. (1996), *Modernity at Large: Cultural Dimensions of Globalization*. Minneapolis: University of Minnesota Press.

Aureli, P.V. (2008), *The Project of Autonomy: Politics and Architecture Within and Against Capitalism*. New York: Princeton Architectural Press.

Barns, S. (2020), *Platform Urbanism: Negotiating Platform Ecosystems in Connected Cities*. London: Palgrave Macmillan.

Berardi, F. (2007), 'Schizo-economy', *SubStance*, 36(1), transl. Michael Goddard.

Borries, von F. (2017), 'Die universellen Ordnungen der Zukunft – Die Headquarter von Apple, Facebook und Google', *ARCH+* 230 (Architekturen der Globalisierung), pp. 208–215.

Bratton, B. (2015), *The Stack: On Software and Sovereignty*. Cambridge, MA: MIT Press.

Brenner, N. (2014), 'Neoliberalisation', in Fulcrum (ed.), *Real Estates: Life Without Debt*. London: Bedford Press.

Cardoso Llach, D. (2015), *Builders of the Vision: Software and the Imagination of Design*. New York and Oxon: Routledge.

Christensen, C.M., Raynor, M., and McDonald, R. (2015), 'What is disruptive innovation?', *Harvard Business Review*, 93(12), pp. 44–53.

Davis, M., Turner, G., and Tan, G. (2019), 'WeWork targets $20 billion to $30 billion IPO value', *Bloomberg*, Deals, 5 September.

Ferreri, M. and Sanyal, R. (2018), 'Platform economies and urban planning: Airbnb and regulated deregulation in London', *Urban Studies*, 55(15), pp. 3353–3368.

Galloway, S. (2017), *The Four: The Hidden DNA of Amazon, Apple, Facebook and Google*. New York: Portfolio/Penguin.

Gillespie, T. (2010), 'The politics of "platforms"', *New Media & Society*, 12(3), pp. 347–364.

Harvey, D. (2006), *Spaces of Global Capitalism*. London: Verso.

Irani, L. (2019), *Chasing Innovation: Making Entrepreneurial Citizens in Modern India*. Princeton and Oxford: Princeton University Press.

Jameson, F. (2005), *Archaeologies of the Future: The Desire Called Utopia and Other Science Fictions*. London: Verso.

Krivý, M. (2018), 'Becoming-platform, the urban and the city', *Mediapolis – A Journal of Cities and Culture*, 24 October. Available at: www.mediapolisjournal.com/2018/10/becoming-platform/.

Lange, A. (2012), *The Dot-Com City: Silicon Valley Urbanism*. Moscow: Strelka Press.

Lash, H. (2019), 'WeWork's starry valuation dazzles landlords, reaffirms doubters', *Reuters*, United States edition, Business News. Available at: www.reuters.com/article/us-usa-property-wework-value/weworks-starry-valuation-dazzles-landlords-reaffirms-doubters-idUSKCN1SG1VD/.

Lefebvre, H. (2003), *The Urban Revolution*. Minneapolis: University of Minnesota Press.

Letter from Mark Zuckerberg (2012), 'Part of the Form S-1 Registration Statement under the Securities Act 1993, as filed with the Securities and Exchange Commission on 1 February 2012'. Available at: www.sec.gov/Archives/edgar/data/1326801/000119312512034517/d287954ds1.htm#toc287954_10.

Mattern, S. (2014), 'Interfacing urban intelligence', *Places Journal*.

Merkel, J. (2015), 'Coworking in the city', *Ephemera: Theory and Politics in Organization*, 15(1), pp. 121–139.

Mooshammer, H. and Mörtenböck, P. (2016), *Visual Cultures as Opportunity*. Berlin: Sternberg Press.

Morozov, E. (2018), 'The case for publicly enforced online rights', *Financial Times*, 28 September. Available at: www.ft.com/content/5e62186c-c1a5-11e8-84cd-9e601db069b8.

Neff, G. (2015), *Venture Labor: Work and the Burden of Risk in Innovative Industries*. Cambridge, MA: MIT Press, pp. 16–17.

'Our Story' (2019), 'Part of the Form S-1 Registration Statement under the Securities Act 1993, as filed with the Securities and Exchange Commission on 14 August 2019'. Available at: www.sec.gov/Archives/edgar/data/1533523/000119312519220499/d781982ds1.htm#toc781982_1.

Piketty, T. (2014), *Capital in the Twenty-First Century*. Cambridge, MA: Harvard University Press.

Platt, E. and Edgecliffe-Johnson, A. (2019), 'WeWork: The "hypothetical" company at the heart of the property market', *Financial Times*, The Big Read Global Property, 2 July.

Price, C. and Littlewood, J. (1964), 'Fun Palace promotional brochure, CCA collection database, DR1995:0188:525:001:023'.

Rogoff, I. (2008), 'Turning', *e-flux Journal*, #00, November 2008.

Sassen, S. (2014), *Expulsions: Brutality and Complexity in the Global Economy*. Cambridge, MA: Harvard University Press.

Sidewalk Labs (2019a), 'The plans', *Toronto Tomorrow*, MIDP vol. 1.

Sidewalk Labs (2019b), 'Urban innovations', *Toronto Tomorrow*, MIDP vol. 2.

Sidewalk Labs (2019c), 'The partnership', *Toronto Tomorrow*, MIDP vol. 3.

Smith, N. (2010), *Uneven Development: Nature, Capital and the Production of Space*. London: Verso.

Spencer, D. (2016), *The Architecture of Neoliberalism*. London: Bloomsbury.

Srnicek, N. (2017), *Platform Capitalism*. Cambridge: Polity Press.

Terranova, T. (2015), 'Securing the social: Foucault and social networks', in S. Fuggle, Y. Lanci and M. Tazzioli (eds.), *Foucault and the History of Our Present*. London: Palgrave Macmillan, pp. 111–127.

Turner, F. (2008), *From Counterculture to Cyberculture: Stewart Brand, the Whole Earth Network, and the Rise of Digital Utopianism*. Chicago: University of Chicago Press.

Wissoker, P., et al. (2014), 'Rethinking real estate finance in the wake of a boom: A celebration of the twentieth anniversary of the publication of the double issue on property and finance', *Environment and Planning A*, 46(12), pp. 2787–2794.

# 9  The aesthetic society: or how I edit my Instagram[1]

*Lev Manovich*

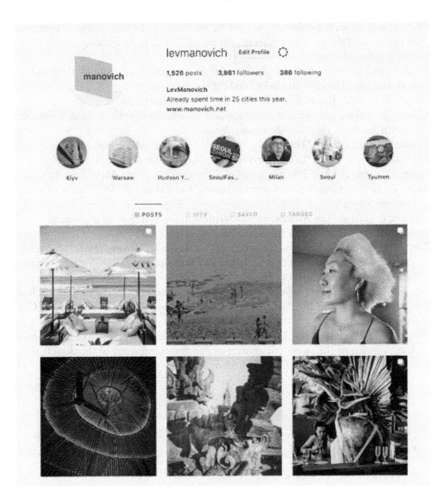

*Figure 9.1* Author's Instagram homepage, 17 December 2019

I caught the tail end of punk, when the Pistols were already disbanded, and less revolutionary but still decent bands like the Stranglers, the Fall and Pete Shelley's Buzzcocks were spitting and being spat on, and shouting out against boredom and bad pop music.

When I walk through that village now, or the town where I live – Totnes – or, indeed, London or Manchester, I don't really see any tribes, except perhaps for raven-haired emos and leather jacketed rockists. What I do see is a single look. It goes by various names, but hipster is the most common. Its dress code is "funny" or "unique" T-shirts, trousers with tight calves, perhaps an ironic tweed jacket, perhaps branded archless pumps and perhaps a WG Grace/Taliban beard.

Chris Moss, "Why don't young people want to be part of a tribe anymore?" (2015)

The dizzying growth of metropolises (megalopolises, rather) as demographers inform us, can only foster the development of "villages within the city". We are, and it is characteristic of the contemporary cities, in the presence of a mass-tribe dialectic; the mass being the all-encompassing pole, the tribe being the pole representing a particular crystallization.

Without the rigidity of the forms of organization with which we are familiar, it ["urban tribe"] refers to a certain ambience, a state of mind, and it is preferably to be expressed through lifestyles that appear and form.

Michel Maffesoli, *The Time of the Tribes – The Decline of Individualism in Mass Society* (1996)

From airport terminals decorated like Starbucks to the popularity of hair dye among teenage boys, one thing is clear: we have entered the Age of Aesthetics. Sensory appeals are everywhere, and they are intensifying, radically changing how Americans live and work . . . Every startup, product, or public space calls for an aesthetic touch, which gives us more choices, and more responsibility. By now, we all rely on style to express identity. And aesthetics has become too important to be left to the aesthetes.

Virginia Postrel, *The Substance of Style* (2004)

## The Rise of Aesthetic Society

We live in aesthetic society where the production of beautiful images, interfaces, objects and experiences are central to its economic and social functioning, as well as the identities of hundreds of millions of people. While aesthetic refinement has been central to all human cultures for thousands of years, the rise of mass production of all consumer goods in the 19th century led to the highest levels of such refinement to only be available to the rich and upper middle class. But after 1990, the growth of global middle class, the emergence of experience economy, the commercialization of "cool," "hip," "avant-garde," and "experimental", new manufacturing methods and new materials, and the adoption of digital technologies, changed this situation. Together, these forces lead to the development of what I call "aesthetic society."

The first author to note was probably Los Angeles cultural critic Virginia Postrel in her 2004 book The Substance of Style (2004). In the following fifteen years, the mass aestheticization of society advanced significantly, affecting many other types of products, spaces, messages, and so on. The sophistication of aesthetics also advanced: today many cutting-edge examples from 2004 appear naïve and simplistic.

For example, consider the design of contemporary mobile phones. As objects, they carry precisions, nuances and aesthetic richness that before was only possible in very expensive objects such as haute couture, where each item is created by hand from start to finish with extreme attention to detail. But in contrast to haute couture, the same phone models are owned by members of the global middle class, as well as by the rich.

The same democratization of sophisticated, refined aesthetic took place in a number of other areas such as hotel design, car design, and presentation of food in restaurants. The interior of many economy cars in 2020 looks more sophisticated then the interior of luxury cars ten years early. Similarly, today, endless inexpensive restaurants feature food presentation that ten years ago would only be available in selected expensive restaurants. Twenty years early, such aestheticized presentation was even more rare, only found in nouvelle cuisine and "molecular gastronomy" restaurants.

The democratization of sophisticated aesthetic began in the 1990s, though a few "design hotels" were already created earlier: Blakes in London (1978), Morgans (1984), Royalton (1987) and Paramount (1989) in New York City. But the movement really began to take off in 1993 when Claus Sendlinger founded Design Hotels group in 1993. It began with a list of 10 hotels, today in 2020, the majority of new hotels which are being built would be called "design hotels" ten years ago. However, this does not mean that the rise of aesthetic society has reached its limits. I believe that this process may continue for many decades. It is always possible to use and mix new materials and offer aesthetic effects that were not possible before. It is also possible to offer more individualized or unique products and experiences in many lifestyle areas.

Look around you. While products, spaces, visual media, and experiences such as eating out have more interesting and refined aesthetics, they are still not individualized. Today examples of mass individualization are still rare, and are also quite limited. Drogerie Market drugstores in Germany allow customers to customize their own personal care products – for example, selecting an existing shower gel and then choosing from a number of fragrance choices, and also creating their own label (Sibol, 2014). NIKE BY YOU (previously called NIKEiD) and miadidas make possible for customers to customize their sport shoes. (Adidas started to customize shoes already in early 1990s but only for selected successful athletes (Baena and Winkelhues, 2016).)

While mass individualization, where each customer can customize a product, is in many ways still mostly a promise today, a different individualization process that started in the 1990s has been fully developed. Before the 1990s, many types of what we today would call lifestyle products and experiences were designed by selecting an established style or template. Most chefs did not try to create dishes that would be unique in taste or presentation – instead they followed the conventions. Hotels were designed according to an existing style and did not stand out by uniqueness of design.

Between 1870 and 1980, experimentation, explicit departure from traditions and rules, and the pursuit of unique style by each creator, mostly happened in the art fields and not in mass culture. But after 1980, mass culture slowly starts to adopt these ideas. The design of storefronts absorbs installation art, music videos absorb experimental film, and fashion enters its "modernist" experimental phase. This adoption of modernism in mass culture puts focus on creating unique aesthetic experiences. Thus, the key idea behind "design hotels" is that each offers an individual design that you will not find anywhere else.

As design society becomes more mature, the value of aesthetic changes. Paradoxically, in this society, aesthetic is both more and less important than in the mass consumer society of the 20th century. It is more important because it matters to more people. For example, as described in Pierre Bourdieu's book Photography: A Middle Brow Art (1965) for most people involved in popular photography, aesthetics was seen as something foreign – reserved for professionals and upper classes. Comparing this to photography on Instagram in the second part of 2010s, we see a big difference. In my Cultural Analytics Lab, we used computational tools to analyze 17 million Instagram photos shared between 2012 and 2016 in 16 world cities. We found that at least in big cities, a significant proportion of users are quite aware about the aesthetic possibilities of the medium, as opposed to only automatically following photo conventions that dictate what and how something should be photographed.

In another example, today, one can look stylish, contemporary, and fashionable without knowing much about fashion trends. You simply visit Zara. Any combination of the items offered at any time is guaranteed to make you look aesthetically advanced.

At the same time, aesthetics matters less than in the 1960s and 1970s – as reflected in a number of surveys of French public conducted by Bourdieu for his books. He correctly theorized in this period that aesthetic taste functions to legitimize class distinctions. The ability to enjoy high culture was associated with more refined sensibility – the privilege of certain classes defined by a combination of education, social capital and financial capital. However, today, the correlations between class and taste have weakened. If Zara can within days translate new looks of most expensive designers into its inexpensive versions, without any (or small) loss in aesthetic refinement, it becomes more challenging for anybody to distinguish themselves through clothing. The same photo filters and photo editing tools are accessible to everybody – in contrast to 1960s when more expensive equipment allowed for more aesthetic control.

Once the sophisticated aesthetic options become available to all classes, they matter less as tools of distinction. This is what I mean when say that in aesthetic society, aesthetics matters less than in previous periods.

One of the differences between the aesthetic society of early 2000s captured in Postrel's book and its more developed current version is the emergence of new platforms and tools that allow normal people to communicate their aesthetic identities without big budgets available only to companies. Perhaps the best example of such platforms is Instagram.

In the following sections of this chapter I will use this example to show how individuals create aesthetic communication using a digital networked visual platform, and also to continue the discussion of the aesthetic society in general. I will use the term instagramism to refer to the aesthetic strategies employed in many Instagram images well as construction of aesthetic identities through these images. (We can also find examples of Instagramism on Facebook, WhatsApp, Snapchat, Tumblr, Line, etc.)

This term suggests an analogy to modern art movements such as futurism, cubism, surrealism, etc. Like these earlier -isms, Instagramism offers its own vision of the world and its own visual language. But unlike modernist art movements, Instagramism is shaped by millions of authors connected by and participating in Instagram and other social networks.[2] They influence each other and share advice on using mobile photo apps to create, edit, and sequence photos to be shared on Instagram. (See also the analysis in Tifentale, 2017.)[3]

The word "aesthetic" is used prominently by Instagrammers and authors of advice posts and videos. For example, a search on YouTube for "instagram aesthetic feed" yielded 7, 200 videos, while a search for the phrase "Instagram aesthetic" on Google yielded 144,000 results (both searches performed on 22 November 2016). The same search on February 12, 2020 29, 2020 returned 1,040,000 results. Looking at Google Trends worldwide for the search term "Instagram aesthetic," we find that these searches begin in the summer of 2014 and their volume gradually rises over next six years.

Why is this the case? All professional design fields – from car design and interior design to interface design and food design – are concerned with aesthetic. But this is not a new situation. The creation of aesthetic objects, spaces, and experiences have always been one of design's goals. However, the word "aesthetic" is not used in design discourse, because we assume that the main goal of design is different – to create functional easy-to-use objects and systems. In amateur arts of the modern period – home photography, home movies, making clothes at home using sewing patterns from fashion magazines, and so on – this word also does not appear. Amateur creators had other goals – following exactly existing pattern, creating a durable object, enjoying the activity itself, etc.

I think that the popularity of the word "aesthetic" in Instagram discourse reflects the key role aesthetic now plays on this platform. The creation of beauty – rather than information – is what successful Instagram accounts aim at. Having a consistent visual theme is seen as a necessary condition for attracting many followers. Another such condition is posting only aesthetically pleasing photos. This is achieved in various ways – applying an Instagram filter to a photo, editing photos in other apps such as VSCO and Snapseed or in Photoshop or Lightroom, and of course, taking aesthetic into account while capturing the photo.

This use of editing software as well as time dedicated to editing each photo separates *Instagram class* from other users of the platform. I am not referring to a class in the economic sense or to a hierarchy of social groups based on wealth, education, prestige or other factors. Instead, I use this term to refer to millions of young people in many countries who use Instagram in systematic ways to create visually sophisticated feeds. Typically, they edit their photos using third-party apps such as VSCO in addition to the basic Instagram app.

Karl Marx's concept of "means of production" is useful here because Instagrammers can be said to own the means of *cultural production*. This means, however, not simply owning mobile phones and apps, but more importantly having the *skills* to use these apps, understanding Instagram's rules and strategies for creating popular feeds, and being able to apply these strategies effectively in practice. Importantly, Instagrammers do not always have to sell their skills to "capitalists" – for the most part, they use these skills to have meaningful and emotionally satisfying experiences, to meet like-minded people, to maintain relationships with other people, or to acquire social prestige.

Using these skills also creates what Pierre Bourdieu calls "cultural capital", which in this case is measured by numbers of followers or respect in the community. This cultural capital can be translated into economic capital if an Instagrammer starts working with advertisers and marketers to promote products in her/his feed or if their followers purchase goods or services via a linked blog or website.

Since content-creation skills and an understanding of digital platforms and styles of expression and communication are what matters here, Instagrammers can also be thought of as *knowledge workers* in a *knowledge society*.[4] However, I would like to propose different terms: *aesthetic workers* and *aesthetic society* (i.e., the society of aesthetically sophisticated consumer goods and services). In such a society, the production and presentation of beautiful images, experiences, styles, and user-interaction designs are central to economic *and* social functioning. Rather than being a property of art, aesthetics is the key property of commercial goods and services (in this sense, "aesthetic society" cannot be equated with Guy Debord's "society of the spectacle").

Aesthetic society values space designers, user-experience designers, architects, photographers, models, stylists, and other design and media professionals, as well as individuals who are able to use social media, including making professional-looking media, and work with marketing and analytics tools. "Using" in this context refers to creating successful content, promoting this content, communicating with followers, and achieving desired goals. And to be successful, this content has to be *aesthetic*.

Aesthetic society is also the space in which urban/social media tribes emerge and sustain themselves through aesthetic choices and experience.

According to Michel Maffesoli, who developed his analysis of the "urban tribe" back in 1980s, the term "refers to *a certain ambience*, a state of mind, and it is preferably to be expressed through lifestyles that favor *appearance and form*" (1996). And this ambience and state of mind are precisely the "message" of Instagramism. Whereas in "classical modern" societies carefully constructed aesthetic lifestyles were the privilege of the rich, today they are available to all who use Instagram, VSCO, or any other of more than 2,000 photo-editing apps, or shop at Zara, which offers cool, hip, and refined styles in its 3,000 stores in 99 countries (2019 data).

## Three types of Instagram photographs: casual, professional, designed

I will look at three popular types of photos shared by people on Instagram and other popular media sharing networks. I call them *casual*, *professional*, and *designed.*[5] The main purpose of casual images is to document an experience or a situation or to represent a person or a group of people. A person who captures and shares a casual photo does not try to control contrast, colors, and composition. (However, she does follow conventions that specify how different subjects should be represented and, in some cases, also dictates visual choices.) Representative function takes precedence over aesthetic function. Historically, these images continue the practices of color "home photography" that developed in the 1950s as the cost of color film processing decreased.

Professional photos are created by people who are explicitly or implicitly aware of the rules of the "professional photography" that also developed during the 20th century. The authors of these photos try to follow these rules, conventions, and techniques, which they are likely to have learned from either online tutorials, posts, videos, or classes. Thus, in my use of the term, "professional" refers not to people who earn a living from their photography but to photographs that accord with a particular aesthetic.

My third designed type refers to photos that adopt an aesthetic referring to a tradition of modernist art, design, and photography dating back to the 1920s. This aesthetic was further developed in commercial fashion, advertising, and editorial photography during the 1940s and 1950s. Note that I use "aesthetic" to refer to a combination of visual style, photo techniques, and types of content, since in Instagram photos they usually go together. These aesthetics (there are more than one) follow their own conventions, but because they have emerged very recently, they may still be less fixed than those of professional photographs. One significant difference between professional and designed images is the treatment of space. Professional photos often show spatial depth exaggerated by composition, blurred backgrounds, and choice of subjects. In contrast, designed photos often create a shallower or flat space with strong two-dimensional rhythms more redolent of modernist abstract art and design. If the landscape and cityscape genres exemplify professional photo aesthetics, still-life and "flat lay" genres exemplify design photo aesthetics.

*Figure 9.2* Examples of *casual*, *professional*, and *designed* image types on Instagram (2015)

*Source:* Each montage shows a selection of photos from a single user in the order they appear in this user's feed

I use the term "Instagramism" to refer to the aesthetics of designed photos on Instagram and other platforms. I propose that the key aspect of Instagramism is the focus on mood and atmosphere rather than the representation or communication of emotions. I also propose that Instagramism is not in dramatic opposition to "commercial" and "dominant" imagery and genres such as the lifestyle genre of photography and videography. Instead, it establishes small and subtle distinctions that set it apart from this imagery in terms of what is shown, how it is shown, and for what purpose. In contrast to the often binary differences between "high" and "low" cultures, or the clear oppositions between "mainstream" culture and "subcultures" during the 20th century as analyzed by Pierre Bourdieu, Dick Hebdige, and others, Instagramism uses alternative mechanisms, and in doing so, it participates in the larger aesthetics movement of the early 21st century that is exemplified by the "normcore" style.

High/low and mainstream/subculture distinctions corresponded to class differences in income, types of occupations, background, and education. In contrast, I see Instagramism as the aesthetic of the new global digital youth class that emerged in the early 2010s. This class partially overlaps with the global Adobe class.

The "Adobe class" is my term for young professionally educated creatives working in design, video, social media, or fashion. Adobe Creative Cloud software dominates the market for design and media authoring. As of September 2016, there were over eight million registered software users worldwide. We can alternatively refer to the Adobe class as the "Behance

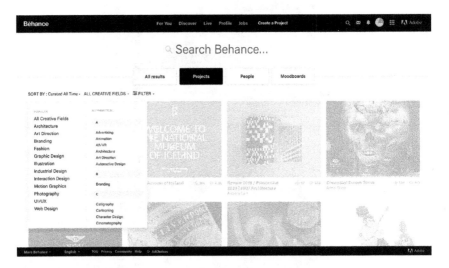

*Figure 9.3* Behance.com home page (accessed December 2019). The pull-down menu shows creative-field categories available for members to share their portfolios.

class". Behance.net is the leading global portfolio-sharing platform. It is owned by Adobe and integrated with Adobe media-creation software, so a designer can directly share her/his work on Behance from Adobe applications. At the end of 2015, Behance reported that it had six million registered users.

Our junior lab researcher Zizi Li contacted twenty-four Instagram users who have feeds of well-designed photos to ask if they had any formal education in art, design, photography, or any other creative fields, or if they worked in any of these fields at present. Half the responders had such education and/or positions; the other half did not.

## Instagramism vs. "normal" photography

Instagramism does not dramatically oppose commercial visual aesthetics. For example, on browsing stock and microstock photography sites such as Shutterstock, 500px, and dozens of others (Schreiber, 2016), we see many photos from the lifestyle and food categories that are very similar to many personal photos on Instagram.

But how is the aesthetic of Instagram designed photos related to the aesthetics of casual and professional photo types? In modern society, aesthetics, styles, and cultural choices often have to define themselves in opposition to each other. In contrast to earlier human societies, which were often completely isolated, modern culture is structural in Saussure's sense. Because many types of cultural "positions" (i.e., aesthetics, ideals, sensibilities, ideologies, interpretations) coexist, their creators and promoters have to define these positions in opposition to each other. More generally, we can say that they are deliberately positioned sufficiently far from one another in a competitive cultural landscape.[6]

So how do you define the aesthetics of designed photos using Instagram affordances? How do we create Instagram *cool*? The answer is by opposing popular image aesthetics (i.e., the types of photo conventions that we think of as normal, mainstream, and popular).[7]

For example, whereas casual portraits and self-portraits (e.g., selfies) tend to show full figures of one or more people arranged symmetrically in the center, designed photos tend rather to show parts of bodies positioned off-center and cut by a frame (think of Degas). They also avoid showing faces directly looking into the camera. (See our discussion of the "anti-selfie" genre in Tifentale and Manovich, 2016.)

Similarly, whereas casual and professional photos favor landscapes and cityscape genres and often exaggerate the perspective and sense of spatial depth, designed photos flatten the space and use large areas empty of any details. (In terms of lenses or zoom levels, this is analogous to the contrast between the wide-angle and telephoto view, which flattens the space.)

Strategies involving frame-cut faces and bodies and flat space align designed Instagram photography with the first generation of "mobile photography" developed by Rodchenko, Lissitzky, Moholy-Nagy, and other New Vision photographers in the 1920s and early 1930s. They created the visual aesthetics of "making strange" by practicing visual strategies that similarly opposed popular taste (i.e., symmetrical compositions, full figures, and faces looking into the camera). Using the affordances of the first compact 35mm Leica camera, which was released in 1925, New Vision photographers developed a different visual language: observing the subject at a 60 to 90 degree angle from below or above, diagonal compositions, showing only parts of objects and people, high contrast, and geometric shadows that flatten the shapes and space and interfere with shape perception. In other words, they were making photography that was defamiliarizing reality, thus creating a visual analog of the *ostranenie* effect described by Viktor Shklovsky in 1917, but in relation to literature. And, like many other avant-garde visual movements of the 1910s and 1920s, they made perception difficult – by abandoning the visual strategies of "normal" photography. That is to say, simply understanding the content of many of their photos required an increased cognitive effort because the compositions and subjects of these photos did not immediately trigger familiar cognitive frames.[8]

Casual and professional photos adopt a set of visual conventions to document events, people, and situations that follow accepted social norms – for example, taking a group photo at meetings, conferences, and trips. Designed photos express an urban/hipster sensibility that opposes these norms. This opposition is constructed using another set of norms – that of contemporary (2010–) design culture. How does this work?

The creators of designed photos find or stage unique moments, feelings, and states of being – in space, in time, with other people, with objects important to them. But rather than directly negating square reality through a strong alternative aesthetics (as hippies did in the 1960s), contemporary Instagram hipsters are often happy to subscribe to the styles of global consumer minimalism. Their Instagram photos and feeds (this term refers to all photos added by a user to her/his account over time) represent our current historical period, in which 20th-century oppositions – art and commerce, individual and corporate, natural and fabricated, raw and edited – are blended together. The Instagram hipster effortlessly navigates between these positions, without experiencing them as contradictions.

## Faces and bodies

Now, let's think about the frequent subjects of designed photos. They are "spreads" or "flat lays": photos of separate objects, parts of a body arranged with the object spreads or separate objects, parts of a body (such as hands holding objects or pointing) with landscapes or cityscapes, a full body positioned toward the edge or corner in a scene.

*Figure 9.4* Examples of visual strategies used in designed photo type

*Source*: Selected photos from the Instagram feed @recklesstonight (Kiev, Ukraine), shared during October–December 2015

Is there any common pattern in these subjects? Yes: it is the presence of the Instagrammer's body in the designed photos. But these representations do not follow mainstream portrait conventions. Instead, they deliberately oppose these conventions by showing hands, fingers, feet, or complete figures in situations: waking up, enjoying a relaxing coffee moment, surrounded by objects, pointing toward the landscape or objects in the cityscape, from the back, and so on. This set of strategies is not found in the commercial and advertising photography published today or earlier in the 20th century, and it also did not exist in New Vision photography.

The original use of the term "hipster" in the 1940s was associated with hot jazz. This association, in turn, allows us to better understand the meaning of hipness in Instagramism. Lives of Instagrammers as presented in their feeds can be compared to the unique improvised experiences of jazz players as opposed to the planned and routine life of "squares".

Today, the enhanced contrast, saturation, and/or colors; the use of diagonals; and the appearance of objects and bodies cut by an image frame in designed Instagram photos are signs of immersion and of life as improvisation. In choosing and representing (or staging and designing) such a style of existence, Instagram authors echo the behavior of the original American hipsters of the 1940s and 1950s:

> The hipster world that Kerouac and Ginsberg drifted in and out of from the mid-1940s to the early-1950s was an amorphous movement without ideology, more a pose than an attitude; a way of "being" without attempting to explain why. . . . The division was *hip* and *square*. Squares sought security and conned themselves into political acquiescence. Hipsters, hip to the bomb, sought the meaning of life and, expecting death, demanded it now.
>
> (Jezer, 1982)

Of course, when looking at many examples of contemporary Instagramism, it is possible to argue that the "life as improvisation" the authors show is completely staged and planned by them. But the reality is more complicated. The boundary between authentic and staged, improvised and planned is not always clear. For example, if an author does some basic edits on the photos, somewhat increasing brightness, contrast, and sharpness, at what point do we declare this photo to be "calculated" rather than "authentic"?

## Instagram themes

As Instagram continued to attract more and more users, and as brands discovered Instagram, many authors learned that they could use their feeds as advertising for their small business or freelance work, as a way to supplement their income by promoting products sent to them by companies, or to completely support themselves by becoming influencers. As a result, the number of photos and feeds that were carefully planned quickly increased. A range of evidence suggests that this shift took place during 2014 and 2015.

One very strong example of this structuration of Instagram is the emergence of strong rules one has to follow to attract a large number of followers. The first rule: develop a particular style and use it for all the photos in your feed.

By 2015, we see even more structure. In addition to the established term "style", the term "theme" starts to dominate how-to advice, posts, and help videos. A theme may combine certain subjects, a particular color palette, and a certain contrast choice.

Using Google Trends and the search phrase "Instagram theme ideas", I found that the global web search traffic for this phrase started to increase in January 2014, and then flattened by June 2015. YouTube has hundreds of thousands of how-to videos about Instagram editing, strategies, and theme ideas. On 19 November 2016, I searched YouTube for a few relevant phrases that appear in video titles. Here are those phrases and the numbers of video returned. (Note that to find only directly relevant videos, I entered the search phrases in quotes.)

"how i edit my instagram photos" – 131,000 videos.
"how i edit my instagram pictures" – 48,600 videos.
"how i edit my instagram photos white theme" – 20,000 videos.
"how i edit my instagram minimal theme" – 6,130 videos.

Many of these videos are very popular, registering hundreds of thousands of views in the few months following their publication. This can partly be explained by the fact that many videos in this genre feature young female authors. But there are also many popular videos that feature young and equally hip male authors. Here are just a few examples of the videos and numbers of views (as of 19 November 2016):

"How I Edit My Instagram Pictures + My Theme", published on 19 July 2016, 421,000 views.
"How I edit my Instagram pictures! | Minimal aesthetic", published on 7 August 2016, 231,000 views.
"34 Instagram Themes", published on 8 June 2016, 187,000 views.

Using a theme does not mean that all photos in one feed should be similar. On the contrary, you have to have enough variety, but this variety also has to be structured. This is the second rule of Instagramism: establish and follow a particular temporal pattern for your feed. Never post similar photos next to each other, but instead alternate between a few types in a systematic way. Create an interesting formal temporal rhythm, alternating between compositions, color palettes, or other variables. And if the goal of your feed is to feature products, place enough photos of other subjects in between product photos.

## Designing photo sequences

The mobile Instagram app allows users to view photos in a few different ways. (Details here refer to the Instagram app interface in the mid-2010s.) The gallery view shows nine photos organized in a three-by-three grid. The order of photos corresponds to the dates and times they were shared on Instagram, with newer photos appearing first. Scrolling down reveals the earlier photos. Clicking on a single photo in a grid brings a new view. It shows a larger version of the photo, along with other information: number of likes, comments, posted date and time. This screen also allows a user to perform a number of functions such as "like", "comment", and "share". (For an analysis of the Instagram interface, see Hochman and Manovich, 2013.) Finally, a user also has another view, which shows all photos shared

*Figure 9.5* Screenshots from YouTube "How I edit my Instagram" videos, captured 24 December 2016

*Source*: In such videos, the presentation often includes shots of an author speaking to the audience while showing photo-editing apps and image gallery, as we see in these screenshots

by all the authors he or she follows. Since this timeline is also sorted by date/time, the photos of a given author appear between the photos of all these other authors.

Since time is such an important dimension of the Instagram interface and user experience, many Instagrammers design their feeds accordingly as aesthetic experiences in time. They employ special sequencing techniques that respond to the ways their photos are viewed by others, which I listed earlier.

Given the two rules for "good Instagram feeds", we can divide Instagram authors into two corresponding types. Some control the characteristics of all or at least most of their individual photos but make no attempt to sequence them in any particular way. Others control both the aesthetics of individual photos and the overall aesthetics of a sequence.

For the latter type of authors (who can be individuals, professional bloggers, influencers, or companies), the sequence aesthetic takes priority over any individual photos. No matter how interesting a particular photo is, the author does not post it if it breaks the established rhythm and theme. The blog post called "How to Establish Your Instagram Aesthetic" (Nadine, 2015) explains this:

> Resist the urge to post things that won't fit in. It might be tempting to post something funny or beautiful that doesn't fit in with the look you've chosen. At some point, you'll have a photo you desperately want to post but it just doesn't work.

A post called "Reimaging Your Instagram Profile" (Dana, 2015) from another blog provides these suggestions:

> *Come up with a theme and stick with it.* Maybe you love colorful and bright photos, or maybe only black and white photos. Maybe you post drawings, or photos of lovely landscapes. *Your formula should help your photos appear as if they are part of a set. Like they belong together.*

One male Instagrammer explained in an interview in 2014 how he used small photo printouts to design the sequence of his photos before starting his Instagram account. He quickly gathered over 50,000 followers purely on the strength of his individual photos and his sequencing. I am highlighting this author because his feed does not include any photos with a popular type of content that used to attract likes and followers, such as spectacular views of exotic landscapes, young females in swimsuits, or pretty female faces. In 2016, it became common among Instagrammers to have two Instagram accounts. One is for the public; the second is private and used to lay out sequences and see if new photos fit the theme and established rhythm before they are added to the public account.

The authors who design both individual photos and their sequences may be considered the true "Instagram professionals". They do not follow the rules of "good photography" and strategies developed well before Instagram for different photo capture and edit technologies, publication and exhibition platforms, and circulation and feedback mechanisms. Instead, they systematically exploit the specific properties, affordances, advantages, and limitations of the medium Instagram.

## Appropriation, subcultures, tribes, mainstream?

In contrast to the influential analysis of the styles of subcultures in Dick Hebdige's *Subculture: The Meaning of Style* (1979), I do not see the Instagram aesthetic of designed photos as a form of symbolic resistance. Young Instagram hipsters do not resist the mainstream; they coexist with it and are not afraid to borrow its elements or show how much they enjoy commercial products and their favorite brands.

Instagramism is not about binary differences from the mainstream. It is about the selection and combination of particular elements drawn from

*Figure 9.6* Examples of sequence strategies used by two Instagram authors (I selected a sequence of 30 photos posted sequentially from each author account)

*Source*: The photos are sorted in the order they appear in the Instagram feed (left to right, top to bottom). The two authors, with their number of followers as of 6 May 2016, are:

@*sex_on_water*. Country: Russia (Saint Petersburg) Followers: 48,000
Self-description: "Evgeniya Iokar. Traveller+Photographer+Blogger+Barista"
@tienphuc. Country: Vietnam (Ho Chi Minh City), Followers: 3,815
Self-description: "Graphic Designer+Photographer" www.facebook.com/kenneth.nguyen2295

different contemporary and historical universes, including commercial offerings.[9]

Our standard model of modern and contemporary cultures assumes that new styles, sounds, art forms, ways of behaving, and other cultural strategies and imaginaries are typically created by small subcultures and then later appropriated by commercial-culture producers, who package them into products sold to the masses. And, indeed, there are numerous examples of such appropriations, narratives in which the part of the original inventor is played by, among others, the European Modernists of the 1920s, the Paris Surrealists of the 1930s, the Beat Generation in late 1940s in NYC, Northern California hippies in the 1960s, hip-hop in the Bronx in the early 1970s, or Williamsburg in Brooklyn in the late 1990s.

Does the Instagram hip generation fit into this model? In my view, Instagrammers are not an avant-garde creating something entirely new, a subculture that defines itself in opposition to the mainstream, or the masses consuming commodified versions of aesthetics developed earlier by certain subcultures. They are more similar to Maffesoli's tribes but exist in the digital global Instagram "city" rather than as "villages" in a physical city.[10] (According to Maffesoli, a tribe "refers to a certain ambience, a state of mind, and it is preferably to be expressed through lifestyles that appear and form".)

If the creation of something new by small subcultures or modernist art movements represents a first stage, and later appropriation and packaging for the masses represent a second stage in modern cultural evolution, then the "cultural logic" of Instagramism represents a third stage: Instagrammers appropriating elements of commercial products and offerings to create their own aesthetics. Instagram and other visual global networks quickly disseminate these aesthetic forms worldwide.

As opposed to the movement of cultural innovation from individuals and small groups to companies and then the masses as described by the appropriation model, we also now have other types of movements enabled by social networks: from individuals and groups to other individuals and groups. The industry borrows as much from these individuals and groups as it influences them. (This logic was already anticipated in the emergence of coolhunting research in the early 1990s. See Brodmerkel and Carah, 2016.)

On Instagram, one operates in a truly global space not constrained by local physical and geographical reality. Although there are many paid photo-editing apps available, both Instagram and enough powerful third-party editing apps are free. Among young people in most countries in Asia, South America, and Eastern Europe today, mobile phone and social media use is as high as or even higher than in the developed Western economies. The same fashion and lifestyle magazines, perfect cappuccino and latte cups, fashion items, and brands of sport shoes can appear in photos from almost anywhere in the world where there are young people who use Instagram. Certainly, because of the differences in income, fewer people in developing countries can afford global brands like Zara or Uniqlo, but there are enough local brands that are cheaper and make products that look equally good.

In physical reality, local norms constrain how people dress and behave. Compare New York's Chelsea and Lower East Side, Seoul's Garosu-gil, and the Harajuku area in Tokyo. You hardly see any color besides black in New York; in Seoul, a white/gray/black palette is the norm; in Harajuku, it is combinations of complementary (warm and cold) bright saturated colors and pastels. Each cultural norm offers plenty of space for variations and individualization – Tokyo street fashion was the most extreme well-known example of such variations in the 2000s. A cultural norm constrains choices only on a few dimensions but not on others. So while my examples focus on only one type of Instagram-designed aesthetics that we found in images from many countries, it would be very interesting to investigate other types of Instagram aesthetics that reflect other local aesthetic norms.

In this chapter I used Instagram example to advance the larger ideas of *aesthetic society* and *aesthetic workers*. This society begins to emerge in the second part of 1990s. Since that time, we see the process of aestheticization advancing relentlessly and systematically. Theoretically, there is no end point at which aestheticization will fully saturate every area of our everyday life and communication – new technologies, new materials and manufacture methods can be always used to create new aesthetics which did not exist before, offer new types of aesthetic effects, and also advance aestheticization though individualization. The fascinating question which this chapter did not address is what changes we might expect in image aesthetics in the future? I believe that we will see further advances – and just as it occurred with image editing that first required expensive computer workstations and eventually migrated to free platforms such as Instagram – these advances will be used by many millions of people rather than only by a few professionals.

## Notes

1  An earlier version of the larger part of this text was published under the title "Designing and Living Instagram Photography: Themes, Feeds, Sequences, Branding, Faces, Bodies", as the fourth part of my book *Instagram and Contemporary Image* (2017). http://manovich.net/index.php/projects/instagram-and-contemporary-image.

2  Photo-editing app VSCO, which is considered the standard among sophisticated Instagrammers, had 30 million active users at the beginning of 2016.

3  A note about two terms that frequently appear in this chapter: "aesthetics" and "class". The words "aesthetics" and "aesthetic" are used prominently by Instagrammers and authors of advice posts and videos. For example, a search on YouTube for "Instagram aesthetic feed" yields 7,200 videos, while a search for the phrase "Instagram aesthetic" on Google yields 144,000 results (both searches performed on 22 November 2016). The same search on Google on 29 January 2020 yielded 1,040,000 results.

4  Peter Drucker coined the term "knowledge worker" in 1957, writing that "the most valuable asset of a 21st-century institution, whether business or non-business, will be its knowledge workers and their productivity". See Drucker (1959).

5 My discussion of these types is based on a quantitative analysis conducted in my Cultural Analytics Lab of 16 million geo-tagged images shared on Instagram in 17 global cities from 2012 through 2016, as well as my own observations as an Instagram user. To be sure, there are other types of images; moreover, since social media platforms, their users, and their content keep evolving, I do not want to make claims about the applicability of my analysis to every geographical location or to periods outside of 2012 through 2016.

6 The metaphor of a landscape containing a number of cultural items situated at particular distances from one another is not my invention. Marketing research uses a set of methods called perceptual mapping to analyze and diagram customer perceptions of relations between competing products or brands. Relative positions and cognitive distances between any cultural artifacts, authors, genres, styles, and aesthetic systems can also be analyzed and visualized using this approach. In many of our lab's projects, we create such maps to visualize the results of computational analyses of characteristics of large sets of cultural artifacts.

7 The term "cool" and the related term "hipster" became popular in the 1960s, when they were opposed to the term "square", which is not commonly used today. See Wikipedia, 2016a).

8 Of course, as these strategies were gradually adopted in commercial design circles such as magazine covers and layouts, they became cultural stereotypes that are predictable and therefore easier to recognize and process cognitively. On the role of stereotypes, "exposure effect", and "cognitive fluency" in the cognitive processing of design, see MacKay (2015).

9 In the contemporary visual creative industry, this remix logic was best realized in my view in collections by a number of fashion designers created between 1993 and 2006, leading figures among whom were Alexander McQueen, John Galliano, and Jean Paul Gaultier.

10 See Bennett (1999) for an overview of the concepts of "subculture" and "tribe" in the sociology of culture.

## References

Baena, V. and Winkelhues, K. (2016), 'Thenext revolution in mass customization: An insight into the sneaker market', *International Journal of Advanced Media and Communication*, 2016(4), pp. 85–104.

Bennett, A. (1999), 'Subcultures or neo-tribes? Rethinking the relationship between youth, style and musical taste', *Sociology*, 33(3), pp. 599–617.

Bourdieu, P. (1965), *Photography: A Middle Brow Art*. Stanford: Stanford University Press.

Brodmerkel, S. and Carah, N. (2016), *Brand Machines, Sensory Media and Calculative Culture*. London: Palgrave MacMillan.

Dana. (2015), 'Reimaging your Instagram profile', 25 January. Available at: www.thewonderforest.com/2015/01/reimagining-your-instagram-profile.html.

Debord, G. (1994/1967), *The Society of the Spectacle*, trans. Donald Nicholson-Smith. New York: Zone Books.

Drucker, P. (1959), *The Landmarks of Tomorrow*. New York: Harper and Row.

Google. (2016), 'Search results', 22 November. Available at: www.google.com/?gws_rd=cr&ei=h78zWPPgDMvbvATu9ImADQ#newwindow=1& q=%22Instagram+aesthetic%22.

Hebdige, D. (1979), *Subculture: The Meaning of Style*. London: Methuen.

Hochman, N. and Manovich, L. (2013), 'Zooming into an Instagram city: Reading the local through social media', *First Monday*, July. Available at: http://firstmon day.org/ojs/index.php/fm/article/view/4711/3698.

Instagram. (2016), 'Instagram today: 500 million windows to the world', 21 June. Available at: http://blog.instagram.com/post/146255204757/160621-news.

Jezer, M. (1982), *The Dark Ages: Life in the United States 1945–1960*. Boston: South End Press.

Kochnar, R. (2015), 'A global middle class is more a promise than a reality', July 15. Available at: www.pewglobal.org/2015/07/08/a-global-middle-class-is-more-promise-thanreality/

MacKay, J. (2015), 'The psychology of simple', 5 November. Available at: https://crew.co/blog/the-psychology-of-simple.

Maffesoli, M. (1996/1988), *The Time of the Tribes – The Decline of Individualism in Mass Society*, trans. D. Smith. Thousand Oaks, CA: Sage Publications.

Manovich, L. (2013), *Software Takes Command*. New York and London: Blooms-bury Academic.

Manovich, L. (2016–), 'Instagram and contemporary image'. Available at: http://manovich.net/index.php/projects/instagram-and-contemporary-image.

Moss, C. (2015), 'Why don't young people want to be part of a tribe any more?', *Telegraph*. Available at: www.telegraph.co.uk/men/fashion-and-style/11624401/Why-dont-youngpeople-want-to-be-part-of-a-tribe-any-more.html.

Nadine. (2015), 'How to establish your Instagram aesthetic', 8 April. Available at: http://blogbrighter.com/establish-your-instagram-aesthetic/.

Pezzini, M. (2012), 'An emerging middle class', *OECD 2012 Yearbook*. Available at: http://oecdobserver.org/news/fullstory.php/aid/3681/An_emerging_middle_class.html.

Postrel, V. (2004), *The Substance of Style: How the rise of aesthetic value is remaking commerce, culture, and consciousness*. New York: HarperCollins.

Schreiber, T. (2016), '22 awesome websites with stunning free stock images', *Shopify.com*. Available at: www.shopify.com/blog/17156388-22-awesome-websites-withstunning-free-stock-images.

Sibol, N. (2014), '4 brands engaging consumers through individualization', imedia-connection.com, November 7. Available at: http://www.imediaconnection.com/article/133414/4-brands-engaging-consumers-through-individualization.

Tifentale, A. (2017, April), 'Rules of the photographers' universe', *Photoresearcher Journal*, 27, pp. 68–77.

Tifentale, A. and Manovich, L. (2016), 'Competitive photography and the presenta-tion of the self', in J. Ruchatz, S. Wirth and J. Eckel (eds.), *Exploring the Selfie: Historical, Analytical, and Theoretical Approaches to Digital Self-Photography*. Palgrave Macmillan, forthcoming. Available at: http://manovich.net/index.php/projects/competitive-photography-andthe-presentation-of-the-self.

Wikipedia. (2016a), 'Hipster'. Available at: https://en.wikipedia.org/wiki/Hipster_(1940s_subculture).

Willett, M. (2015), 'Everyone's obsessed with 'knolling' their stuff and putting the photos on Instagram', businessinsider.com, May 14. Available at: http://www.businessinsider.com/instagram-flat-lay-trend-knolling-2015-5.

YouTube. (2016, November 22), 'Search results'. Available at: www.youtube.com/results?search_query=instagram+aesthetic+feed.

# 10 Publics or post-publics?

## Contemporary expression after the mobile phone

*Ravi Sundaram*

## Introduction

In her widely circulated book *Cruel Optimism* (2011), Lauren Berlant suggested that the precarious but affect-driven energies of the neoliberal epoch have transformed collectivity, producing a "desire for the political". This desire for the political refers to a form of collective attachment that is neither oriented toward particular ends, nor valued for its transformative effect. In the neoliberal present, people seek to maintain the process – the ongoingness – of attachment as such. At the core of Berlant's question is a transformation of collectivity in the post-media landscape where new data-led infrastructures dominate our lives and mobile gadgets now connect us in real time, creating new intensities and spurts. The widespread proliferation of digital platforms and mobile phone apps since 2008 have foregrounded new questions of political subjectivity worldwide. Online and device-led participation increasingly stands in for the political/collective, transcending the phenomenologies of the 20th-century crowd.

## Street crowds to calculative infrastructure: the "new masses"

More than a century ago, European writers warned about the dangers of irrational street crowds. For early writers like Gustav Le Bon and Gabriel Tarde, large crowds were prone to irrationality and hypnotic suggestion, posing dangers to the enlightened bourgeois public sphere. In the figure of the mass, the crowd represented a dangerous excess, excitable, violent. In Tarde, forces of imitation and contagion make crowds a particularly vital and unpredictable force (Borch, 2012; Jonsson, 2013). Weimar crowd theorists moved beyond arguments of a dangerous collective crowd psychology. Georg Simmel and Siegfried Kracauer situated crowds in the rhythms of capitalist modernity – expressive of a new sociality and industrial repetition. In Kracauer's *Mass Ornament* (1995), published in the 1920s, synchronized forms of collective behavior are presented as akin to mechanized production, rendering the mass as increasingly functional to capitalist ratio. By the mid-1940s, critical theory's argument for the growing rationalization of collective energies intimated in *The Mass Ornament* seemed to have come full circle. In the widely circulated chapter on culture industry in their *Dialectic of Enlightenment* written in 1944, Max Horkheimer and Theodor Adorno suggested that industrial media played a key role in homogenizing diverse populations into consumers. In their now-familiar argument, mass culture produced docile subjects, framed by false needs that were created by media corporations (2002). The larger implication of the culture industry thesis was that the earlier street crowd had been significantly reassembled by media infrastructures. By the 1960s, it was argued that post-war populations were tamed by the post-war boom and mass television, which dispersed the dangerous energies of the industrial crowd. Later referencing crowd theory, Peter Sloterdijk argued that the televisual principle had replaced the Fuhrer principle: programming now produced docile individual subjects; mass media provides a privatized venue for collective discharge (cited in Borch, 2016). Remarkably, a century ago, Gabriel Tarde had suggested that the rise of print publics offered a way out from the dangerous proximity of street crowds, a form of "contagion without contact". In this argument, publics were "less extremist" than crowds, which were defined by an "animal" quality (Borch, 2012, p. 59). The imitative connections afforded by print contrasted with the dangerous proximity of crowds. For Tarde, print publics offered the possibility of rational discussion and deliberation – all hallmarks of the Enlightenment individual. Print publics were presented the "instantaneous transmission of thought from any distance", diluting the dangers of crowd psychology and potential anarchy (Tarde, 1969).

In 1985 Jean Baudrillard published his widely circulated essay, "The Masses: The Implosion of the Social in the Media". Almost anticipating the digital future, the essay argued that" "we will never in future be able to separate reality from its statistical, simulative projection in the media" (1985, p. 579). Overinformed, the masses become an "obese" part of the silent majority. He goes on, "For the masses are also made of this useless hyperinformation which claims to enlighten them, when all it does is clutter up the space of the representable and annul itself in a silent equivalence" (p. 580). Baudrillard's essay was an obituary of older forms of politics based on contingent public speech. Condemned to permanent participation, "the masses" have been absorbed by a late capitalist strategy of transparency.

In the last two decades, marked by the spread of the internet, the figures of the mass, the crowd, and the public have re-emerged, with various incarnations: first as a radical potential[1] (Seattle, Tahrir Square, Occupy) and then as a dark demonic drive (right-wing populism, the new fringe). In hindsight, it is clear that new forms of collectivity are increasingly shaped by informational infrastructures, which are central to the production of value: economic, cultural, and political. This is the landscape of the "new masses" (Baxman, Beyes and Pias, 2016), where public affect is defined by a dynamic, calculative infrastructure that has spread worldwide in the past two decades. Since the rise of internet infrastructures and neoliberal governance, calculative infrastructure has significantly shaped the new collectivities and suggests a disjunction with the older discussions of the crowd in the 1930s.

## Calculation as generative infrastructure

Calculation has dramatically reinserted itself into contemporary debates, offering many things at the same time: a revitalization of urban policy through transparency indicators and real-time dashboards (Mattern, 2015) and a modulation of governance through device-led participation rather than contingent political speech (Gabrys, 2016; Kelty, 2017). Emerging calculative infrastructures have generated a volatile mix of actors: data intermediaries and server farms spread worldwide, managerial technocrats, and older state employees affected by audit culture. There are shifting interface zones for subaltern populations and migrants, along with para-legal networks of hardware, money transfer, and ID documents. Calculation offers us a diagnostic of the contemporary, its atmospheric shifts, and its technical affordances. Ian Hacking (1990) famously referred to the "avalanche of numbers" in the 19th century, which made populations, landscapes, and networks legible to government. Various documentary practices like the cadastral map, census registers, and health records were combined with enumerative/recording technologies like the fingerprint and photography. Social security numbers and ration cards followed in the 20th century. The performance of sovereignty emerged through the play of documentary artifacts, calculative technologies, and media storage systems. Calculative strategies in the social city of the 19th and early 20th centuries were geared toward an orchestration of flows: of humans, technical artifacts, and species. The proliferations of statistical techniques as well as the rise of recording technologies like typewriters, stencil duplicators, and filing systems allowed information to be indexed, retrieved, and transmitted (Yates, 1993).

Since 2005, we have seen the unprecedented transformations of these calculative infrastructures, which increasingly shape everyday life. Global landscapes are now covered by a sensory infrastructure, where value is drawn from experience (Sundaram, 2015). This new infrastructure includes not just computational systems, data networks, and sensing devices, but millions of mobile phones. Media infrastructure since 2005 has shifted toward the transformation of experience based on personalized media gadgets. The scale of this shift is already apparent before our eyes. A few decades ago, many of these would have been Western monopolies. Today, this picture is only partly correct. A growing plurality of urban populations in Asia, Africa, and Latin America have now got regular access to mobile devices, which act as computational and sensory data points. Many new location technologies are being retailed and even researched in India and China, with Africa being one of the global pioneers in mobile money (Gahigi, 2017).

These transformations have placed a great sense of strain on governance, which for the most part was not designed for this new flux. Post-colonial governance, for example, operated within a code that functionally separated the social/informational and the media spheres. Welfare/information was the domain of governance, while regulators and courts managed public affect. Governmental power periodically filtered and differentiated two orders of circulation: of people and things and of public affect. In the contemporary conditions where calculation and sensory expression appear blurred, the old hierarchies seem unsustainable. Confronted by media-enabled populations for which it had no place, the post-colonial design has been subjected to great fissures. After the spread of low-cost media devices and mobile phones, unregulated forms of media (audio, video, images) began to rapidly circulate from a population hitherto seen solely as social and political actors within India's post-colonial design.[2] As low-cost media spread through inexpensive cellular phones and populations became producers and proliferators of media, the boundaries of the social and the political went through considerable turmoil, and the older institutional sites of media lost their old monopoly. In effect, we have a radical multiplication of the calculative and the sensory, unanticipated by post-colonial design and sovereign power. This network power manifests in what Benjamin Bratton calls a new global Nomos, where sovereignty is dispersed in transnational and corporate bodies (2014a). Orit Halpern (2014) has traced the development of a "communicative objectivity" in the 1950s where information and cybernetic theory connected calculation, prediction, and aesthetics. Contemporary calculative infrastructures are significantly expressive (Thrift, 2012).

This is a radical restatement of measure itself, bringing in the formerly incalculable. This expansion of calculation creates new affordances and capacities. In this expanded map of measure, state bodies have long lost their monopoly over calculation. Data analytics companies promising new granular calculation now regularly contract their services to urban bodies. Private biometric ID contractors work in India and Africa, urban transportation data is often with Google and Uber, and an increasing body of routine evidence in minor urban criminal trials is stored in data servers thousands of miles away owned by social media companies like Facebook. Mark Hansen suggests that the 21st-century data-intensive turn has produced a "feeding forward" of subjectivity, displacing humans as unique addressees of media. In the new operational present, humans are shaped by processes outside their control and knowledge, a radical reengineering of consciousness as it existed in the Western imagination. Consciousness stands "humbled", existing only to modulate other forms of "sensory prescensing" (Hansen, 2015).

Calculative infrastructures enable an atmospheric media bringing together humans, machines, and artifacts. The mobile phone is increasingly the preferred machine in the new landscape of measure, perhaps more so in the South. Mobile phones combine calculation, surveillance, location, transmission, and public affect. Central to the design of the mobile phone is the conception of the body as a sensory motor, constantly interacting with the environment. Very early on, designers realized that audio communication was too limiting for a device like the mobile phone. The initial text messaging has now been joined by audio, video production and circulation, reading, writing, and storage. For most media-enabled populations in the South, the mobile phone is the first computational device. The phone is also the operative camera and recording device, the storage of intimate and public memory, all in all a powerful means of public expression, entertainment, and communication. Mobile phone apps set up an "interfaciality" that embeds users in a larger circulation engine. Writes Bratton, "In connecting one thing to another by remote control, by action at a distance, the interfacial thing unfolds out toward the world of other things in looping cybernetic circuits of relay and interruption. It doesn't fold in, it explodes out" (2014b).

This outward expressivity is generative in every sense. We witness the emergence of provisional infrastructures of agility, where subaltern populations move in and out of the circulation engine. Bluetooth-enabled phones create provisional networks of communication; removable memory cards swap and top up media in neighborhood shops. This loop shapes much of contemporary circulation, wherein media objects move in and out of infrastructures, attach themselves to new platforms of political aesthetic action, and are drawn to or depart from the spectacular time of events.

## Curated collectivity?

Vast technological infrastructures owned by transnational corporations have reassembled global populations fairly rapidly since 2005, offering new forms of connection through personalization. Personalization is integral to the economy of experience in the web since 2005, transforming the way information is gathered and shared. Three elements are integrated in this process of personalization: the search, user-generated media, and a model of surveillance that is the new normal. This model is premised on the constitutive instability of online subjectivity. As users are invited to permanently engage in machine-like activity (sharing, posting, updating their profiles), there is an assumption that identity is constantly changing, each trail producing a stream of data to further personalize public action. These individual data trails are created by all online business companies, Indian or transnational, and are available (in many cases) for use by political parties and advertising companies, which tailor campaigns in response.

These forms of attachment are often unrecognizable from earlier models of the collective, while amending and intervening in collective projects of the political. A larger and open question is a transformation of collectivity in the post-media landscape. In some of the gloomier readings, Web 2.0 collectivities are measured up and seen wanting against older modernist models of stranger sociality, radical contingency, and a political tied to public speech (Dean, 2009). Unsurprisingly we have a familiar catalogue of negatives: a receding public in the midst of permanent publicity, a solidarity dispersed by permanent personalization, a compromised politics scarred by online media events, memory archives now hostage to large transnational media corporations; the desire for attachment is periodically exploited skillfully by right-wing movements worldwide – India and Turkey serving as notorious examples. The recent rise of violent internet right-wing groups and fake news seems to suggest the final breakdown of liberal models of public speech. The utopian possibilities of network culture that dominated the writings of Michael Hardt and Antonio Negri but a decade ago seem to have receded. However, the question of the political remains, as a form of contingency and potential that manifests in the affordances of network culture and data infrastructures. Do new forms of collectivity restate some of the fears of classic crowd theorists, where expansions of affect without deliberation drives populist and right-wing mobilization? I want to enter this debate from the vantage point of ongoing fieldwork in India, focusing on the interface between mobile phone application and multiple infrastructural affordances. Mobile phone media circulation, notably through software applications like WhatsApp, offers important insights into the nature of collective formation in the contemporary. Central to my argument is the movement between multiple time-space and infrastructure zones, as media circulates and collective formations assemble and melt away. The atmospherics of digital media culture generate a somatic collectivity in public events yet, remarkably, also quite rapidly fragments into other, smaller formations. To expand my argument, I will examine some of the trajectories of public expression and the constellation of events after the mobile phone. These trajectories have been volatile. Mobile media has been cited as a player in many events: censorship and surveillance, communal riots, and sexual assault.

## Infrastructure: mundane and volatile

Expressive of recent times, a WhatsApp message went out from India's rural development ministry to state that "no more" funds would be available for NREGA (a major welfare program), and current funds would have to be used "judiciously".[3] When challenged about using an unofficial platform for formal communication, the ministry clarified that this was an "informal" message. The WhatsApp message was by no means exceptional for governmental communication. The mobile platform has become a significant player in the communication between government and populations. The government has encouraged citizens to file police complaints and report traffic violations, railway enquiries, and municipal complaints through WhatsApp. Police officials use the platform to communicate in crisis; there are internal departmental networks that run on the platform. WhatsApp is a private messaging service owned by Facebook; user data is stored in servers outside India. It is an off-the-web application, not searchable like a web page: i.e., there is no public record like a website. As a private chat application, WhatsApp's main function is communication between mobile phone users, voluntary groups, using text, video, and audio. The platform is a ubiquitous record of banal pleasures and functionality: rapid chat sessions; interaction among friends, families, political groups, and small business. Equally, the platform is a major player in communal mobilization, hate speech, and vitriol. In short, there is a remarkable situation where state officials, private individuals, and social/political groups share a similar volatile infrastructure, blurring and confusing partitions of public and private. Media periodically overflows in from one channel to another, leading to unanticipated consequences: the exposé of police torture or political secrets, a leaked intimate video. This is partly a result of the deliberate design of much of contemporary new media, where value is generated through the "making public" of personal expression. The trend toward the personalization of expression unites much of contemporary digital communication, while causing periodic disjunctures and crisis. The separation of intimate and public life was the basis of much of recent Western social theory, the foundation of much of legal doctrine and case law. What we have is an unanticipated situation for social theories of publicity, where the older partitions seem to be increasingly unworkable. The contradictions have affected all institutions of sovereign power: the police, the state, and the courts, which now struggle to deal with evidence increasingly far removed in California servers.

## The circulation engine

Post-colonial governance was driven by a model where populations were kept away from the dangers of "sensuous provocation". It is this interface that has been rendered inoperable in the last two decades beginning with the video era. Media have moved from being just a distinct infrastructural site (a cinema hall, a radio station) to a condition of life itself, marking expression in all walks of life (Sundaram, 2009).

In much of the non-Western world, this disjunctive infrastructure goes back to the emergence of video cassettes in the 1980s. The circulation of video altered the materiality of cinema itself in the South, by generating new infrastructures and aesthetics and creating networks of trans-regional circulation (Larkin, 2008; Lobato, 2012). But for the past decade or so, a personalized media gadget, the phone, has dominated the circulation engine. It would be no exaggeration to say that for poorer populations of the Global South, the phone is the first accessible computing and media infrastructure. This explains the rapidly growing numbers of low-cost smartphone users among the poor in the last few years. The rise of the cellular phone in the South is concurrent with the design of Web 2.0, with a premium on user-driven media, aggregated through platforms like Facebook, YouTube, Instagram, and Twitter. We have the rise of aggressive new media capitalism unimaginable in the wild days of the video era. (Alibaba and Flipkart are two of China and India's fastest growing companies.) The phone is a significant player in developing models of user-driven infrastructure and "citizenship" based on transparency and permanent publicity. We also have a massive rollout of a security infrastructure like biometric ID's all over Asia and Africa, which is on route to integration with cellular phone operating systems.

## Post-publics: curation and disjunction

In the current landscape, carefully curated experiences are drawn from user profiles that are silently gathered by social media algorithms when users go online – leading to personalized connections, search predictions, a vast surveillance engine of circulation. As users are invited to permanently engage in machine-like activity (sharing, posting, updating their profiles), the idea was that identity is constantly changing, each trail producing a stream of data to further personalize public action. These individual data trails are created by all online business companies, Indian or transnational, and are available (in many cases) for use by political parties and advertising companies. Significantly this move signals a transformation of internet time as imagined by social media. Circulation has taken command, within a temporality of ceaseless transit, a seeming culture of the indeterminate that resists representation. We are caught in "a state of animated and animating suspension that forces itself on consciousness" (Berlant, 2011, p. 5). The clarity of closure is impossible; life is a series of updates, number of friends/likes, and the constant stream of information – of travel, of political opinion, of individual popularity. Search engines "rank" pages, individual stardom, and political spectacle. "In this public culture of temporality", writes Carlo Caduff, "the present is perceived as a series of disruptive events. The spectacular and the catastrophic rather than the structural and the chronic have become the characteristic marks of this present" (2014, p. 11). In this culture of temporality, the event is transformed and is exhibited as a series of short spurts. This temporary capture of a fast-moving temporality is now part of news television: the periodic spectacle, the 24-hour news loop similar to "viral" online events.

Remarkably, at the same time, the political campaign increasingly casts itself in intimate vernacular terms, addressing the new generation of media-enabled users. In India, the Hindu nationalist party election campaign of 2014 included a "selfie with Modi" slot, aimed at mobile-enabled voters, who were encouraged to send their selfies to the Narendra Modi campaign, which later became part of a collage of Modi's face. Baishya (2015) suggests that this selfie campaign was a project of "vernacular multiplication"; even while it connected an everyday practice, it produced the leader as a man of austerity and action. The strategy here is to produce new forms of agglomeration, by multiplying in many networks. This is the business model of information capitalism since 2005; it is hardly surprising that high-profile political campaigns like that of the Hindu nationalist leader Narendra Modi in 2014 were led by Indian advertising brand managers like Piyush Pandey of Ogilvy. The Modi campaigns also used Twitter in the 2014 election to produce a new form of virality. In his comparative study of the Obama

2008 and Modi 2014 Twitter campaigns, Joyjeet Pal (2015) shows that while Obama's model was more open and expansive (650,000 followers), the Modi campaign was selective with just 1,000 followers. Yet the Modi campaign had the ability to retweet its messages:

> Modi had only twice tweeted messages that had more than 10,000 retweets, whereas Obama had 40 tweets in the same period that reached the same figure. In other words, although Modi had less than a seventh of the followers, Obama has far less ability to turn messages gigantically viral. Modi was significantly more able to get a consistent social media buzz about what he had to say.
>
> (2015, p. 7)

This form of recognition connects to the process of personalization integral to mobile phone users in a social media world. The issue here is not a personalized address by a political leader, but the ability to intervene in an affective infrastructure where value comes from multiplication and connection. The curated campaign does not define all public affect – populations may also inhabit a disjunctive sensory infrastructure, traversing the multiple spatial zones of the digital and analog, online and offline. In 2013, a Mumbai artist collective CAMP followed a local ship of sailors from Kutch in Western India across the region, as they comingled with other sea proletarians from Baluchistan, Iran, and Sind. The project video *Gulf to Gulf to Gulf* tracked the movement of commodities, local ships, and sailors across the contemporary turbulent geographies of the Indian Ocean: Somalia, Aden, Sharjah, Iran, Pakistan, and Western India. In *Gulf to Gulf to Gulf*, the sailors mobile phone videos generate connections between sailing routes, the death and life of ships, and work time and dreamtime, expressive of the poetics of infrastructure that the anthropologist Brian Larkin has written about (2013). The videos produced by the sailors in *Gulf to Gulf to Gulf* express an inter-medial junction, connecting disparate histories of cinema, music, and the emergent subjectivities of media-enabled subaltern populations. The grainy textures of analog video, mixed with popular music, nevertheless emerge from a personalized digital device – a feature phone. The sailors used a particular Nokia phone model with a powerful Bluetooth signal and removable memory cards, useful for sharing videos and music. Despite being produced in the Web 2.0 social media era, the sailors' media is shared almost entirely off network through Bluetooth connections. This is a remarkable infrastructure of agility and possibility. Even as this peer-driven network recalls the utopianism of the early internet by bypassing media industry filters, it also signals conditions of possibility for poorer populations in the non-Western world. Here, provisional networks form around temporary connections: Bluetooth sharing of media by sailors, urban proletarians, and migrants, serviced by local neighborhood shops and networks.

## The violent event

What happens when complex ecologies of connection are projected onto a larger landscape, involving many protagonists? On 5 March 2015, thousands of young men in Dimapur in Eastern India broke into a prison and lynched a Muslim man accused of sexually assaulting a local woman. In the widely circulated image of the Dimapur lynching, we see a large surging crowd of men surrounding the victim's tortured body and straining to capture the moment on their mobile phone cameras. But this is equally a crowd of 8,000 men, observers, voyeurs, and torturers, prosthetically augmented by the infrastructure of the phone and connected to networks. As many have shown, in new media the experience of "liveness" produces a sense of taking us out of ordinary time (Chun, 2016). To "participate" is to touch the real through circulation. Even as the mobile-enabled crowd produced thousands of phone images that capture a sense of "being there", their real power is in rapid movement and endless proliferation across other networks. This is a dynamic loop: the murderous crowd in the street, the white-hot expansions of lynching images in multiple space-times, again returning to the crowd in motion.

In Dimapur, for instance, local police inquiry claimed that almost "all those" who attended the rally had responded to messages seen on two blogs, Naga Blog and Naga Spear. "Visuals were used to stir passions", said the local police, in a language familiar to colonial and post-colonial censors. Blog administrators claimed they had deleted comments rapidly (*The Indian Express*, 2015). A later investigation showed (unsurprisingly) that the rapid comments had come from across the country. Equally unsurprisingly, the messages and subsequent images of the event mostly spread through the personalized phone message application WhatsApp.

In *Software Takes Command* (2013), Lev Manovich argues that software is a meta-medium, synthesizing previously separate media and anticipating not-yet-invented media. Software is the cultural interface through which we negotiate the world; the ever-updating model of software makes it a candidate and agent for the contemporary culture of temporality. New media is new because of the permanently extendable possibility of software techniques. By privileging formal techniques over any context, Manovich's argument can appear limited; however, his notion of "deep extendibility" gives us unintended insights into the ecology of WhatsApp. From a messaging service, WhatsApp has integrated audio/video calls and rapid video circulation via cloud servers. Just about every smartphone user in India has WhatsApp and uses it to share images, text, and video and to make free audio calls. In India, as across the world, there are user groups that act as communication platforms for family, business, and political and social networks. Ever since WhatsApp incorporated rigorous near-unbreakable encryption for messages and audio calls, most political activists in India have shifted to its platform to avoid local police surveillance. As a vehicle of personalization, pleasure, and connectivity, WhatsApp has emerged as a significant player in the trans-actions between aesthetics and politics. This vitality of software applications like WhatsApp has become a metaphor for the power of new media in general, uniting political activists of the right and left. WhatsApp has become a vehicle for much mediated communication, in governmental departments, political parties, and educational institutions. WhatsApp's incredible reach makes it a crucial player in the comingling of street crowds and online agglomerations, wetware, and software. The old fears about the uncon-trolled energies of irrational crowds impinging on post-colonial citizenship have now shifted to mobile phone circulation. Almost everywhere in India, WhatsApp-driven media have been cited as players in violent conflicts. Here ficto-graphic atrocity stories (images, sounds, videos) circulate and attach themselves to sites of violence; in many situations, for instance, "fake" vid-eos have been held out as reasons for disturbances in various cities, leading to the intimidation and killing of minority populations. Michael Warner (2002) points to the "fruitful perversity" of all acts of modern publicity. Once initiated, these acts abandon intended audiences and face the risk of dispersal, misuse, and escape. Here, media ostensibly shared between private WhatsApp groups suddenly explodes in a burst of circulation and becomes volatile within rapidly developing events. Technically this is "private" com-munication enacting forms of publicity associated with large events. This is a kind of private-public, or even post-public, both terms failing to capture conceptual challenges to the contemporary posed by the shifts of the last decade.

William Mazzarella suggests that post-colonial censorship's "performa-tive dispensation" was to play both police and patron, to filter authorized and unauthorized sensuous transgressions (2013). The circulation of phone media nevertheless poses new problems for the performance of post-colonial sovereignty, whose authority is typically linked to the nation-state. Web-based Facebook or YouTube pages or Twitter handles can be successfully shut down only after a legal process that takes 48 hours. WhatsApp does not go on the web; its circulation is entirely between private user networks, though it may overflow into other environments during moments of cri-sis: social mobilization, communal riots, or a murderous crowd attacking minorities or migrants. This is the bleeding edge of publicity, where the movements of information and the movements of street crowds appear puz-zlingly blurred as in the police inquiry in Dimapur. This is the terrifying wager of corporealized technologies like the mobile phone: every action is now potentially public and is now available for instant circulation.

## Riding the circulation engine

Faced with new swarms of media-enabled crowds spilling into political pro-tests or communal conflict, the regime has undertaken a radical step, the suspension of all mobile internet infrastructure in parts of the country for short periods of time. The remarkable part of this strategy is that the main legal instrument for this prohibition has been section 144 of the colonial-era Indian penal code, used to prevent crowd agglomeration, or gatherings of more than four persons. Confronted with a swarm of mobile shadows, the regime turns them into a crowd, the only template available for the language of the law. The crowd in the street and the allegedly immaterial swarm are now fused into one.

The second strategy is to pin culpability for the circulation of material. This is being done through arrests of WhatsApp moderators for content that has allegedly led to violence. In Jammu and Kashmir, WhatsApp groups have been asked to register with the government. This is an ingenious attempt to displace the materiality of the WhatsApp group to treat it like a print newspaper, where the rules of legal prohibition apply, and sovereign power can play its familiar role – as censor and patron. The third strategy is one of temporary capture rather than outright prohibition of networks. This long-term technique is to inhabit and temporarily slow down the circulation engine. In India, police cyberlabs in various city departments monitor social media activity. For WhatsApp circulation in India, the police try and join local groups and keep a window open with local community and activist groups. When crisis emerges, the police attach themselves to agglomerating crowd energies, hoping to divert its drive or dissipate it. If this is successful, the police begin the transition to judicial time: the FIR, a possible charge-sheet. The effort is to displace the materiality of the media from the digital to paper (FIR) with a slower temporal order and a familiar terrain.

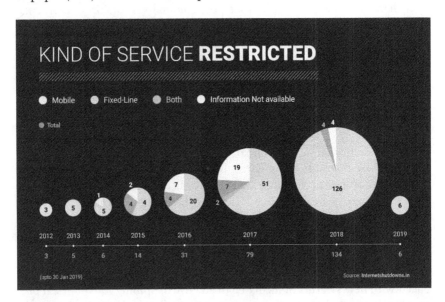

*Figure 10.1* Internet shutdowns in India, 2019

*Source*: Software Freedom Law Centre in India (SFLC.in)

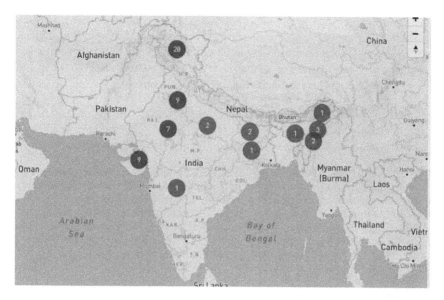

*Figure 10.2* Kind of service restricted

*Source*: Internetshutdowns.in

Many events display rapid switching modes, from the initial rush of the WhatsApp media to the paper filing systems crucial to legality. Again, this is also between different orders of time: the rapid movements around the event and the slower cycle of judicial time. In the changing environments of private-public media, there are different combinations of people and technologies, as the initial event gives way to a constant redistribution of forces. We move from the "private" world of WhatsApp to unstable negotiations between police and a crowd in formation, then to the slower landscape of the law and paper infrastructures.

## Conclusion

How do we imagine collectivity in an era of mobile digital networks? As I have shown, atmospheric infrastructures have significantly transformed public affect, with radical spatial effects. Wendy Chun writes that "Crisis is new media's critical difference" (2016). The very performativity of networks becomes visible in crisis, the volatile, addictive live forwarding of media and the sense of inhabiting the time of an event. As WhatsApp group updates expand exponentially during crises, they leak and attach to other environments, political events or platforms, and media infrastructures like paper. This volatile mobility provokes familiar questions of media theory, the nature of the mobile sensorium, the techniques of navigating this treacherously addictive world. The late Miriam Hansen once called for a political ecology of the senses in the wake of digital media, which would engage with conditions of "apperception, sensorial affect, and cognition, experience and memory" (2004). If the encounters between cinema and mass crowds resulted in so many pioneering ideas of media theory, it is entirely possible that the best work on contemporary media mobility is yet to come.

## Notes

1 Michael Hardt (2006), at the end of the first decade of the internet economy, claimed that the idea of the multitude was preferable to the concepts of the mass and the crowd. For Hardt, crowds and masses suggested passive agglomerations demanding manipulation, while multitudes retained singularities and differences. Remarkably, the very elements of digital infrastructure that Hardt and Negri had pinned their hopes on would transform significantly in the social media turn and Web 2.0.
2 The circulation of privately collected media is not specific to India. From prisons to schools, streets, and hospitals, privately produced videos have emerged to make their way into public events and court battles worldwide.
3 Sethi, Nitin. "Using WhatsApp, Centre Asks States to Stop Creating MNREGA Work". The Wire, 24 October 2016. http://thewire.in/75537/government-uses-whatsapp-toask-states-from-stop-creating-work-under-mgnrega/.

## References

Baishya, A. (2015), 'Selfies|# NaMo: The political work of the selfie in the 2014 Indian General Elections', *International Journal of Communication*, 9(1), pp. 1686–1700.

Baudrillard, J. and Maclean, M. (1985), 'The masses: The implosion of the social in the media', *New Literary History*, 16(3), pp. 577–589.

Baxmann, I., Beyes, T. and Pias, C. (2016), *Social Media-New Masses*. Berlin: diaphanes AG.

Berlant, L. (2011), *Cruel Optimism*. Durham, NC and London: Duke University Press.

Borch, C. (2012), *The Politics of Crowds: An Alternative History of Sociology*. Cambridge: Cambridge University Press.

Borch, C. (2016), 'Crowd mediation: On media and collective dynamics', I. Baxmann, T. Beyes and C. Pias (eds.), *Social Media – New Masses*. Zürich: Diaphanes AG, pp. 23–34.

Bratton, B. (2014a), 'The black stack', *e-flux Journal*, 53.

Bratton, Benjamin H. (2014b), 'On Apps and Elementary Forms of Interfacial Life: Object, Image, Superimposition'. *The Imaginary App*, Ed. Paul D. Miller and Svitlana Matviyenko (Cambridge, MA: The MIT Press, 2014), pp. 3–16.

Caduff, C. (2014), 'Sick weather ahead: On data-mining, crowd-sourcing and white noise', *The Cambridge Journal of Anthropology*, 32(1), pp. 32–46.

Chun, W. (2016), *Updating to Remain the Same: Habitual New Media*. Cambridge, MA: MIT Press.

Dean, J. (2009), *Democracy and Other Neoliberal Fantasies: Communicative Capitalism and Left Politics*. Durham, NC: Duke University Press.

Gabrys, J. (2016), *Program Earth: Environmental Sensing Technology and the Making of a Computational Planet*. Minneapolis: University of Minnesota Press.

Gahigi, M.K. (2017), 'Mobile money is only just starting to transform some of Africa's markets', *Quartz Africa* [Online]. Available at: https://qz.com/africa/1039896/m-pesa-mtn-orange-others-lead-africas-mobile-money-revolution/ [Accessed 28 October 2019].

*Gulf to Gulf to Gulf* (2013), Film directed by *CAMP* (Shaina Anand and Ashok Sukumaran). Available at: https://indiancine.ma/BBRJ/info.

Hacking, I. (1990), *The Taming of Chance* (Vol. 17). Cambridge: Cambridge University Press.

Halpern, O. (2014), *Beautiful Data: A History of Vision and Reason since 1945*. Durham, NC: Duke University Press.

Hansen, M.B.N. (2004), 'Why media aesthetics?', *Critical Inquiry*, 30(2), pp. 391–395.

Hansen, M.B.N. (2015), *Feed-Forward: On the Future of Twenty-First Century Media*. Chicago: University of Chicago Press.

Hardt, M. (2006), 'Bathing in the multitude', in J. Schnapp and M. Tiews (eds.), *Crowds*. Stanford: Stanford University Press, pp. 35–42.

Horkheimer, M. and Adorno, T.W. (2002), *Dialectic of Enlightenment*, ed. G. Noerr. Stanford: Stanford University Press.

Jonsson, S. (2013), *Crowds and Democracy: The Idea and Image of the Masses from Revolution to Fascism*. New York: Columbia University Press.

Kelty, C.M. (2017), 'Too much democracy in all the wrong places: Toward a grammar of participation', *Current Anthropology*, 58(S15), pp. S77–S90.

Kracauer, S. (1995), *The Mass Ornament: Weimar Essays*. Cambridge, MA: Harvard University Press.

Larkin, B. (2008), *Signal and Noise: Media, Infrastructure, and Urban Culture in Nigeria*. Durham, NC: Duke University Press.

Larkin, B. (2013) 'The politics and poetics of infrastructure', *Annual Review of Anthropology*, 42, pp. 327–343.

Lobato, R. (2012), *Shadow Economies of Cinema: Mapping Informal Film Distribution*. London: Bloomsbury Publishing.

Manovich, L. (2013), *Software Takes Command* (Vol. 5). New York: Bloomsbury Publishing A&C Black.

Mattern, S. (2015), 'Mission control: A history of the urban dashboard', *Places Journal*. Available at: https://placesjournal.org/article/mission-control-a-historyof-the-urban-dashboard/.

Mazzarella, W. (2013), *Censorium: Cinema and the Open Edge of Mass Publicity*. Durham, NC and London: Duke University Press.

Pal, J. (2015), 'Banalities turned viral Narendra Modi and the political Tweet', *Television & New Media*, 16(4), pp. 7–10.

Sundaram, R. (2009), *Pirate Moderni: Delhi's Media Urbanism*. Routledge Studies in Asia's Transformation. New York: Routledge.

Sundaram, R. (2015), 'Post-postcolonial sensory infrastructure', *E-flux Journal*, #64, April.

Tarde, G. (1969), *On Communication and Social Influence: Selected Papers*. Chicago: University of Chicago Press.

Thrift, N. (2012), 'The insubstantial pageant: Producing an untoward land', *Cultural Geographies*, 19(2), pp. 141–168.

Warner, M. (2002), *Publics and Counter-Publics*. New York: Zone.

Yates, J. (1993), *Control Through Communication: The Rise of System in American Management*. Baltimore: Johns Hopkins University Press.

# Index

Note: page numbers in *italics* indicate a figure.

For Product Safety Concerns and Information please contact our EU
representative  GPSR@taylorandfrancis.com
Taylor & Francis Verlag GmbH, Kaufingerstraße 24, 80331 München, Germany